"A wonderful resource for those searching for ideas to bring mindfulness to their own lives as well as to their students. The voices and expertise of classroom teachers resound throughout this rich volume." —**Mark T. Greenberg, PhD, Pennsylvania State University**

"At last: a book about mindfulness meditation for teachers—and thus for students—that preserves the depth and the wisdom of its Buddhist roots. And a practical one at that, full of elegant suggestions that today's stressed youngsters ought to jump at. It will do much good."
—**Guy Claxton, PhD, *What's the Point of School?* and *Building Learning Power***

"The contributions of Thich Nhat Hanh and Katherine Weare to the field of contemplative pedagogy are many. With this important book they bring not only their own depth of experience to the task, but also that of hundreds of teachers to aid teachers and students everywhere in attaining genuine happiness through the practice of a mindful and compassionate education." —**Arthur Zajonc, PhD, *The Heart of Higher Education***

"This book is both a joy to read and a very practical resource for teachers who want to pass on the practice of mindfulness to their students. Grounded in research evidence and in the experience of teachers who have travelled this path before, it shows the transformative power of mindfulness to bring education to its senses. A must for any teacher in any setting who has ever wondered if what they are doing could be done with more fun and less effort."
—**Sarah Stewart-Brown, PhD, Warwick Medical School, UK**

"This book should not only be a required reading for teachers and educational personnel, but also for those who are concerned about the future of our children. The contemplative practices and experiential exercises . . . are indeed capable of fostering more resilient, happier and compassionate teachers and pupils, and thus have the potential to change the world."
—**Rony Berger, PsyD, The Center of Compassionate Mindful Education, Tel Aviv University; Ben Gurion University; The Center for Compassion and Altruism Research and Education at Stanford University**

"What an important book! Thich Nhat Hanh is a global leader dedicated to bringing mindfulness, happiness, well-being, and peace to educators, students, and society. He has keenly felt the responsibility of helping young people ...and has dedicated his whole life to the mission of communicating timeless, universal values in an accessible way. Katherine Weare is an educator with decades of experience in bringing well-being and mindfulness into schools and universities. . . . To have these two co-authoring this book is a wonderful and precious gift to us all." —**Vidyamala Burch, *Mindfulness for Health* and *Mindfulness for Women***

"For educators everywhere who yearn for wisdom and partnership in their courageous efforts to form young hearts and minds in an increasingly fragmented world, this book is a trustworthy and wise companion . . . It is essential reading for all those interested in mindfulness in education today." —**Robert W. Roeser, PhD, co-editor of *Handbook of Mindfulness in Education***

"In this outstanding book, Zen master Thich Nhat Hanh, with his profound teachings and deep practices, and Professor Katherine Weare, with her considerable experience of emotional education, child development, and mindfulness in education, collaborate to provide a step-by-step detailed sequence of mindful practices for everyday activities such as breathing, walking, eating . . . Beautifully written, highly accessible, knowledgeable and deeply practical, this book will be an invaluable to teachers and students alike." —**Paul Gilbert, PhD, OBE, Centre for Compassion Research and Training, University of Derby, *The Compassionate Mind***

"'Mindfulness is a path not a tool.' Thich Nhat Hanh, Katherine Weare, and the Plum Village teachers illuminate this path with precision and clarity. Enlivened with the diverse and precious experiences shared by those who walk the path in their classrooms and lecture halls across the globe, this book is an extraordinary offering to all educators and their students." —**Christine Burke, PhD, Australian Catholic University**

"*Happy Teachers Change the World* is an enormously valuable compendium of mindfulness practices for those working in education." —**Richard Burnett, Mindfulness in Schools Project, UK**

"Bursting with wisdom and compassion in an era when our teachers and students need it more than ever, this book is a gift to the future of our communities and larger society. [It] reminds us that the best way to cultivate happy, mindful children is to cultivate happiness and mindfulness in the adults around them...Nhat Hanh and Weare teach us exactly that, drawing deeply on both science and spirit to nourish the seeds of mindfulness in ourselves and future generations, truly changing the world." —**Christopher Willard, PhD, *Growing up Mindful* and *Child's Mind***

"When I first read this book a single word came up over and over, 'beautiful.' The book's intention; the potential to change the culture of schools, to affect the trajectory of young people's lives; the confluence of ancient wisdom and contemporary education practice; the clarity of the writing—beautiful. I hope this proves to be a seminal text for educators around the world with an interest in how best to support the learning and well-being of young people and those who teach them." —**Willem Kuyken, PhD, Oxford Mindfulness Centre, University of Oxford[It]**

"This wonderful book gives us wise insights and tools to integrate mindfulness into education, in order to enhance the full human-beingness of teachers, students, and parents. [It] allows us to teach best what we most need to know—the art of living." —**Nimrod Sheinman, ND, Israel's Center for Mindfulness in Education, The Center for Mind-Body Medicine, and Mindful Schools, Israel**

HAPPY
TEACHERS
CHANGE the
WORLD

HAPPY TEACHERS CHANGE the WORLD

a guide for cultivating mindfulness in education

**Thich Nhat Hanh
and Katherine Weare**

Foreword by Jon Kabat-Zinn

**PARALLAX
PRESS**

BERKELEY, CALIFORNIA

Parallax Press
P.O. Box 7355
Berkeley, CA 94707
parallax.org

Parallax Press is the publishing division
of Unified Buddhist Church, Inc.

Cover and text design by Debbie Berne
Illustrations by Br. Phap Ban

Thanks to Yvonne Mazurek and Elli Weisbaum
for assistance in preparing the book.

Author photograph Thich Nhat Hanh © Richard Friday
Author photograph Katherine Weare © Katherine Weare
Printed on 100% post-consumer waste recycled paper

Note: This book is intended for teachers, children, and individuals
of all physical and mental abilities, including those with limited
mobility and/or vision and hearing. Please feel free to modify
the language to suit the situation you're in and the needs of the
people involved. You can add "move" when the text says "walk,"
"straighten up" when it says "stand." When it talks about being in
touch with the earth while walking, you can add, "I'm aware of my
connection with the earth through the legs or wheels of my chair,"
and so on.

ISBN: 978-1-941529-63-8

Library of Congress Cataloging-in-Publication Data is available
upon request.

2 3 4 5 / 20 19 18 17

contents

appendices

foreword

JON KABAT-ZINN

What you have in your hands is a uniquely important gift—we could equally well say, *transmission*—from Thich Nhat Hanh late in his remarkable life. As you will see, it is a product of his deep affection for the young and his enduring appreciation of the necessity of a wise and kind education for future generations. On every page, you can feel the honoring of those who take on this calling, so often unrecognized, and the enormity of what they do every day in the service of shaping, transforming, and healing this world of ours from the bottom up, generation by generation— namely teachers. It is equally the product of an inspired collaboration with coauthor Professor Katherine Weare, an educator and mindfulness teacher, who has been studying the effects of mindfulness training in education for many years, and an advisory team of writers, Thay's senior students, from the Plum Village community. Together they have crafted a multifaceted and highly user-friendly training manual for teachers that can be used to bring mindfulness in a variety of ways into your classroom and into your own life.

Mindfulness is a practice that can help students of all ages tune their instrument of learning. By that, I mean their entire being—body, mind, heart, and brain as well as their relationships among themselves as learners, and thus, a social/environmental dimension that is also crucial to optimal learning and inquiry. Cultivating the very capacity to pay attention is foundational. Teachers need their students to pay attention to and inquire with discernment into what is most important. It really helps to purposefully develop that capacity as a skill—one which can ignite and sustain a lifelong curiosity and love of learning, as well as an effective and insightful grasp of whatever specific material is being studied. Increasingly, teachers around the world are coming to this realization.... Why not teach their students the *how* of paying attention and of deep listening rather than simply exhorting them to pay attention, as so often happens in the classroom when the teachers themselves are stressed beyond their limits? The approach to mindfulness offered in this volume is a natural pathway for developing that capacity.

Mindfulness is all about paying attention and about the awareness, inquiry, discernment, and wisdom that arise from careful and care-filled attending. Deep listening and attentive reflection are linked to learning to trust one's own perceptions and experiences. They tap into imagination and creativity to facilitate peeling back the outer layers of appearance to reveal the underlying processes at work, and then, coupled with the requisite social skills also developed through the practice of mindfulness, sharing those moments of both insight and frustration openheartedly in a classroom community with others.

Awareness (mindfulness) is a natural human faculty that is probably not as appreciated within educational circles to the degree that thinking is appreciated. Yet the two in combination are demonstrably more powerful than thinking by itself. Awareness is bigger than thought, in that it can hold any thought, recognize it *as a thought* rather than a fact, and thus facilitate an inquiry into whether it is true, complete, accurate, and germane to or perhaps obscuring of the matter at hand. This is an essential skill for developing critical thinking, and, interestingly, also for cultivating emotional intelligence and thus, a greater effectiveness in regulating one's emotions and emotional reactions. When thinking is complemented by awareness, it is a more powerful and vetted thinking, giving us greater confidence in what we know, and also, hopefully, recognizing what we don't know, an equally important domain of education, creativity, and life.

Although the authors are clearly and unapologetically grounded in an ancient and venerable Buddhist tradition from which mindfulness received its most elaborate and precise articulation thousands of years ago, they have gone to great lengths to frame their work in a universal, wholly mainstream, and secular way. That is not so difficult to do, as the essence of mindfulness is in fact universal—what many of us have come to think of and experience as "a way of being" and "a way of being in relationship with what arises," and thus, a deep inquiry into relationality itself. Much of education is predicated on doing and on acquiring knowledge. A lot of students get lost along the way and don't necessarily see the relevance of what they are required to learn to their lives. The irony is that when our learning and our interest are grounded in the domain of being, the domain of embodied wakefulness, the doing (and the learning) that arise out of that "non-doing" is far more robust and nuanced and effective. This is attested to by the up-swelling of the mindfulness in schools movement throughout the world, as more and more teachers are finding it necessary to ground their classes in full presence from the very beginning *as a practice*, rather than merely "taking attendance," which may denote that the student's body is in the room, but, ironically, not necessarily the student's mind and heart. The universality of this approach is also evident from the many non-Buddhist teachers from all around the world who are practitioners of mindfulness and who have contributed anecdotes and recommendations to the book based on their own classroom experience. As the authors also point out and cite, there is a growing and already fairly robust scientific evidence base for the efficacy of *training* the basic faculties of mind (all the senses, and awareness itself, as well as the emotions of kindness and compassion), even from an early age, so that they can both catalyze optimal learning and ignite an ongoing curiosity about life itself.

Schools and universities have long recognized the importance of PE (physical education) and sport, since the benefits of movement and exercise across the lifespan, starting in childhood, are well established. Yet we all know that thinking and talking about exercising or moving is not enough. For the true benefits to accrue and be experienced, you have to actually exercise your body and its muscles and bones—pretty much every day. PE and sport also bring down stress levels from too much mental focusing over too long a period of time, and allow the students an occasion to restore both mental and physical balance. In a similar way, mindfulness training in the schools can be thought of as a kind of MT (mental training) or ME (mental education) where the muscle of mindfulness is being awakened, exercised, and strengthened through ongoing practice.

The world is changing so fast that we don't actually know what intellectual foundations and skills will be most important to acquire for the coming generations. But we certainly do know that to be creative, love one's work, navigate the digital/analog divide, and experience a lifetime of learning, it will be essential for young people of all ages to develop the skill of being present. This includes learning how to befriend and trust one's own inner experience, and learning how to navigate the inner landscape of mind, body, and heart, and the outer landscape of learning with others. Tapping into one's own capacity for creativity and imagination across the lifespan in this way is an essential prescription for success, well-being, and yes, as the title of the book suggests, happiness.

One of the major principles here is that mindfulness needs to be incorporated into the life of the teacher before he or she can effectively bring it into the classroom. If you are a teacher and are new to mindfulness, this book shows you with great precision how to go about developing your own mindfulness meditation practice, as well as how to creatively bring it into your classroom in the service of your students and their well-being, emotional intelligence, and joyful learning. Please note that there is no one right way for going about it. The beauty of this approach is that it gives you a range of options to experiment with, and ultimately reminds you that it is your own creativity, nurtured by your meditation practice, which provides those endlessly novel and creative opportunities. In a very real way, your students will call that wisdom and discernment out of you. They will be your greatest mindfulness teachers.

The virtue of this approach is that it can come directly out of your love of teaching, and out of your aspirations for your pupils and students to thrive, shaped and informed by your own intuitions and expertise, all grounded in your own moment-to-moment mindfulness practice. As far as I can see, wonder, learning, and insight just keep growing out of that nurturing soil.

One of Thay's early books to have a major impact in the West was called *The Miracle of Mindfulness*. Here, in this book, is the miracle made real. I offer my own personal gratitude for this inspiring contribution to making our world a better and more loving and compassionate place.

Jon Kabat-Zinn
Berkeley, California
February 22, 2017

letter to a young teacher

THICH NHAT HANH

Dear Colleagues,

I am a teacher and I love my job, and I know very well that you love your job too. All of us want to help young people to be capable of being happy and of making those around them happy.

Our mission as teachers is not just to transmit knowledge, but to form human beings, to construct a worthy, beautiful human race, in order to take care of our precious planet.

I am very fortunate because the people—especially the young people—with whom I work and live have the same ideal. They want to learn to transform themselves so they can live happily and help others live happily too. So, every time I walk into my classroom there is happiness and mutual understanding between teacher and student, and a brotherhood and sisterhood which makes the work of teaching and studying much easier.

I always get to know about the life of my students. I tell them about my own difficulties and dreams so that communication between us may always be possible. We know that the children—the students of today—have a lot of suffering in them. This is often because their parents suffer. Their parents cannot communicate with each other, and it is not easy for the parents and children to communicate with each other either. There is a sort of loneliness, a kind of vacuum in the child, and the child tries to fill up this emptiness with video games, movies, television, food, drugs, and other things like these.

You know this all too well.

There is an enormous amount of suffering in young people, and this makes the work of teaching a lot more difficult. We ourselves, as teachers, have difficulties too. We try our very best, but the environment, our family, and the colleagues we work with have a lot of suffering in them.

If we as teachers, along with our colleagues, are not happy, how can we expect the children to be happy? This is a very important question! We may not yet have enough patience, understanding, freshness, or compassion to be able to confront all this suffering. There is a certain spiritual dimension we need to help us to transform and to begin to help the people around us—our family members, our partner and, then, others—to transform. If we succeed in this practice we become more pleasant and compassionate.

Bringing Our Mind Back to Our Body

The first step is to come back to yourself—the way out is in. Come back to yourself to be able to take care of yourself: learn how to generate a feeling of happiness; learn how to handle a painful feeling or emotion; listen to your own suffering, so that understanding and compassion can be born and you will suffer less. This is the first step and, as a teacher, you have to be able to do this. You have to begin with yourself. We have practice methods to help us do this, and we can practice these together joyfully.

Through mindful breathing we can bring our mind back to our body and take care of our body first. After you have done this for yourself, you can help others to do the same. When you have not changed yourself it is very difficult to help the other person change so that he or she will suffer less. With more peace and gentleness in yourself, you become more pleasant and that is why you can much more easily help the other person to suffer less.

There is tension and pain in our body. With the practice of mindfulness, you can come back to your body, recognize the tension and suffering which is present in the body, and breathe in such a way that you can let go of this suffering. A half hour or even five minutes of practice can already change the situation.

Mindfulness is a kind of energy that helps us to be fully present in the here and the now, aware of what is going on in our body, in our feelings, in our mind, and in the world, so that we can get in touch with the wonders of life that can nourish and heal us.

The Art of Living

The practice of mindfulness is the practice of joy. It is an art of living. With mindfulness, concentration, and insight you can generate a feeling of joy and happiness whenever you want. With the energy of mindfulness you can also handle a painful feeling or emotion. If you do not have the energy of mindfulness you will be afraid of being overwhelmed by the pain and suffering inside.

Mindfulness is always mindfulness of something. When you practice breathing in and out mindfully, that is called mindfulness of breathing. When you practice walking mindfully, that is called mindfulness of walking. When you eat your break-fast mindfully, that is called mindfulness of eating. You do not have to sit in the meditation hall to practice mindfulness. You can do it when taking a shower, while driving a car, when at school or working on a project, and in your relationships with other people; and you can practice mindfulness whether you are standing, walking, sitting, or lying down. The energy of mindfulness generated by awareness of breath-ing, or awareness of your steps while walking, helps bring your mind home to your body, and when mind and body are together you are well established in the present moment. Life with all its wonders, with all its refreshing and healing elements—joy, happiness, and peace—is available only in the present moment. The past is already gone and the future is not yet there; the present moment is the only moment in which you can be truly alive.

Mindfulness always helps increase concentration, and mindfulness and concen-tration together can bring insight. When you breathe in mindfully, concentrating on your in-breath, you may discover simple but essential things, like the insight that you are alive and that you have a body. "I know I have a body"—that is already insight! I am alive, I am free, I am present in the here and the now. "Breathing in, I know I am alive, and to be alive is a miracle—the greatest of all miracles." When you breathe in, you know you are alive—because someone who is dead cannot breathe in anymore. As you breathe out, you can already celebrate the fact that you are still alive. Your lungs are strong enough for you to enjoy your in-breath; your feet are strong enough to walk, and allow you to touch the earth with every step. So many conditions for happiness are available. With mindfulness and concentration, insight continues to arise.

Stop Running

There are so many conditions of happiness. We don't need to have more. If we were to take a pen and write down the conditions of happiness that we already have, one page would not be enough, two pages would not be enough—even ten pages would not be enough. Writing down our conditions of happiness is an important meditation.

When you recognize the conditions of happiness you already have, you can be happy and joyful right in the here and the now. Many people mix up happiness with excitement, but excitement is not exactly happiness. When you're excited, there's not enough peace in you, and the happiness isn't real. Mindfulness is a kind of practice that helps us to understand what true happiness is—it's not something made with objects of craving like fame, power, wealth, and sensual pleasures, but is made with understanding and compassion.

True happiness means that you don't need to run after anything anymore. There's a feeling of satisfaction being in the here and the now, when you recognize you have so many conditions for happiness, wherever you are. If you can do that, you can generate a feeling of happiness and joy at any time. We can create joy and happiness not only for ourselves, but also for other people. You remind others with your mindfulness—it can be contagious. You remind them that we are in a wonderful world, that they can touch the wonders of life that are available, and that can make them happy. If you're joyful, happy, and aware, you light up the lamp of happiness and joy in others, because in each of us there is a seed of mindfulness, a seed of awareness. This is an art, and it's not difficult. As a teacher, you can perform that miracle in just a few seconds, and you can make the students in your class happy.

Deep Communication

Nowadays people use many means of communication, like cell phones, television, and computers, but communication has become very difficult between partners, father and son, and mother and daughter. It's not because you have a lot of electronic devices that you improve the quality of communication. If you do not understand yourself, if you cannot be in touch with yourself, if you do not know what is the cause of your own suffering, fear, and anger, you cannot communicate with yourself. And when you cannot communicate with yourself, how can you communicate with another person?

That is why going home to yourself to get in touch with your body, your feelings, your perceptions, and your suffering—understanding yourself—is crucial before you can help another person. That is why we propose that teachers and students sit together to tell each other about the suffering inside. We should have the time—we should be able to afford the time—to do that. True communication should be done on that level: understanding the suffering inside, understanding the suffering in the other person. We need to teach this to the younger generation.

Deep listening and loving speech, practiced with our students, helps remove the obstacles between teachers and students. If the students understand your suffering, they will not continue to make you suffer anymore. If we understand their suffering, we will know how to help them to suffer less. Together we improve the quality of teaching and of learning, and the classroom becomes a very pleasant place to be for everyone. It is possible to be happy together as teachers and students.

Mindfulness practice applied to listening and speaking can help us restore communication with ourselves because we can learn to listen to our own suffering. We don't have to try to get away from ourselves; we don't have to cover up what is unpleasant in us. We try to be there for ourselves, to understand ourselves, so that we can transform. If you know how to listen with compassion and love you can help the other person to suffer less. You know that suffering is in you, but in him or in her there is also suffering. When you see the suffering in the other person you don't blame or accuse them anymore. Instead you want to help him or her to suffer less. But how can you recognize the suffering in the other person if you do not recognize the suffering in yourself? That is why the practice of mindful listening to our own suffering is very crucial. Compassion will arise in us and we will suffer less. After that we can look at the other person and we will know how to help them to do as we have done. Listening to him or her with compassion will bring relief in just half an hour or one hour. That is the practice of mindful listening.

Coupled with mindful listening is the practice of loving speech. We try to tell the other person the truth about the suffering in ourselves and in him or her, using gentle speech to help the other person to open his heart. The way we speak helps the other person to recognize the suffering in him or herself, and in you. All these are practices of mindfulness—mindfulness of listening and mindfulness of speaking.

The teacher and the students can then apply the practices of mindful listening and speaking in sharing sessions. They need to listen to each other first. The teacher should be able to sit down and listen to the suffering of the students. And the students can come to know the difficulties and the suffering of the teacher and of their fellow students. After they have listened like this, their behavior will change. The whole class can practice sitting down, breathing, and listening to each other. This is not a waste of time—on the contrary it leads to mutual understanding. Students and teachers will be able to collaborate with each other in making the learning and teaching a joy for both. We can imagine a teacher sitting down with a student to talk about the suffering of the young person. The teacher has developed the capacity to listen with compassion and help the student to suffer less. Until now there may have been no one who could understand the suffering of that young person. His father and mother are so busy, and because of that this young person is so angry. Now we have a chance to sit down and listen to his suffering—the teacher may be the first person who knows how to sit down and listen to him. If the young person feels that his suffering is understood by someone, he will suffer less. So the practice of compassionate listening helps connect the teacher with the student, builds trust, and removes the anger and fear between teacher and students.

Administrators and head teachers need to understand that when sessions of deep listening are organized in schools, teachers and students will have more energy and focus for teaching and learning. Without these practices, teachers can make students suffer and students can make teachers suffer, and the gap widens between the two generations. The practice of using deep listening and loving speech to restore communication and to promote understanding and collaboration between teachers and students should be included in all teacher-training courses.

The Art of Handling Happiness and Suffering

Sometimes we believe that happiness is not possible right here, right now. This belief has been handed down to us from our parents and our ancestors. That is why we always try to run into the future to get more conditions of happiness. We don't believe that we already have more than enough conditions for happiness. Every breath, every step taken in mindfulness helps us to stop this running. We have the habit of running into the future to look for something, even during our sleep, and this habit energy is very strong. The practice of mindfulness means to become aware of our habit energy, to recognize it, and smile to it. When we can do this, the habit energy cannot push us to run anymore.

The art of handling happiness and suffering is very important. That is what we want teachers to teach in school so they may suffer less in their family, with their friends, and in their relationships with their students and colleagues, in their community, and in the world—and so they can also help their students to suffer less. If we try to run away from our suffering, we have no chance to understand and transform it. We can even speak about the goodness of suffering. If we know how to embrace our suffering, to hold it tenderly, and to look deeply into it, then we will be able to generate the energy of compassion and understanding, which are the foundation of true happiness.

The Insight of Interbeing

My students and I have come up with five mindfulness trainings that can be considered to be a kind of global ethic. They do not have to be the precepts or the commandments of any religion, and anyone can adhere to them or verify the value or truth in them. These trainings can help us to practice mindfulness all day long: to protect life, to practice true happiness, true love, deep listening and loving speech, and mindful consumption. If we follow these trainings, we are able to handle our suffering and our happiness, restore communication, and help the family, the community, and the world to suffer less. These trainings are very concrete practices, and not theory. Practicing like this we can have a lot of joy, happiness, and peace.

This ethic is based on the insight of interbeing.

"Interbeing" means that you cannot be by yourself alone—you have to inter-be with everything else. Suppose we look at a rose deeply with mindfulness and concentration. In a short time, we discover that a rose is made of only non-rose elements. What do we see in a rose? We see a cloud, because we know that if there is no cloud there will be no rain and no rose can grow. A cloud is a non-rose element that can be recognized in the rose. The sunshine, which is crucial for a rose to grow, is also a non-rose element that is there in the rose. If we remove the cloud and the sunshine from the rose, there is no rose left. Continuing like that we see many other non-rose elements within the rose, including minerals, the soil, the gardener, and so on. The whole cosmos has come together to produce a wonder called rose. A rose cannot be by herself alone. A rose has to inter-be with the whole cosmos. That is the insight we call interbeing.

Happiness is the same. Happiness is a kind of rose: it is made of only non-happiness elements. If you try to throw away all the non-happiness elements you will never have happiness. It's like when you grow lotus flowers—you need the mud. Looking deeply into the lotus flower, you see the mud. You cannot grow lotus flowers on marble. A lotus is made only of non-lotus elements, and happiness is made of non-happiness elements. That is the nature of interbeing. Everything is in everything else. We cannot really run away from one thing to grab onto another thing, because things are inside of each other, not outside of each other. We must abandon our dualistic way of looking at things.

From this insight, we see clearly that happiness is not an individual matter. If we understand our suffering, and we are skillful enough to make good use of our suffering, then we can create happiness. That is the vision of interbeing: happiness and suffering inter-are.

When we look at our planet, we see that humans are also made only of non-human elements. Looking into ourselves, into our body, we see that we are made of non-human elements: minerals, animals, plants, and so on. If we remove all these non-human elements, the human race disappears. That is why to protect humanity, you must protect the non-human elements. That is the deepest kind of ecological teaching. The five mindfulness trainings are a kind of behavior, a kind of lifestyle, that is based on this insight of interbeing. They are a very concrete expression of the practice of mindfulness. If we ourselves, and the young people, live according to these five trainings, then happiness is possible, compassion is possible, healing is possible. A schoolteacher should embody that kind of mindful living, that kind of compassion and understanding. This will help the young generation tremendously in their transformation and healing.

Nothing can be by itself alone. Everything must rely on everything else to exist. The insight of interbeing helps us to remove the notion of a separate self, and that helps us to remove the complexes that are at the ground of suffering. You don't compare yourself to anyone anymore. Most suffering is born from wrong perceptions like this, and that is why restoring communication within ourselves and with others is crucial to reducing suffering.

A Community of Interbeing

Everyone can practice mindful breathing to release the pain and tension in his or her body. Anyone can practice mindful breathing or mindful walking to touch the wonders of life in them and around them, to recognize that they have enough conditions of happiness to be happy right here and right now. Everyone can practice mindfulness to be able to take care of a strong emotion, like fear, anger, or despair. Everyone can practice compassionate listening and loving speech to help restore communication and to bring about reconciliation.

Let's dream about building a community among the colleagues and personnel of our institution. There must be two, three, or four people with whom you can communicate better, right? You should talk with them first about the happiness and suffering you see in yourself and in your school.

These people will see your transformation and healing: you are fresh, compassionate, and smiling. You can talk with them, and get together more often with them to be able to continue the practice, not only on your own or as a family, but as a community. Building a community of practice is absolutely necessary! You can do walking meditation together, drink tea together, have a session of total relaxation together, and, by doing so, create a small community consisting of happy teachers. And it is these happy teachers who will change the world.

With this little community, you will be able change the whole institution. You can write a letter, saying: "We are a group of people who have changed our lives, at home and at work. We think that if you could join us that would be wonderful." Your colleagues can then start to taste this peace, brotherhood and sisterhood, and relaxation for themselves.

We cannot go on with things as they are now. If teachers are unhappy, if they do not have harmony and peace with each other, how will they help young people to suffer less and to succeed in their work?

Every teacher should be a community builder. The teacher has a noble, beautiful, and respectable job, but without a community he or she cannot do much. So, dear friends, please make good use of this book, written and compiled together with educator and mindfulness practitioner Katherine Weare and my students. In it, teachers who have been touched by this practice tell us how they water the seeds of mindfulness in themselves and others to create happy teachers, classrooms, schools, and universities. Please share it with your colleagues. The teachings and methods presented here have been used in our retreats for educators and in work in educational settings around the world; Katherine uses her insight and experience as a teacher to present them in a way that makes them clear and easy for you to put into practice right away in your own life as well as in your classrooms, schools, and universities.

May we have the time and the opportunity to practice all of this together soon. I wish you a good and happy practice!

Thich Nhat Hanh
Plum Village, France
October 2014

preface
a vision for education
THE PLUM VILLAGE COMMUNITY

happiness is possible

When Zen Master Thich Nhat Hanh picked up his calligraphy brush in a simple wooden hut on a hill in southwest France in 2011 and wrote the words, "Happy teachers will change the world," it was not just wishful thinking. It was a powerful insight based on the evidence of a lifetime of spiritual practice and teaching.

Thich Nhat Hanh has devoted his teaching career to creatively applying the power of mindfulness to the challenges of our times. The goal of education is to provide an environment where both students and teachers can grow and blossom, learning skills to lead happy, healthy, creative, balanced, and meaningful lives. When a teacher knows the art of transforming difficulties and cultivating happiness in daily life, then it will benefit their family, colleagues, and students right away. Thich Nhat Hanh has said that the greatest talent of all is "the talent of knowing how to be happy." And "happiness," he says, "is a habit that each of us needs to learn."

In this book, Thich Nhat Hanh and his community in Plum Village, France, and at centers all over the world, offer inspiration and guidance for educators at all levels of education, in a practical, nonreligious, and nonsectarian way. Aware that happy teachers make happy students, this book offers mindfulness practices to help educators and their students become more in tune with themselves, bringing awareness to body and mind, to be able to reduce tension and develop confidence, clarity, compassion, ease, and joy. An educator who knows how to take care of body and mind, how to cultivate joy and happiness, how to reduce stress and handle difficult emotions, is someone who displays resilience and compassion. Such a teacher will be able to help his or her students do the same.

The focus of this book is to offer effective methods for educators to apply mindfulness in their own daily lives and the lives of their colleagues and their students, helping to create a more loving, peaceful, and supportive learning environment where there is mutual trust, communication, and understanding in classrooms, schools, and universities.

mindfulness is a path not a tool

Thich Nhat Hanh has demonstrated that the true practice of mindfulness cannot be devoid of a spiritual or ethical dimension. For this reason, in Plum Village the practice of mindfulness is taught not as a tool, but as a path. Mindfulness is a way of living that we are always cultivating and deepening. Mindfulness is not a means to arrive at an end; it is not a tool for us to use to get better outcomes later—whether those outcomes are greater happiness or improved grades. Along the path it is possible to touch happiness, peace, and well-being right away, in every moment of our mindfulness practice, even if we are a beginner. This book therefore draws on the ethics underlying true mindfulness practice, offering us a guide on to how to build a happy, healthy, and compassionate community within our classrooms, schools, and universities.

As Thich Nhat Hanh said in a talk to teachers at a retreat at Plum Village in June, 2014,

> Administrators may be attracted to mindfulness because they think it will improve academic performance and prevent teachers burning out. But the practice of mindfulness can do much more. The practice of right mindfulness can help both teachers and students suffer less; they will be able to improve communication and create a learning environment that is more compassionate and understanding. Students can learn very important things, such as how to handle strong emotions, how to take care of anger, how to relax and release tension, how to restore communication and reconcile with others. What's the use of learning if that learning doesn't bring you happiness? The practice of right mindfulness can bring about a deep change both in the classroom and the wider education system, so we can educate people in such a way that they can be truly happy. If, while doing so, the students can learn more easily and quickly, and educators can avoid burning out, that is also wonderful.[1]

a lifetime of teaching

Thich Nhat Hanh is respected throughout the world for his inspiring teachings and bestselling writings on the art of mindfulness. He was a leading pioneer in bringing mindfulness to the US and Europe, giving lectures on mindfulness at the universities of Princeton, Columbia, and Cornell, as early as the 1960s. From the war in Vietnam to his global teaching career, which he continued tirelessly until his stroke in 2014, Thich Nhat Hanh has continually sought innovative ways to apply the practices of mindfulness, concentration, and insight to contemporary challenges. His key teaching is that, through mindfulness, we can learn to live happily in the present moment—the only way to truly develop peace and happiness, both in oneself and in the world.

Born in central Vietnam in 1926, Thich Nhat Hanh became a novice monk at the age of sixteen. In the 1950s, amidst the turmoil of war, Thich Nhat Hanh and his friends began to explore how to apply the essence of the teachings and practices they had learned into the fields of politics, economics, education and humanitarian work. They published radical magazines, taught new courses at institutes, and even founded an experimental new school for children in the central highlands on the Dalat plateau. They started the School of Youth for Social Service (SYSS), a grassroots relief organization with thousands of students, based on the principles of nonviolence and compassionate action, and the Van Hanh Buddhist University, which offered a groundbreaking new curriculum for young monastics. With each endeavor, Thich Nhat Hanh was determined to explore how wisdom, compassion, and true community could be cultivated in education and in society.

In 1966, after daring to make a tour of the US and Europe to call for peace in Vietnam, Thich Nhat Hanh was exiled. He continued his tireless efforts to call for peace and traveled widely in the US and Europe, speaking personally with politicians and leading a Vietnamese delegation at the Paris Peace Talks. From a distance, he continued his work supporting the SYSS and leading programs to bring aid to war victims and to sponsor orphaned refugee children. He was nominated for the Nobel Peace Prize in 1967 by Dr. Martin Luther King. In the 1970s, he led a program to rescue boat people from the high seas in Southeast Asia. Mindfulness practice supported Thich Nhat Hanh's engaged action, and he wrote his classic text, *The Miracle of Mindfulness*, in 1975 in the midst of these efforts.

mindfulness and community

As refugees in France, Thich Nhat Hanh and his Paris Peace Talks team were first based in a small apartment in Paris, then at a small rural farmstead in the Forêt d'Othe, before they eventually found and purchased a dilapidated farm in southwest

France. There, the Plum Village community started to bloom and to open its doors to visitors eager to discover meditation and the art of mindful living. Thich Nhat Hanh began to give lectures and retreats for families, teachers, businessmen, politicians, scientists, psychotherapists, war veterans, police officers and, beginning in 2003, for Israelis and Palestinians.

Since its founding in 1982, the Plum Village community has grown into what is today the West's largest international mindfulness and meditation practice center, with over two hundred residential monastics and thousands of guests every year. As Thich Nhat Hanh became more internationally renowned, he was invited on teaching tours around the world. He has addressed the United States Congress, the parliaments of the UK, Northern Ireland, and India, UNESCO, the World Bank, and the World Parliament of Religions. In the last fifteen years he has founded residential monastic practice centers in California, New York, Vietnam, Paris, Hong Kong, Thailand, Mississippi, Australia, and Germany. There are now over 2,000 local mindfulness groups in the Plum Village tradition meeting regularly in towns and cities around the world. Over sixty of these are groups of young people in the Wake Up Movement, actively engaged in contributing to a healthier, more compassionate society.

When in 2008 Thich Nhat Hanh began developing an international training program for teachers to bring mindfulness into educational contexts such as schools and universities in Europe, North America, and Asia, it was a natural continuation of his lifelong efforts to make education meaningful, joyful, and transformative for teachers and students alike. With extensive experience leading retreats for over thirty years, Thich Nhat Hanh and his community have developed and refined a rich, creative, and effective range of practices for transmitting mindfulness to educators and young people. In the course of his teaching career, Thich Nhat Hanh has used the imagery of a poet, the insight of a Zen master, and the playfulness of a child to develop creative ways to share mindfulness teachings and practices with children and young people, their parents and teachers. In 1987, in a retreat in Santa Barbara, California, he devised his famous four-part "Pebble Meditation" for children, now a classic meditation exercise popular around the world. He has used a plant of corn to teach children about interbeing, and the story of a cloud to teach them about impermanence, dying, and continuation, and the story of his two hands and a hammer to teach them about inclusiveness and nondiscrimination. He has shown that even the youngest children can learn to cultivate love and understanding—the core elements at the very foundation of ethics.

wake up schools

In 2008, as part of his response to the urban riots that had shaken France in previous years, then-President Nicolas Sarkozy launched a new policy of "civic and moral education" in French schools, to help contribute toward a more ethical society. But it soon became clear that many teachers were not sure what to teach in those classes.

"We have some suggestions," said Thich Nhat Hanh at the time, and he instructed his students to submit a proposal to the President on the kind of "applied ethics" Plum Village had already been sharing with children, teens, and teachers since the 1980s. For Thich Nhat Hanh, learning how to relax, how to be truly present and mindful, how to concentrate, how to cultivate compassion, and how to practice loving speech and deep listening, are all concrete, teachable practices of "applied ethics" that have the capacity not only to tackle the roots of violence and injustice but also to bring profound, enduring happiness and well-being to individuals, schools, families, and society.

Since Wake Up Schools was set in motion in 2011, Thich Nhat Hanh and the Plum Village community have led Educators Retreats and training programs several times a year in the US, France, Germany, Spain, the UK, Bhutan, Canada, Korea, Hong Kong, Thailand, and India. Teacher training is now being developed; the first stage of the Wake Up Schools training enables teachers to embody the practice, and the second stage focuses on sharing mindfulness practices with their students and school communities. (You can find details about how to contact Wake Up Schools and the practice centers in "What Next" at the end of the book.)

In September 2008, Thich Nhat Hanh and his students led a groundbreaking training retreat for over five hundred teachers in Dehradun, in the foothills of the Himalayas of northern India, developing these ideas further. When he met Sonia Gandhi a few weeks later in Delhi, education and teacher training were at the top of their agenda. Thich Nhat Hanh continued to develop his teachings on Applied Ethics, and in 2011 announced a new initiative to develop and share these Plum Village practices more widely. "Wake Up Schools," as it came to be known, offers training that has its roots in Plum Village teachings and insights and is nonreligious and nonsectarian.

Today Wake Up Schools operates from Plum Village in France, and offers retreats, training programs, classroom content, and a community network to support the happiness, personal development, and well-being of teachers, administrators, students, and parents. Wake Up Schools is guided by Thich Nhat Hanh's students and is sustained by an active international community of educators and volunteers who are long-standing mindfulness practitioners in the Plum Village tradition.

The Wake Up Schools program aims to provide an ethical foundation for teachers, promote an atmosphere of concentration and social-emotional learning in schools and universities, and support teachers' mindfulness and well-being. The program recognizes that educational environments are becoming ever more stressful, with increasing demands placed on teachers and staff; meanwhile, social and economic pressures have brought new challenges to family life. This makes it very important for educators to be able to cultivate their own happiness, mindfulness, and well-being, so they can help children and young adults develop the skills they need to handle challenges and pressures and to find more joy in their daily life right now. By embodying mindfulness, concentration, joy, and peace, educators can bring happiness, stability, and clarity to their community. With the energy of mindfulness and compassion, the classroom, the school, or university can become like a family where students, especially those from disadvantaged backgrounds, can have a second chance. Gradually, educational communities can become agents of personal and social growth for students, teachers, and the world.

This whole book is inspired by Thich Nhat Hanh's vision of bringing happiness, well-being and peace to educators, students, and society. Thich Nhat Hanh has taught dozens of retreats for educators around the world, and eagerly oversaw the initial stages of work on this book, up until his stroke in November 2014.

During these Educators Retreats Thich Nhat Hanh delivered many hours of talks and question and answer sessions, which inspired the hearts and minds of the thousands who attended. Here, for the first time, educators have an opportunity to profit from the transcripts of those teachings, edited into extracts that form the core of the book by a team of monks and nuns who worked closely with him in these retreats. They have distilled the essence of Thich Nhat Hanh's teachings, experience, and vision that he was so keen to share, and which forms a vital part of his legacy for the world.

The Plum Village community
Plum Village, France
October 2016

preface
the plum village contribution to the field of mindfulness in education

KATHERINE WEARE

I have the privilege of being coauthor of this book and an educator by profession. As such, I hope here to bring an educator's perspective to the study of mindfulness and to the Plum Village approach. After starting my professional career as a teacher in high school, for forty years I have been involved in development and research in the fields of well-being, happiness, mental health, and social and emotional learning, in schools and universities. I added an interest in mindfulness, compassion, and contemplative studies to my research and practice about fifteen years ago. My own route to mindfulness was inspired by trying to cope with an episode of serious illness, which moved rapidly to the realization that mindfulness could transform my relationship with myself and with the many, mostly self-inflicted, challenges of my overstuffed life. It is gratifying to see this whole field, from well-being to mindfulness, now becoming more mainstream, in some parts of the world at least.

how this book came about

Meeting with the Plum Village lay and monastic community at the Educators Retreat in London in 2012, I was struck by the depth, breadth, and authenticity their approach brings to this whole field, and delighted to be invited to help write this book. Here I would like to sketch out the intentions of the book, the educational landscape to which it relates, and to explore what I feel the Plum Village approach is adding to this rapidly moving and expanding field of human enquiry and endeavor.

This book sprouted from a seed planted when a large gathering of keen students of Thich Nhat Hanh, many of them very eminent practitioners, packed into a small room during an Educators Retreat in London in April, 2012. We were discussing what the lay community could do next to best support the development of Thich Nhat Hanh's vision of mindfulness in education. We were all aware of how mindfulness and contemplative approaches in education—in schools and increasingly in universities—were growing exponentially across the world, as reflected in the proliferation of research, programs, training, publications, and conferences.

The Plum Village community was already involved in a great deal of activity around mindfulness and applied ethics in education, with a strong, largely word-of-mouth, reputation for seminal, inspirational, and authentic work, through their Educators Retreats in particular. Within all this activity there was as yet no definitive written guidance from Thich Nhat Hanh or the community on how best to help teachers cultivate mindfulness in their own lives, as well as in their classrooms in schools and universities, using a clearly authoritative and canonical approach. We became determined to put this right.

The initial intentions for the book were modest. A small group of monastics and laypeople identified what the community felt constituted the core practices of the Plum Village approach. We planned a simple set of laminated "recipe cards" summarizing step-by-step how to practice them oneself and teach them to others. They aimed to be succinct and useable for those new to the teachings. (These principles of brevity and practicality remain at the heart of the core practices in Part One. A set of practice sheets summarizing the core practices can be found in Appendix A.)

Once we began, the vision and aspirations for the book grew steadily until it became the substantial guidebook you now have in your hands.

We noted the valuable resource that are the words and vision of Thich Nhat Hanh, in particular his talks, which held audiences rapt at the Educators Retreats. These had not yet appeared in print and we were keen to include them in the book. You will find them at the start of the book, and at the beginning of each of the chapters in Part One.

using examples from teachers

We also wanted to support Thich Nhat Hanh's inspirational vision by responding to the many requests for practical guidance from teachers on developing mindfulness in their own lives, as well as in their classrooms, schools, and universities. We completed the step-by-step accounts of the practices, but became more ambitious. Convinced that there was a great deal of solid work happening that we could marshal to support teachers, we decided to inform our guidance with a systematic exploration of how the teachings had already impacted the lives and work of the teachers who were practicing in the Plum Village approach. Harvesting these experiences was a foray into the unknown that turned out to have unexpectedly rich rewards, and which profoundly shaped the nature and content of the book.

Initially we identified and contacted around seventy experienced practitioners who had been involved in the Plum Village approach to education over many years, and asked them to share their stories with us. Some stories they had already published in *The Mindfulness Bell* (the official magazine of the community) but most accounts were kindly written afresh or told to us in interview. We also conducted an online survey in French, English, and Spanish with those who had signed up to receive information about Wake Up Schools, and posted the invitation to the survey on the Mindfulness in Education (MiEN) listserv and the Wake Up Schools website. We trawled *The Mindfulness Bell* for further articles on practicing in educational contexts. We gathered responses after various Educators Retreats and training courses across the world. Some communities, such as in Italy and India, we engaged through word of mouth and email. Essentially we reached out to anyone in education, right across the world, wherever we had a lead and a contact. We received a wealth of responses, and around one hundred fifty people are finally quoted in the book. All who responded are listed at the end of the book, although a few wished to remain anonymous, and we could not use everything we received.

Thich Nhat Hanh is often called "Thay" by his students and you will read this in some of the examples. The word originally means "teacher" in Vietnamese, but has in effect become his nickname.

We sought first-person stories, reflections, and illustrative examples of how the teachings of Thich Nhat Hanh and/or Plum Village had touched teachers' lives and their teaching. We queried the teachers about the effect of mindfulness on themselves and their students, how they taught the practices, whether they had managed to work with colleagues across the school and university and reach out to parents, and what resources they found useful. We asked them to stick only to what they could attribute clearly to the Plum Village tradition, not to mindfulness more generally or other approaches.

The process took two years. As the replies came in, we categorized them by a process of content and thematic analysis, and over time the replies themselves shaped the structure and content of the book. So the resultant book is not abstract speculation, but a reflection of the solid reality, from the ground up, of what is actually happening to teachers in schools and universities, which we can clearly attribute to the inspirational and highly practical teachings of Thich Nhat Hanh and the Plum Village community.

what the plum village approach brings to the educational landscape

It has been my role in coauthoring this book to attempt to lead our efforts to set the vision of mindfulness and the examples from the teachers into a framework of practical guidance on how to cultivate mindfulness in our lives and in our everyday work in schools and universities. As an educational practitioner and academic, I was able to help us bring together our thinking on linking the Plum Village approach to mindfulness with ongoing educational concerns, interests, and research evidence. We developed this guidance and chose these areas not just on the basis of theory and research, but also on the actual responses of the teachers we contacted.

In the following introduction to the practices, I will explore what, in my view, the Plum Village approach brings to the overall picture of mindfulness in schools and the surrounding educational landscape. These are very much my personal reflections as an educator, but, while they do not pretend to represent any kind of official Plum Village view on mindfulness in education, they have been reached after considerable contact with the teachings and lengthy discussions with those involved in the approach. I offer them in the hope they will help our understanding of the context in which this approach has become so popular, valuable, and accessible to teachers in today's world.

a shift in focus toward positivity and well-being

The world appears to be facing a crisis in mental health, particularly among the young. Across the globe, mental health problems are the leading cause of non-fatal illness, contributing around a quarter of the total disease burden.[1] Depression, anxiety, self-harm, suicide, and violent, aggressive behavior would appear to be on the rise, coupled with a less dramatic but pervasive sense of stress and dissatisfaction. Addressing this epidemic is made difficult by the shame and stigma that surround mental illness: people find it hard to talk about for fear of being thought weak or feeling blamed or ostracized.

How can we manage our unhappiness and stress, and, more positively, how can we achieve greater happiness? This is the perennial human question. Given how long we have striven to solve this puzzle and the apparently increasing mess we appear to be in, it is clearly not an easy one to answer. However, the growing science of happiness and well-being[2] is offering us some clues. Recent shifts in thinking and growing research evidence very much resonate with the wisdom represented by Thich Nhat Hanh and the Plum Village approach.

There is a new emphasis on the positive in approaches to human development. It is discernible in the increasingly widespread use of terms such as "well-being," "positive psychology," "positive mental health," "thriving," and "flourishing." This positive shift recognizes that the focus of enquiry has for too long concentrated almost entirely on what is *wrong* with people by way of mental health difficulties and suffering, rather than also exploring what is *right,* including the strengths and resilience that can help us address these problems.

Those who work in education are talking increasingly about the expanding role of universities and schools, away from a narrow focus on academic learning only, to a more expansive view of what helps people to thrive and flourish, based on the cultivation of sound human values and solid secular ethics. They are using words such as "pro-sociability," "connectedness," "mental, emotional and social health/learning/skills," "emotional intelligence," "character," "values," "morals," "ethics," "non-cognitive/soft skills," "life skills," "well-being," and "happiness." Research is establishing a clear link between this agenda and academic attainment.[3]

cultivating happiness to alleviate suffering

Thich Nhat Hanh and the Plum Village community bring a skillfully balanced approach to address the ongoing riddle of achieving human happiness. As Thich Nhat Hanh acknowledges in his letter at the start of this book, "With mindfulness, concentration, and insight, you are capable of generating a feeling of joy and happiness whenever you want. With the energy of mindfulness, you can also handle a painful feeling or emotion. If you do not have the energy of mindfulness, you will be afraid of being overwhelmed by the pain and suffering inside."

Thich Nhat Hanh has a realistic view of the darker side of humanity, lurking as "seeds" of potential anger and violence in our "store consciousness" alongside the seeds of potential happiness and goodness. The outcome depends on which seeds we "water." Research on evolutionary psychology is suggesting that the human race appears to have not been dealt the best of hands by our evolutionary past, and that many of us are fundamentally prone to some slants of mind such as a "negativity bias" that cause us to tend toward rumination, pessimism, worry, anger, over-planning, and hypervigilance. These tendencies may have once kept us safe as a prey species surviving in dangerous environments, and allowed the gloomiest and most aggressive among us to pass on our genes, but they no longer serve us well in helping us to get along together or meet the modern challenges of a pressurized and hyper-connected age.[4] If we are to live a happy and compassionate life we need to take positive action.

We cannot restlessly strive or buy our way from suffering to happiness. Positive frames of mind are not reliably achieved through ever more acquisition, higher status, and achievement, nor even by "good things" happening to us. Once we have enough for our basic needs, adding more does not bring a commensurate rise in emotional well-being.[5]

The core message of the Plum Village approach—that we need to cultivate authentic happiness from within—turns out to be well founded. Research suggests that happiness can be reliably developed by increasing our sense of connection with others, cultivating altruism and compassion, savoring the present, accepting with equanimity what cannot be changed, and building a sense of meaning and purpose in our lives. It is also enhanced by mindfulness, as we see later in the chapter when we look at the evidence.

A concern for cultivating the well-being and happiness of the whole person in education is not a modern invention—Aristotle is reputed to have said that "Educating the mind without educating the heart is no education at all." But it has gone out of favor, as schools are asked to focus on matters of the intellect and on chasing test results, often driven by an agenda of national economic growth and standing within a competitive global economy. Now, across the world, teachers in an increasing number of mainstream schools and universities are starting to feel this trend has gone too far and are taking steps to broaden their mission. They are attempting to do more to foster the skills and states of mind that will help their students and teachers develop as fully rounded human beings, in touch with their emotions, skilled at making relationships, with a sense of responsibility and purpose that helps them flourish, thrive, and be happy in the present. The Plum Village approach is fitting in very well in supporting this shift of emphasis to a more holistic approach.

You will read in this book accounts of visionary teachers, and even of a number of whole schools, who are putting the cultivation of happiness and well-being at the heart of their teaching, with the help of mindfulness, and inspired by the Plum Village approach. Many are finding that such a move enhances academic learning and that there need be no conflict between these intentions. We explore the links between mindfulness and learning in chapter ten.

the growth of mindfulness meditation

The tradition that inspired Thich Nhat Hanh to create what is now a firmly secular approach to the cultivation of human happiness has a direct lineage of 2,500 years of practice and study in the countries of Asia. The 1970s saw a wave of interest and activity in bringing mindfulness and meditation practices to the West. Within these developments, the pioneering work of Thich Nhat Hanh in the US and Europe and the publication of his accessible and popular *The Miracle of Mindfulness* in 1975, was highly influential, as is outlined in the earlier preface on the history of mindfulness by the Plum Village community.

Beginning in the late 1970s, Jon Kabat-Zinn, supported by others, led the way in exploring the scientific basis for meditation and in making mindfulness meditation highly accessible. This approach focused particularly on the development of short courses, which in turn enabled mindfulness to be constructed as specific "interventions," which have the advantage that they can easily be subjected to western scientific research methods, most notably the randomized control trial.[6] Over the last thirty years or so, mindfulness-based interventions, under titles such as Mindfulness-Based Stress Reduction (MBSR), and accompanied by a growing evidence base, has spread into all kinds of contexts, beginning initially in the health sector, and now moving into almost every conceivable social, occupational, and personal context, including schools and universities. Mindfulness meditation for children and young people has spread rapidly in some parts of the world, and we now have a wealth of programs, interventions, and accompanying research in educational, health care, parenting, and community settings.

Bringing mindfulness to the breath, the body, to movement, eating, and walking, as well as to cultivating an attitude of open-minded and kindly curiosity about our own experience, are all practices that are now widely taught. They are all practices that Thich Nhat Hanh has inherited and honed and taught for his long lifetime, before mindfulness became popularized, a popularization to which he has indeed contributed greatly. Now that the practices have attracted a great deal of scientific attention, we have a rapidly developing evidence base that suggests mindfulness meditation is of considerable practical use.[7]

I will attempt to give an overview of the scientific evidence base for the effectiveness of mindfulness meditation. I am an academic by trade, so my cautious tone may well contrast with the current hype for mindfulness we sometimes read, particularly in the popular media. In the Plum Village spirit of "no need to hurry," let us celebrate what we know so far about the benefits of mindfulness meditation, without claiming to know more than we do, and remain content to know there is still a long path ahead.

the benefits of mindfulness for teachers

Mindfulness programs for teachers are developing rapidly, some connected with school- and university-based programs and some with teacher education.[8] In a recent authoritative *Handbook of Mindfulness in Education*,[9] half the chapters are concerned with developing the personal mindfulness of the educators themselves, to further their own happiness and well-being, not just so they can teach mindfulness to students. The basic wisdom of the Plum Village approach, that we begin with the teacher, is increasingly being recognized.

Research with teachers echoes the solid evidence base that has built up over the last thirty-five years on the effects of mindfulness meditation in general. In adults, mindfulness meditation has impacts on a very wide range of mental and physical health problems, especially on depression and anxiety, on social and emotional skills, on learning and cognition, on lived experience and performance of various kinds, and on many indicators of quality of life and well-being in a wide range of settings. The research base is summarized in a recent review by Khoury et al.[10] Studies consistently show a clear link between the amount of practice students are prepared to do and the degree of benefit they gain. The accumulated findings on the effect of mindfulness with adults are now generally accepted as convincing, so we can be reasonably certain that we are on stable ground, scientifically speaking.

The evidence that follows next on the specific value of mindfulness meditation for teachers comes from a recent review of this area.[11] It is as yet a small evidence base, and so we should treat it with caution, but it is growing rapidly.

Teachers who study mindfulness tend to experience fewer mental health problems, such as stress, depression, and anxiety. They report greater well-being, including a sense of calmness, life satisfaction, self-confidence, and self-compassion. They show an increase in kindness and compassion for themselves and for others, with greater empathy, tolerance, forgiveness, and patience, and less anger and hostility. Their cognitive performance improves, including their ability to pay attention and focus, make decisions, and respond flexibly to challenges. They make better teachers, showing higher levels of classroom management and organization, with a greater ability to prioritize, to see the whole picture, and to be more self-motivated and autonomous. They are more attuned to their students' needs, and achieve more supportive relationships with them. They also tend to have better physical health, including lower blood pressure, declines in cortisol (a stress hormone), and fewer reported physical health problems and days off work.

The examples offered by the teachers cited in this book touch on all of these areas of benefit. You will hear about increased self-care and self-compassion, of greater empathy and attunement to others, of an enhanced ability to take things slowly, to let things go, and to keep a balanced perspective, and of reduced stress and negative judgment of oneself and other people.

the benefits of mindfulness for children and young people

Promising results are also emerging from research on mindfulness with children and young people, in a range of settings including health care and education. The evidence base is again still relatively small and we have a very long way to go, but it is a good start. The results below are again taken from a recent review.[12]

When taught well, mindfulness can improve the mental, emotional, social, and physical health and well-being of young people. These effects are particularly strong in reducing mental health problems, especially for children with more serious levels of difficulty.[13] Mindfulness can reduce depression, stress, anxiety, reactivity, and difficult behavior. It can improve well-being, and bring about greater calmness, relaxation, and sleep. It increases the ability to manage emotions, and increases self-awareness, self-esteem, and empathy. Mindfulness also has a clear impact on academic achievement,[14] improving learning by contributing to the development of cognitive and performance skills and executive function. It seems to help by enabling young people to pay greater attention, be more focused, think in more innovative ways, use existing knowledge more effectively, improve working memory, and enhance planning, problem solving, and reasoning skills. So far no adverse effects (examples of harm) have been reported.

In our investigations for this book we were not able to ask students directly—that is work for another time—but the reports of changes in students in the testimony of the Plum Village teachers supports many of these findings. You will hear stories of students being calmer, more relaxed, happier, less depressed and anxious, more in control of their thoughts and behavior, kinder towards themselves and others, expressing gratitude and compassion, better able to alleviate their own suffering and cope with the challenges of learning and examinations, peer relations, and family life.

the evidence from neuroscience on the impact of mindfulness on the brain

There has been a surge of neuroscience research around mindfulness meditation. We now know that the structure and function of the brain is by no means fixed in childhood, and brains remain "neuroplastic"—that is, changeable—throughout our lives. An increasing number of brain imaging/MRI studies are suggesting that mindfulness meditation reliably and profoundly alters the structure and function of the brain to improve the quality of both thought and feeling. To simplify drastically a highly complex subject, mindfulness meditation appears to reshape some vital neural pathways, increasing the density and complexity of connections in areas associated with cognitive abilities, such as attention, self-awareness, and introspection, and with emotional areas connected with kindness, compassion, and rationality. It decreases activity and growth in those areas involved in anxiety, hostility, worry, and impulsivity.[15, 16] Although the most striking changes are observable in long-term meditators, mindfulness interventions of just a few weeks have shown clear and visible impacts on brain function and performance.[17]

These findings echo the first-person examples you will read from teachers who contributed their accounts of their experience of the effects of Plum Village meditation. They talk of feeling that they know themselves and their own habits and motives better, experience more compassion and less hostility and judgment toward others, have an increased ability to be calm and patient, are less impulsive, and experience greater rationality with a better sense of perspective.

plum village and the research evidence

The kind of meditative practices explored by the research are essentially the same as some Plum Village core practices, focusing on such practices as mindfulness of the breath, of sitting, walking, eating, the body, movement, and cultivating kindness and compassion toward others and toward ourselves. As I have indicated, the details of the effects of mindfulness described in the research literature closely echo the first-person accounts of the Plum Village teachers about their own experience and that of their students. So while we have not yet specifically published scientific evidence coming from the Plum Village practices themselves (although some is now in progress) we can have reasonable confidence that positive effects will be likely to flow from engagement with Plum Village meditative practices, so long as we build our practice slowly and steadily.

a solid ethical purpose

As mindfulness meditation has become more popular a concern has arisen not to dismiss the overall ethical system from which it evolved, which was intended to help people live their whole life with compassion and kindness, freed from over-obsession with possessions and achievements. The Plum Village approach provides us with a clear and useful example that manages to be not only strictly secular, popular with ordinary teachers, and of practical use, but also explicitly based in ethics. This approach attracts thousands of people, not only because it is engaged in helping us deal with our twenty-first century challenges, but also because it is clearly inspired by a deep ethical and social purpose, which many who come to it find a compelling feature.

The practices offered in this book do indeed help all of us, including teachers and students, become calmer and more focused to work and learn more effectively. But more fundamentally they are also and quite explicitly a path of human transformation intended to bring about a more equitable, sustainable, and compassionate society. Thich Nhat Hanh tells us, in his letter at the start of this book, that he sees the goal of education as being to "form human beings, to construct a worthy, beautiful human race, in order to take care of our precious planet." Realizing this clear ethical purpose through our mindfulness practice, our lives, and our teaching and learning, is a thread that runs strongly through this book, including in the lived examples offered by the teachers.

a broad-based, contemplative approach

Thich Nhat Hanh sets out his own vision of mindfulness very clearly in his "Letter to a Young Teacher" that begins this book. His deep and broad use of the term *mindfulness* is rather different to the narrow way in which the term is often used in modern contexts, and closely parallels the term *contemplative practices*. Contemplative practices have been defined as "the ways that human beings, across cultures and across time have found to concentrate, broaden, and deepen conscious awareness as the gateway to cultivating their full potential and to leading more fulfilling lives."[18] It is proving particularly fruitful in higher education, where its style and language fit well within academic culture, giving rise to a thriving field of research, courses, and publications.[19] Contemplative education includes many areas in addition to meditation and compassion, such as volunteering, social action, creativity, art, poetry, and mindful movement, and overlaps considerably with the broad, socially engaged nature of the Plum Village approach.

deepening social and emotional learning

Social and emotional learning (SEL) is a term that relates strongly to mindfulness. SEL has a solid evidence base, including links with improved academic learning as well as with well-being, which has helped it to become more prominent in many mainstream schools and universities. SEL aims to help us learn the skills of understanding and managing ourselves and our feelings, and relating to other people. CASEL,[20] a large US network which is very active in this field, suggests that there are five areas of skill development: self-awareness, self/emotional management, responsible decision-making, relationship skills, and social awareness/empathy.

There has been a good deal of discussion on the relationship between SEL and mindfulness. Given its aims and areas of skill development, SEL can be a natural supportive home for mindfulness, while the embodied nature of mindfulness practice grounds the sometimes goal-oriented, wordy, and cerebral tendencies of SEL.[21] Mindfulness is often seen as the "missing piece" or "key" that can help ensure that the ambitious aims of SEL are realized, not just in words, thoughts, and future intentions, but in the here and now, impacting on hearts, bodies, and actions.

You will read of Plum Village teachers who are already successfully integrating these two areas. The broad and engaged nature of the Plum Village approach makes it particularly well placed to bring SEL and mindfulness together in synergy. Its clear focus on ethics, gratitude, and mindful consumption addresses the skills of responsible decision-making, directly and explicitly. The relational practices of sharing, listening deeply, and loving speech directly cultivate core skills for relationships and social awareness. The more meditative practices of awareness of breath, body, and the embodied practice of embracing of strong emotions develop an ability to remain calm and present, grounded and with focused attention.

a comprehensive, whole school approach

In his "Letter to a Young Teacher" Thich Nhat Hanh talks of the vital importance of building a *"community of practice,"* and in their preface the Plum Village community reminds us, "the goal of education is to provide a whole environment where both students and teachers can grow and blossom, learning skills to lead happy, healthy, creative, balanced, and meaningful lives."

This emphasis on cultivating mindfulness within one's community and work environment, and not just in the individual classroom, relates strongly to the increasing interest across education for what is variously called a "school- or university-wide approach," a "comprehensive approach," or a "whole school or university approach." These terms attempt to capture the importance of symbiosis, of working systematically right across the organization, of creating a supportive central culture and ethos, ensuring that all parts work together in a coordinated, cohesive, and coherent way. It is a concept that has been applied with some success to many issues which have been found to work best when integrated at a whole school/university level such as health, well-being, safety, equity, and violence prevention. The Plum Village approach is wise to emphasize the community approach to mindfulness from the outset, which, as we will see in chapter eleven, is starting to give rise to schools where a whole school approach to mindfulness is becoming a reality.

It has been my privilege, with help from many valued colleagues, to weave the various elements and the teachers' stories into what we hope is a coherent narrative. We have tried to bridge the inspirational words of Thich Nhat Hanh and the core practices of Plum Village with the world of schools and universities, linking them to the everyday concerns of busy teachers and pressured students, and to the surrounding social and educational context.

We hope that we have provided an adequate setting for the twin brilliant diamonds that are the teachings of Thich Nhat Hanh and the lived examples and reflections of our teacher colleagues, and that the resultant book will be both inspirational and of practical use to you the reader.

All of us involved in producing this book wish you joy in reading—and more importantly, using—this book.

Katherine Weare
Somerset, UK
December 2016

PART ONE

CORE PRACTICES

Peace is every breath.
THICH NHAT HANH

one
the breath

in this chapter

- Explore how helpful awareness of our breathing can be to bring us back to the present moment, help us handle our emotions, and become calmer, focused, and in touch with what is happening in our mind and body.

- Learn step-by-step instructions and practical guidance for the core practice of getting in touch with the breath, and some variations on the practice.

- Hear some thoughts and suggestions from practicing teachers on cultivating mindful breathing in our daily lives and in our teaching and learning.

breathe, you are alive!

THICH NHAT HANH

Mindful breathing brings our mind home to our body so we can establish ourselves in the here and the now, fully present to live each moment of our daily life deeply.

Teachers should master the practice of mindful breathing before they can offer it to their students. This can be very joyful and pleasant to do. When we are able to enjoy mindful breathing, it can bring joy and help us to handle painful feelings and emotions. When teachers can do this, they can naturally help their students to do the same.

Even very young students can often be victims of their strong emotions and painful feelings. If they do not know how to handle these painful feelings and emotions, they will suffer. We can, as teachers, breathe in and out and generate the energy of mindfulness to help our students suffer less. This is a very beautiful thing to see. If you understand their suffering and listen to their suffering, you can tell them, "I have also suffered, but I practice like this and now I suffer less. Would you like to learn how to do it?" And they will listen to you. Communication like this between teacher and students transforms the class into a community. When students are happy and relaxed, the work of teaching and learning becomes much easier.

Do not wait until a strong emotion comes to begin the practice. We should begin the practice of mindful breathing right away, and then after a few weeks we will be used to the practice.

Mindfulness of breathing is very practical and everyone can do it. It is not complicated, and it brings a lot of calm and happiness right away. To begin the practice is simple: "Breathing in, I know I am breathing in. Breathing out, I know I am breathing out." You identify the in-breath as an in-breath, and the out-breath as an out-breath. When you breathe in, you know this is an in-breath: you are aware that an in-breath is taking place. When you breathe out, you know that an out-breath is taking place. When you use your mind to identify the in-breath and out-breath there is no more thinking. "Breathing in, I know this is an in-breath"—that isn't thinking. That is recognizing what is going on: your in-breath and your out-breath. You can enjoy your in-breath and your out-breath.

As we breathe in, we pay attention to our breath only—our breath becomes the only object of our mind. If we are truly focused and mindful of our breath, we release everything else—the past, the future, our projects, our fear, and our anger—because the mind has only one object: the breath. There is regret and sorrow concerning the past, and fear and uncertainty concerning the future. We release all of that in just one or two seconds because we are focusing our mind on our breath. Breathing in, mindfulness sets us free. In that moment, if we need to decide to say or do something, we do it better because we have enough freedom. We are not under the influence of anger or fear.

The effect of this practice can be very deep. When you pay attention to your in-breath and go home to your body, you can get the insight: "Oh, I have a body! I'm aware that I have a body." When your mind and body are together, you are truly in the present moment—the here and the now—ready to live your life. If we know how to be in touch with our body and connect with our body, we will connect with Mother Earth and the whole cosmos.

Please do not underestimate this easy exercise. Even if you have practiced mindful breathing for ten or twenty years, this remains a wonderful practice, and you will continue to get more and more benefit from it.

Next we practice following our in-breath and out-breath all the way through: "Breathing in, I follow my in-breath from the beginning to the end. Breathing out, I follow my out-breath from the beginning to the end." There is no interruption in our mindfulness during the time of our in-breath and out-breath. By focusing our attention entirely on the breath, we cultivate concentration: not a millisecond is lost; you are entirely with your breath, and you dwell very solidly in your breath. To be solid, to be stable, means you are free from the past, you are free from the future, and you have the capacity to be in the here and in the now.

During the time of breathing in, many kinds of insights may come to us like "Breathing in, I am alive!" We can celebrate the miracle of being alive just by breathing in. That is happiness already. We do not have to go and look for happiness elsewhere. We just sit, breathe in, and enjoy the fact that we are alive.

If we practice mindful breathing while walking, we may recognize it is a wonder that we are alive and that we are making steps on this beautiful planet. With this insight, happiness can come right away. Happiness is not made of money, fame, and power, but just by mindfulness of breathing. By following and enjoying our in-breath and out-breath all the way through we cultivate more concentration, because mindfulness and concentration are of the same nature, like water and ice.

When mind and body are apart, we are not truly there. When we spend two hours with our computer we can forget entirely that we have a body, and when the mind is not with the body we are not truly alive. We are lost in our work, in our worry, in our fear, and in our projects. So, mindful breathing can help us to bring the mind and body together. When we do this, it is a moment that we are truly alive. When mind and body are together we can touch the wonders of life inside us and around us, and that is life.

When we are with our body, not only do we touch the wonder that is our body, but we may realize that there is something in our body that needs care and attention to transform, perhaps tension or pain. By living in forgetfulness, we have allowed tension and pain to accumulate in our body. We have a lot of stress. Modern life has caused a lot of tension and stress to accumulate in our body.

With the practice of mindful breathing, we can release tension in the body. "Breathing in, I release the tension in my body." When we breathe in and come back to our body, we may notice that this tension prevents us from being relaxed, peaceful, and happy. Seeing this, we become motivated by a desire to do something to help our body to suffer less. While breathing in and breathing out we allow the tension in our body to be released. That is the practice of total relaxation. As we practice more we find it is very pleasant.

Caught up in the pressures of our daily lives it can often feel as if we do not have any time to practice mindfulness. Breathing in and out mindfully, letting go of our thoughts and becoming grounded in our own body, however, takes only one or two minutes. We can practice all day long and benefit right away, whether sitting on the bus, driving a car, taking a shower, or cooking breakfast. We cannot say, "I have no time to practice." We have plenty of time if we know where to look. This is very important. When we practice and we get relaxation and joy, our students profit. To practice mindful breathing is an act of love. We have peace, relaxation, joy, and we become an instrument of peace and joy for others.

getting in touch with our breath

Why practice getting in touch with our breath?

- To experience the breath as a friend that is always there to help us return to ourselves in the present moment and create moments of peace throughout the day.

- To increase our ability to concentrate, focus, and pay attention to what is happening here and now.

- To calm and anchor body and mind to help manage difficult emotions and impulses.

- To relax and help relieve stress and tension.

- To increase the ability to recognize how we are feeling.

- To help unite body and mind.

- To help us be more present and "there" for others, to enable us to listen more deeply and communicate more empathically.

Mindfulness is always mindfulness of something, and the breath is an easily available object for our attention. It is with us wherever we go, always there as a source of stability, always available in the present moment, a safe place we can go to become more solid and stable. Whatever the "weather" in our minds—our changing thoughts, emotions, and perceptions—the breath is with us like a faithful friend, connecting us to our body and to the present moment.

Mindful breathing can help us focus. By bringing awareness to our breathing we can gently bring our wandering mind back to the present moment. Whenever we feel carried away, or overwhelmed by a strong emotion, or caught up in our worries or plans, we can come back to the concrete experience of our breath to help collect and steady our mind, bringing it back to the here and now.

Mindful breathing is not complicated. We do not need to try to control our breathing. We simply focus on the sensation of the flow of air in and out of our body, perhaps aware of our belly rising and falling, or the sensation of breath in the nostrils or chest. We just come into contact with the breath as it is. We may feel how light and natural, how calm and peaceful our breathing is, or we may notice it is short, shallow, and agitated. Just being aware of our breath, without judging or trying to change it, can help us be more aware of how we are feeling. With our awareness focused on it, the breath often naturally becomes slower and deeper and we may become more relaxed and peaceful. Whatever happens, there is no need to try to change or force anything—simply continue to be aware.

At the end of the chapter we explore how we can apply and teach mindful breathing through examples from practicing teachers. They talk about why and how they use the breath, and how they feel it helps themselves and their students. Breathing practice is often supported by listening to the bell and/or sitting practice, so you may find the guidance and illustrations from the next two chapters helpful: "The Bell of Mindfulness" and "Sitting."

Over time, we can get more in touch with our breath, so it can become a thread of mindfulness through all our daily activities—while we are dressing, brushing our teeth, washing up, taking a moment before we answer the telephone, or as we talk to people. Mindful breathing is a simple precious gift, which has the capacity to transform our lives.

. . . . .

8

There is a summary of this practice and all other core practices at the end of the book.

For more detailed instructions on using the bell, see chapter two, "The Bell of Mindfulness."

core practice

getting in touch with our breath

The following instructions are for a short foundational practice that will take a few minutes. Once you have mastered this, there are suggestions for longer practices/variations below. They can be used to teach yourself or as the basis of a script to read aloud.

We suggest you might use a bell in this practice. We say we "invite" the bell to sound rather than using the harsher terms of "ringing" or "striking" the bell. We are inviting the bell kindly to share with us the sound it already has within. As Thich Nhat Hanh explains: "We never say 'strike' the bell, because for us the bell is a friend who can wake us up to full understanding."

Invite the bell at appropriate moments. You will find guidance on using the bell in the next chapter.

Materials and Preparation

- A teacher experienced in breathing meditation.
- Chairs, cushions, mats, etc., according to how you want people to sit.
- Bell and inviter (optional but strongly recommended).

1. Prepare

Find a comfortable, relaxed, and stable sitting position. This can be on a chair, on a cushion, or anywhere you feel comfortable. You might like to imagine you are sitting like a mountain, solid and stable.

Sense the contact with the floor, the ground, the chair, or the cushion.

Invite the students to close their eyes or keep them open with their gaze gently resting on the floor in front of them.

Invite the bell (if you wish) to begin. Otherwise gently start the instructions below.

Reluctant or anxious people can find starting the meditation with eyes open helpful, so make sure you offer the choice.

2. Notice You Are Breathing

Take a few moments to gradually become aware that you are breathing. There is no need to change anything. Be aware of, notice, and recognize the breath, just as it is.

People usually find it difficult not to change the breath at first, and young children in particular may become noisy with it. Encourage them to let their awareness follow the normal rhythm of their breath.

3. Follow the breath

As you breathe in, follow with all your attention the whole length of the in-breath—as it comes in through your mouth or nose, passes down through your throat, and fills your lungs. As you breathe out, follow with all your attention the whole length of your out-breath—the feeling of the air leaving your lungs, passing through your throat, and coming out through your mouth or nose. If you become distracted and lost in thought, just notice this and gently bring your attention back to the breath.

Remind yourself and your students from time to time that when their mind wanders, which it naturally will, to come gently back to the breath. With practice, we start to see more clearly when we are lost in our thinking and when we are directly aware of the physical sensation of the breath.

4. Feel the Breath in the Belly

Put your hands on your belly and see if you can become aware of it rising with the in-breath and falling with the out-breath. No need to change anything.

This stage is optional.

Just stay with noticing the sense of the in-breath and the out-breath, feeling the hands and belly move, even if only slightly.

Notice the length of the breath, and the gentle transition between the in- and out-breath.

When people have a lot of habitual tension they often breathe with the top of their chest only, and their belly may go in, instead of out, on the in-breath. Don't assume anything about what you or your students may notice on first starting this practice.

5. End

You might like to end by inviting the bell.

Invite the students to take three mindful breaths to finish and then they may gently open their eyes and stretch.

—

variations on getting in touch with our breath

Breathing practices can also be done lying down or standing. You can note what difference the position of your body makes to the feeling of your breath.

Finger breathing—this practice can help us keep our attention focused by connecting breathing with a simple movement.

Mike Bell, a former classroom teacher from the UK, describes it like this: "You start with the index finger of one hand resting on the wrist of the other hand, just below the thumb. Breathing in, slide the finger up the thumb. Breathing out, slide the finger down the other side of the thumb. Breathing in, slide the finger up the first finger; breathing out, slide the finger down the other side of that finger, and so on."[1]

Put your finger under your nose for a while and see if you can feel the breath and become aware of the difference between the in-breath and the out-breath—in temperature, moisture, quality, and so on.

Note where in the body you feel the breath most clearly right now. Note whether this changes at different times. See if you can become more aware of the sensation of the breath in different parts of the body—such as the nostrils, back of the throat, chest, or abdomen. See if you can gradually become aware of subtler sensations, such as the breath in the back of the rib cage.

Use the breath to gather helpful information about your state of mind. Gently note what your breath is doing and where your mind and body are right now, what that might tell you about your current feelings and preoccupations, and whether there is any shift after the practice.

Become aware of the length of the in- and out-breaths. You could count the seconds. Notice how their length varies with your state of mind. Notice how the breath tends naturally to become longer as you practice for a longer time or more often.

Note: Some people can find what they can think of as "smiling to order" feels inauthentic and uncomfortable—pediatrician Dzung X. Vo explains later in this chapter on page 15 how he teaches this to skeptical adolescents.

Combine the breath with a smile. For every out-breath you could smile a little bit more until you have a gentle smile on your face and a sense of relaxed smiling openness in your body.

Gently add in the idea of counting, e.g., "one" before an in- and out-breath, then 'two' for the next breath and so on, up to ten. Notice when the mind wanders and gently start the count again at one, so that you acknowledge that your mind has wandered.

There are several **Plum Village songs about the breath** that you and your class might enjoy. We make suggestions in chapter ten. Lyrics and music can be found at www.wakeupschools .org/songs.

Recite—to yourself or aloud—one of the verses in rhythm with your in- and out-breath.

> Breathing in, I know that I am breathing in.
> Breathing out, I know that I am breathing out.
> Breathing in, I am calm. Breathing out, I smile.

Over time you can shorten one line into the words, "In" as you breathe in, and "Out" as you breathe out.

Your students could write up these verses and memorize them, or illustrate them with a picture, getting in touch with their breath from time to time as they do so. They might like to compose their own "breathing in / breathing out . . . " poem.

looking deeply: reflection questions
for breath practice

These are some questions for you to reflect on yourself or to use with the students after any practice, either during in-class sharing or just by letting the questions settle in the mind. Use them sparingly—it is not a checklist!

- How do I feel right now? What is happening right now in my mind/body? (e.g., calm, clear, relaxed, tense, anxious?)

- How is my breath? (e.g., slow, deep, light, fast?)

- What happened for me during this practice, in my mind, body, and breath? Did anything change? (e.g., calmer, more agitated, more present, mind clearer?)

- How easy was it to keep my mind on the breath?

- How did the practice feel? (e.g., strange, good, enjoyable, difficult, boring?)

Add other questions as appropriate. Keep them few, simple, open, nonjudgmental, encouraging, and accept all kinds of responses including "negative" ones and "I don't know." If students wander off into theorizing, gently bring the sharing back to what they have really experienced.

mindful breathing in our lives and our teaching

Most people who practice mindfulness quickly come to appreciate how central the breath is to being fully present in mind and body. They experience getting in touch with the breath as a transformative practice, a foundation to which, once they have learned it, they find they naturally return time and again.

The following are some reflections by teachers on their experience of the impacts of mindful breathing.

What's been most helpful for me is becoming aware of my breathing, seeing my breath and my breathing as my friend. My breathing is my refuge—in moments of joy it intensifies my joyful feeling; in moments of sadness or anger it soothes and lightens my anxiety. My breathing also helps me prepare for challenging events, by connecting my mind and body and helping me feel more grounded. —SALLY ANNE AIREY, COACH, FRANCE

Sometimes simply being with the breath shifts worried moods and misguided perspectives.

I find the simplest practices can often bring great benefit to me. Sometimes when I worry too much about work, simply spending forty minutes resting my mind with my breath, brings a sense of ease, calm, and relief, and a very different perspective, allowing me to reengage with life with more clarity and self-compassion. —MICHAEL BREADY, MINDFULNESS TRAINER, UK

Breathing and relaxation are closely connected.

The most useful thing I learn from Thay is "Breathing in, I know I am breathing in. Breathing out, I am breathing out." Why is that so? Because the moment I realize it, I feel the tension that is in me, and I am free from that tension. —CHAU LI HUAY, MIDDLE AND HIGH SCHOOL TRAINER, SINGAPORE

Mindful Breathing Can Help Us to Teach Better

Staying in touch with our breathing when in the middle of the busy, demanding, and stressful challenges of a teaching day can help us stay centered. You can find many ways to gently integrate mindful breathing into your daily routine, without needing to make major changes or add extra time. You might make it a habit to breathe mindfully in (and out) whenever you turn to the classroom board. One teacher observes how helpful it is to focus on the breath when things get tough,

I've noticed that I hold my breath, which is something I do when a situation is difficult or I feel emotional. So instead of holding my breath, I try to breathe through those situations. I found that really helpful.

Chau, a middle and high school teacher trainer from Singapore, tells a story of being in the unenviable and challenging position of a "freelance" or substitute teacher who works in schools on a temporary basis and so has no time to build up relationships with classes. Chau found using the breath to stay grounded to be a more effective method to keep rowdy classes under control than punitive methods, such as shouting.

> I taught in government schools for two years as a "freelance." The students (of whom there are forty in a class) are very noisy, and their attention is so short. I know that instead of shouting or being angry or scowling, I can be a quiet revolution by just coming back to my breathing and walking mindfully into the classroom. They do sit up and take notice!

Teaching Mindful Breathing to Our Students

Sequencing Our Teaching of Mindful Breathing

Mindful breathing is the first core practice we teach in this book, as it is foundational. Peggy Rowe Ward and her husband Larry from the US are both long-standing practitioners and mindfulness trainers. In the program they developed at an international school in Thailand they began with mindfulness of the breath and taught a simple a routine involving just five breaths. This short practice proved so effective it spread into many different parts of the school.

> Working as consultants to the American Schools of Bangkok, we recommended that we begin our journey with a very short simple practice that we called "Take Five." Take Five was the practice of taking five mindful breaths. We were given just a few minutes at the morning all-school assembly. We took five mindful breaths. In this way, we began the school day by stopping and calming ourselves. Then the practice of Take Five spread as we integrated it into multiple learning activities, sports activities, and assessment testing.

Christine Petaccia, an American occupational therapist, describes a longer sequence of breathing practices, which she has carefully adapted to the capacities of her classes of vulnerable children with special needs.

The students I teach have special needs, but I have developed a sequence through activity analysis that works for any child. We start by talking about bringing the body and mind together, and about how the body and speech affect the mind and vice versa. We then lie on our backs and listen to a number of chimes or a singing bowl, about ten chimes. Then we progress to watching a breath move in and out (maybe with a toy on their tummy to see it move, or maybe by having them watch the teacher). I remind them to breathe a normal relaxed breath, and then they try three breaths, then five, then they count how many breaths in ten seconds, twenty seconds, and so on. I relate their breathing to ocean waves coming in and out.

The next step is to try the sequence of breathing while sitting in a chair. This is more advanced and can be a challenge for children with disabilities due to physiological breathing patterns. I point out the relaxed feeling they may have experienced from the breath awareness sequence they did while lying down, and then I ask them to invoke that feeling on the exhale. I then explain that we will take that breath when I invite the bell.

I also use breathing for children who have fluency issues such as stuttering and attention difficulties. The students often speak too quickly and without thinking, so they learn to take a mindful breath to collect their thoughts prior to answering questions or sharing.

"Lots of Fun Ways" to Teach

The breath is a reliable anchor because it is always there, but some young people may, as a result, feel that this practice is somewhat boring. To keep the idea of awareness of the breath fresh in young people's minds it can help to find lively and varied ways to teach it.

For Dzung X. Vo, a pediatrician in Canada trying to help teens with mental health issues, teaching mindful breathing is where he starts his whole program. He adds in a focus on cultivating friendliness and kindness with a smile.

I introduce experiential mindfulness practice very early on. I have great trust in the inner wisdom of adolescents, and I have found that when they have the opportunity to experience the benefits of mindfulness for them-selves first-hand, they are even more open-minded and open-hearted than adults. As an introduction, I will usually offer a short (two- or three-minute) guided mindful breathing practice, using Plum Village-inspired language to invite not only attention to breathing, but also smiling. I explain that smiling doesn't mean "faking it," or "pretending to be happy if you're not." (Adolescents are very sensitive to inauthenticity.) Instead, I explain, "Smiling means bringing kindness and friendliness to the awareness of your breathing." You can bring kindness and compassion to any moment, whether it is a pleasant moment or a difficult moment.

Alison Mayo, a preschool teacher in the UK, has a wealth of "fun ways" to offer her younger classes:

Working with very young children, I have found that they need lots of fun ways to explore and feel what breath and breathing are, so they are well prepared for the introduction of the bell and breathing practice. Ways we have done this include blowing out candles, blowing bubbles, making model sail boats and blowing them across a water tray, placing fingers under nostrils, hands on their bellies, lying down relaxations with toys on their tummies, role-play blowing up balloons, bee "hums" and chanting, and even running around and feeling what happens when you are out of breath.

Mindful breathing can in turn make the mundane more interesting. One of Jenna Blondel's young adult students in the US managed to create a mindful breathing practice out of his daily task of sweeping the floor.

We share in class how our practice is going. Students share ways that they've discovered to work with their breath outside of meditation in the class. One student, a diesel mechanic, reported that he had figured out how to bring mindfulness to his work by sweeping the floor—he coordinated his breathing with the sweeping, and it became Sweeping Meditation!

Breathing Can Help Our Students Calm Down
Students often find that the calming effect of mindful breathing can be a powerful support to help them with their stress. This can be particularly apparent at exam time as pediatrician Dzung X. Vo reports.

I remember another teenager who sometimes had panic attacks when she tried to take exams. She said, "I would sit down in front of the exam, and all of a sudden I would freak out, and I couldn't remember anything that I had learned!" After learning to take a moment for a breathing space, she reported back: "I sat down to take the exam. Before I started, I closed my eyes, and I did a breathing space. I could feel myself starting to freak out, but I kept with the practice. When I opened my eyes, I could think more clearly, and I was able to finish writing the exam."

Jennifer Wood, a high school teacher and student advisor in the US, also recommends breathing as a way of relieving test anxiety, noting that, "Simple breathing (in/out three times, for example) is effective before and after tests and when students are in transition."

Students find many daily aspects of school and university stressful. Sometimes all that is needed to help is for the teacher to breathe along with them.

One student who arrived in my counseling office was so upset she could barely breathe due to some incident that had happened to her friend. I was able to help her calm down just by simply sitting and breathing with her, in, out, and slowly she calmed down. Minutes later, with a "Thanks, Sir!" she left smiling and calm. —DEREK HEFFERNAN, HIGH SCHOOL TEACHER, CANADA

We can sometimes work most effectively by simply embodying ourselves what we want our students to do and encouraging our students to practice along with us. Pascale Dumont, an elementary teacher in France, helped a small child who had been labeled "uncontrollable" to relax and calm down by sitting, meditating, and breathing with him on her lap. (In France, bodily contact between students and teacher is allowed at the teacher's discretion, but this may not be possible in your context.)

Victor was a "little guy." He couldn't sit still in class. The teacher had to isolate his desk, facing the board, at the very front. One day, we had gathered all the students in the big hall for a choral concert. His teacher had assigned him to me because he was uncontrollable; it was unimaginable to have him sing with his class. So I took him by the hand to attend the show. We sat down. To better enjoy the show, I asked him to sit on my lap. He moved a lot so, instinctively, I put my hands on one another, as I usually do while I meditate, and my hands met his belly. It relaxed a little. And then, spontaneously, he gently laid his two little hands in mine, as if he'd found a cozy little nook. I let him be and began to meditate. During the length of the school concert, I sensed his body gradually release and become very relaxed, calm, peaceful. His back seemed to be embedded in me. Our breathing was one.

Christiane Terrier, a retired high school teacher and mindfulness trainer in France, talks about how she routinely breathed with her agitated and panicking high school students before lessons to help them calm down.

When students are in the hallway before entering the lesson, I suggest to them we breathe together for a moment, like a game. Their agitation decreases and we can quietly begin the class. This short practice encourages them to be ready to learn. Students sometimes have stress or panic attacks in the classroom or in the hall. Even if we do not know the student personally we tell him we are there for him and breathe with him. "I breathe, I become calm, I breathe, I smile." Often just a few breaths change the situation, and the student becomes serene and smiling.

Taking Care When Our Students Are Challenged by Mindful Breathing

Focusing on the breath can bring up tension and strong emotions. Some students may have problems with the breath—for example, those with strong anxiety or with asthma or similar breathing difficulties. It is sensible and safe practice to keep the practice invitational and light, and suggest to all students that if they feel anxious at any time that they can forget about the breathing and just move their attention to a different part of the body, such as the feet on the floor, the feeling in their hands, or their bottom on the chair. Stay particularly aware of, and in visual contact with, any students you are particularly concerned about; keep your own eyes open to spot any students having difficulties, while still participating in the practice for yourself. If students have strong or even "negative" reactions in the reflections and discussion, respond with calm, kind curiosity in the moment and have a word later with any you are concerned about.

It may help prevent any anxiety and tension to teach mindful breathing in ways that are not always intense or serious, as Sara Martine Serrano, an experienced special education assistant from Switzerland working with disabled children, suggests,

I was working with twelve-year-old, mentally disabled children whose potential is very diverse. The first problem I encountered was breathing. I noticed that the in-breath and out-breath created tension in their upper body and breath retention. So, I explored other methods to practice with the breath.

First, I playfully invented a story that mentions a feather or a sheet of paper. I placed one of these in the hand of the child to whom I was telling the story, asking the child to blow gently on his sheet or feather just enough to make it rise or tremble, then asked them to gradually increase the volume of their breath to see the feather fly. The child's attention was not placed so much on the breath as on an outside object, while all the while working on his breath.

**Listen, listen, this wonderful sound
brings me back to my true home.**
THICH NHAT HANH

two
the bell of
mindfulness

in this chapter

- Explore the importance of "inviting the bell," to create a moment of mindfulness, to stop and become more present, and to treasure our time and our life.

- Choose the most appropriate bell for your classroom situation.

- Step-by-step instructions and practical guidance for two core practices i) inviting the bell ii) listening to the bell, with some variations.

- Reflect on ways to integrate the bell of mindfulness into our daily lives and into our teaching, with examples and suggestions from practicing teachers.

an ambassador for peace and happiness

THICH NHAT HANH

We want to treasure every moment of our life; we want to treasure every minute. We don't need to forget time; we don't need time to go quickly. We don't *want* time to go quickly, because time is life.

Every second has in itself many jewels, and each minute—each second—is itself a jewel. When you look into the jewel of this very second you see the sky, the earth, the trees, the hills, the river, and the ocean—so beautiful! We don't want to kill time. We want to profit deeply from each moment that is given us to live. The bell of mindfulness helps us to do so.

Without mindfulness, you waste your time; you do not live your life deeply. The bell helps us to go back to ourselves and produce the energy of peace and joy.

The bell is an ambassador of peace and happiness in our home or classroom. We use the phrase "inviting the bell," and not "hitting" or "striking" the bell, because we aim to treat this ambassador with respect, inviting it to share with us the wonderful sound it already has within. When we see that the bell is an ambassador of peace and happiness, we can breathe in mindfully and become aware that the bell, the ambassador, is there. When we breathe out, we smile to his excellency, the ambassador. Breathing in and out like that brings you peace and relaxation.

This chapter will help you prepare to be a good bell master. You begin by holding the bell and inviter (or stick) and practicing breathing in and out deeply two times while reciting silently a short verse. The first line of the verse is "Body, speech and mind in perfect oneness." While you breathe in you recite that line silently, and you bring your body, mind, and speech together in concentration.

> Breathing in, "Body, speech, and mind in perfect oneness, "
> Breathing out, "I send my heart along with the sound of this bell."
> Breathing in, a second time, "May the hearers awaken from forgetfulness,"
> Breathing out, "And transcend the path of anxiety and sorrow."

While you recite this poem silently and breathe in and out, you bring in the energy of peace, relaxation, and mindfulness. In this way, you become qualified to be a bell master. When we are not peaceful, calm, or happy enough, we should not invite the bell. If we are peaceful, the sound will transmit this quality of peace.

The first thing we do after reciting the poem is to wake up the bell. You produce not a full sound but a half-sound, by touching the inviter to the edge of the bell and holding it there. This wake-up sound warns everyone in the classroom that a full sound is about to be produced. When everyone has enjoyed one in- and out-breath, stopped their thinking and talking, and is ready to receive the sound we produce, we invite a full sound of the bell for the first time.

See the illustration on page 27.

After inviting the bell, we should allow people to have enough time to enjoy three deep in-breaths and out-breaths. Be generous, because this is the time to produce peace and happiness. The length of everyone's breath varies, and as bell master you may want to allow four in- and out-breaths. Especially when a child is acting as bell master, they should allow an extra in- and out-breath after each sound of the bell. If we are young, then our in-breath and out-breath will not be as long as the in-breath and out-breath of those who are adults, who are already used to the practice.

While breathing in we can say, "I listen, I listen." We invite all the cells in our body to join us in listening very deeply. We allow the sound of the bell to penetrate every cell of our body to help our body relax. There are billions of cells in our body, and they are breathing in together. That is why when we say "I listen, I listen," it really means "We listen, we listen." Billions of cells are listening at the same time. They come together to produce the collective energy of listening. We do not listen as an individual, we listen as a community: the community of cells. This is called *deep listening*. Listening like this will bring peace and relaxation to our body and to our feelings at the same time. When we have feelings that are not peaceful, it is very good to listen like this, and we will be able to calm our feelings.

We know that all our blood and spiritual ancestors are fully present in every cell of our body. We may like to invite all of them to join us in listening to the bell so they may come alive again. We think that our ancestors are no longer alive, but when we look deeply we see that that is not true. They are always alive in every cell of our body. We can get in touch with them at any time we want. We can talk to them. We can invite them to walk with us, to breathe with us and to listen to the bell with us. When you hear the bell, you may like to invite all your ancestors in you to join you in listening. Listening like that can be very transforming and healing.

When we breathe out we say, "This wonderful sound brings me back to my true home." Our true home is in the present moment, where life is available. So, while breathing out and listening to the bell, we get away from the past, the future, and our projects, and establish ourselves in the present moment, in touch with the wonders of life in us and around us. Wherever we go, if we have mindfulness, that place is our true home.

We breathe in and out three times before we invite the bell to sound for a second time. With three sounds of the bell we have a chance to breathe in and out nine times.

In the morning, before going to work or to school, you may like to sit down and listen to a sound of the bell—alone, or together with the whole family. If we produce three sounds of the bell, then we have a chance to practice nine times of breathing in and breathing out. When a group of people breathes together like that, the energy of mindfulness and peace can be very powerful, healing, and nourishing. If children are sitting with us they can feel that energy. We do not need to wish each other to have a good day. We can make the day good by a having a good beginning to it. The same goes for the evening. We may like to gather the children around the bell, and practice mindful breathing to relax their bodies and feel each other's presence, before they go to bed.

During the day, any time we feel that the atmosphere is not peaceful enough—if there is anger, restlessness, or difficulty breathing—we can invite the bell to sound, so that the whole classroom can relax, breathe, and restore peace and happiness. You may even like to program a bell of mindfulness into your computer, so that every fifteen minutes you can stop working, listen to the bell, and come back to enjoy your in- and out-breath.

the bell of mindfulness

Why invite and listen to the bell?

· To experience a gentle, pleasant way to create a moment of mindfulness—to stop and enjoy the present moment.

· To be aware of our breath and of how we are feeling right now.

· To calm, rest, and relax the body and mind.

· To improve the atmosphere—in a classroom, meeting, or communal meal— bringing about more happiness, peace, relaxation, and focus.

· To help build a sense of connection with others.

using the bell in our lives

You can use the bell to support every aspect of your mindfulness practice, including mindful breathing, sitting meditation, mindful walking, and mindful eating.

We can all do with a refreshing reminder to come home to ourselves in the present moment, to take time for ourselves. Our mind, even while practicing mindfulness, can often become distracted and take us away to the future or the past, and get caught up in worrying and planning. We easily get out of touch with our true feelings, with what our body is telling us, and with what is happening in the real world. The bell can help us to cut through our busy thinking, bringing us back gently, kindly, and with understanding to be in touch with what is happening in the present moment.

Sometimes it's easy for our mind to come back to the present moment; at other times we may be overwhelmed by a difficult or strong emotion. In either case, we continue to practice being gentle with ourselves and present with whatever happens. Sometimes this means just to be at peace with our agitated mind, with patience, kindness, and maybe with a touch of kindly humor.

Over time we can gradually choose to identify regular "bells of mindfulness" throughout our everyday lives—regular little punctuations of mindful breathing—such as red traffic lights, the first three rings of the telephone, climbing up or down a flight of stairs, or while closing a door. We can use these as opportunities to remind us to stop briefly and come back to the present moment.

take time to learn the skill

Inviting the bell should not be done automatically, but in mindfulness. Learning to invite the bell takes some personal preparation, practice, and skill, for ourselves and for our students. This can be something fun to learn. It is not as easy as it looks to invite the sound you want! Don't pressure yourself and others to do it perfectly. Skill in inviting the bell comes with experience.

The quality of the sound depends on the state of mind and body of the person who invites it: producing a warm, steady tone needs a gentle touch, so it is important first to be calm in body and mind, as best you can, and to enjoy the experience. You, the teacher, can learn to invite the bell yourself before sharing this with your students. It can be a wonderful practice to give you a sense of calmness and ease.

guidance on choosing a bell

- Small Japanese bells, called rin gong, are bowl-shaped and pocket-sized (useful if the class meets in different places) and produce a beautiful sound. They come with a stick (called an "inviter" to remind us that the sound is already present in the bell; we just need to provide the final condition—the movement of our hand—to invite the sound to come out) and a cushion for the bell to sit on.

- Bigger brass singing bowls are wonderful for the warm full sound they produce. The extra volume of sound created by larger ones can be helpful for a larger class size, assemblies, walking outside, and so on.

- You can download the sound of a mindfulness bell on your computer or smartphone to have as a backup to the real thing. There are several apps that produce the sound of a mindfulness bell. One is available from the Plum Village website, www.plumvillage.org.

- If using a bowl feels too "religious" for your context, a single bar chime or triangle may be more appropriate—though it may not have the same quality of sound, or feel as special as inviting the bell. The section at the end of the chapter gives examples from teachers of the many different bells they have used.

in the classroom, remember

- Treat your bell with care and encourage students to do the same. Use it only for mindfulness practice, and with respect.

- Practice calming your mind and being able to offer a relaxed smile, maintaining your own concentration throughout, so you can embody the practice as you invite the bell.

- Take care not to use the bell as a disciplinary device. You transmit to everyone whatever emotion you are experiencing when you invite the bell. If you are feeling angry or irritated, calm these emotions in yourself by breathing and smiling with acceptance before inviting the bell.

- Make sure the practice remains authentic and fresh by using a range of practices, words, and images to inspire and guide yourself and the students.

. . . . .

At the end of this chapter we explore using the bell with some stories from practicing teachers who talk about what bell they choose and why and how they use the bell in their own lives and in the classroom.

Inviting the bell always goes together with mindful breathing, and often with sitting practice, so you may find the guidance and illustrations from chapters 1 and 3 helpful.

core practice

inviting the bell

Materials and Preparation

- Bell and inviter.

- A teacher with a sense of relaxation, fun, and openness to learn this new skill.

A summary is available in appendix A on page 292.

1. Prepare

Get settled and focused. Sit up with your back straight but relaxed.

Hold your hand out horizontally with your elbow bent and your palm facing up, letting the bell sit in the palm of your hand. Make your hand as flat as you comfortably can, with as small a point of contact between your hand and the bell as possible so that your hand doesn't dampen the sound of the bell. If you find it difficult to produce a clear sound in this way, you may like to move the bell to the tips of your fingers which are pressed together and vertical.

2. Wake Up the Bell / Invite a Half Sound

First breathe in and out mindfully at least two times to come back to the present moment. Enjoy your breathing.

Holding the inviter (stick) upright and parallel to the rim of the bowl, gently but firmly bring it into contact at an angle of 30 degrees. When it comes in contact leave it against the bell so that it dampens the sound, making a "half sound." This is called "waking up the bell."

The "half sound" is a clear, audible but dampened and non-ringing sound that is used to "wake up" the bell and "wake up" the listener to the fact a full sound is coming, before inviting the full sound.

3. Make the Full Sound

The full sound is clean, strong, and clear.

Breathe in and out mindfully once.

Holding the inviter with the thumb, fore, and middle finger, use an upward sweeping motion so it gently strikes the outside of the bell, just below the rim. Approaching the bell with the inviter pointing upright, or horizontally and parallel to the rim of the bell, gives a clear, gentle sound. With practice and a bit of experimentation, keeping it light, fun, and relaxed, you will find the way.

4. Listen to the Bell

You may also like to use any of the practice variations listed at the end of the following "listening to the bell" practice.

Breathe in and out, mindfully and naturally, three more times, letting the sound of the bell penetrate every cell of your body.

core practice

listening to the bell

A summary of this practice is available in appendix A on page 292.

This practice gives you basic instructions for listening, and is followed by suggestions for ways to extend this practice.

Materials and Preparation

- A teacher practiced at inviting the bell.
- Bell and inviter.

1. Prepare

Find a comfortable and stable sitting or standing position. You may like to think of sitting "like a mountain," or "like a prince/princess."

2. Invite a Half Sound of the Bell

Sit up straight and breathe in and out mindfully two times to calm your mind and body. Invite a half sound of the bell.

3. Invite the Full Sound

You may also like to choose one of the practice variations below.

Breathe in and out mindfully once more, focusing fully on your in- and out-breath.

When you feel ready, invite a full sound of the bell. You can do this once, twice, or three times.

Allow for three full in- and out-breaths between each full sound of the bell.

Verse for Listening to the Bell (Optional)

> Listen, listen.
>
> This wonderful sound
>
> brings me back to my true home.

—

variations on listening to the bell

Do any of these practices as many times as feels right, slowly, with clear pauses and reflections between. Just use one or two practices per session or lesson.

- Notice as thoughts arrive, and then see if you can gently let them go and bring your attention back to the sound of the bell and the awareness of your in- and out-breath.

- Allow the sound to penetrate every cell of your body.

- Use the sound to help you get in touch with your center, a place where you feel safe, solid, and secure.

- Pay attention to the sound until you no longer hear it.

- Invite students to move around the room, to stop when they hear the bell and to breathe, starting to move again when they no longer hear the bell, or after three breaths. (This may work better than sitting for younger and more active students.)

- Invite students to count how many breaths they take (in/out = one). Invite them to open their eyes when they can no longer hear the bell and raise their hand and fingers to show the number of times they breathed.

You may like to recite quietly this verse before the bell is invited in order to help prepare your or your students' minds, or after the bell has been invited to help stay focused. Silently recite one line to yourself with the in-breath, the next with the out-breath, and then next line with the next in-breath and out-breath.

looking deeply: reflection questions for the bell of mindfulness

Here are some questions for you, the teacher, to reflect on yourself or to use with the students, either during in-class sharing or by just letting the questions settle in the mind. Use them sparingly—it is not a checklist!

- Did the bell help me find my calm center, my "island within"? Or did I feel anxious, or irritated? What happened for me?

- Was I able to return my mind to the bell/breath when thoughts arose?

- Was it difficult or easy to remain focused on the sound of the bell?

Add other questions as appropriate. Keep them simple, open, nonjudgmental, encouraging, and accepting of all kinds of responses including "negative" ones and "I don't know." Gently bring the sharing back to present real-life experience.

the bell of mindfulness in our lives and in our teaching

Using the Bell to Support Our Own Practice

Denys Candy, a university program director and consultant, finds the bell an invaluable way of bringing peace and refreshment into his busy life. He shares a warm image from his Irish childhood to express the refreshment the bell brings to him.

I have found it helpful to invite the bell at different times throughout the day and week. I call this befriending the bell. Inviting a bell upon waking or last thing before going to sleep, while taking a break from a keyboard or phone, or simply at random, reminded me that peace was available then and there. Slowing down with the bell brought me back to a refreshing breath. That breath then opened up other practice options such as smiling a half smile, further amplifying my joy. As a boy in Ireland when I awoke refreshed after an extra-long sleep, my parents would say, "you had a nice lie-in." Inviting the bell is like permeating my day with nice lie-ins.

Inviting the bell is not as easy as one might think. John Bell, a senior teacher in the Plum Village tradition who has worked for decades with out-of-school youth in the US, has discovered that there is a fair amount of skill in inviting the bell effectively.

> I've spent a lot of time with this bell. I know it well. I know that there are many ways this bell can sound. I know that there are certain conditions under which it sounds the most beautiful. For example, it sounds different at different points on the rim. I've also learned that if I use this lower part of the "inviter" stick rather than up here near the top, it sounds better. I've also learned that if I use an upward motion on the rim of the bell it sounds better than a downward motion. Certain conditions allow the bell to sound its most beautiful, to fulfill its true nature.

John has learned that he and the bell "inter-are": the bell is sensitive to the state of the person inviting it. He suggests below that this is a reminder to be aware of the state of our mind and body when we invite the bell.

> Another lesson of the bell is that since the bell and I are in a relationship, how I am affects how the bell sounds when I invite it. If I am angry it might sound louder than the situation calls for. If I am feeling depressed, it might be too soft to focus the attention of the hearers. If I am distracted and not being mindful of the motion of the inviter, it might land poorly and produce a harsh sound. So, the bell and I inter-are. If I am not mindful, the bell will not be able to offer its best. So, as teachers, taking good care of ourselves in healthy ways is related to our ability to take good care of our students.

John's insights remind us to take better care of ourselves when we find, on reflection, that we are not in a calm and settled place as we guide the practice.

Using the Bell with Students . . .

Once they are practiced at inviting the bell and using it to support their own mindfulness, many teachers enjoy moving on to use it in their classrooms. Denys has some useful practical tips.

1. Relax and take care of your own practice. Don't worry about what people may be thinking. (e.g., "This is weird.")

2. Take time to explain bell practice in full and rehearse it with participants a couple of times. Ask people to sit up straight and relaxed in their chair, feeling their feet on the earth; give permission for people to close their eyes if they choose; recite a verse, such as, "Breathing in I, know I am breathing in; Breathing out, I know I am breathing out."

3. Practice trust: trust your own presence and practice, trust the group to enjoy mindful breathing, and trust the bell to evoke the energy of mindfulness for all.

We refer to the bell often, as it is immensely helpful as a support to the many practices suggested in this book: breathing, sitting, moving, walking, eating, and being with ourselves and others.

. . . to Structure the Lesson in a Gentle Way

Some teachers have found it helpful to invite the bell at regular intervals—perhaps two or three times within a one-hour lesson—once students are familiar and comfortable with it, to give the students an opportunity to stop and breathe. This can induce a little more calm and focus, and help everyone to enjoy the moment. Every twenty minutes is a good guide; don't overdo it.

We should take care not to undermine the gentle invitational quality of the bell by using it as a means of classroom control. Alison Mayo reminds us,

> We teach children about why and how we breathe, and introduce them to
> the vocabulary for describing what they feel. I feel it is very important that
> children are introduced to the bell-breathing as being an enjoyable and
> calming thing, and that the same bell should not be used for classroom

control/getting the children to be quiet. We sound the bell and "enjoy a
quiet breath" before singing our thank you song at snack time, and also
during our "carpet-time."

Teachers sometimes use the bell to mark a transition, such as at the start and end
of a lesson. It gives everyone in the class the opportunity to pause and breathe, to
take stock, and to move mindfully into the next part of the day instead of rushing
mindlessly on. Betsy Blake Arizu, a retired high school teacher and counselor from
Florida, suggests the following.

Listening to the sound of the bell—really listening and feeling the sound in
one's body—is a wonderful way to relax and bring one's awareness to the
present moment. It's a great way to begin a meeting or a classroom lesson,
or for starting and ending a mindful awareness practice.

Over time the young people can become very attached to the bell; it often becomes a
class bell, with the young people choosing a place or home for it and making suggestions for its use. To Ross Young's class of younger children in the UK, it has become
the class "pet."

I explain to the children that our bell likes a "kiss" before it is rung, to wake
it up. We see it as a class "pet" or "friend" that can be taken home by a different child each day and rung in the morning and before bed. We let it "sit"
with a different member of the class each day who looks after it.

Alison Mayo finds that students enjoy being asked to invite the bell at appropriate
moments, and learn the skills and attitudes of becoming what you might like to term
a "bell master."

The children love to invite the bell themselves, and one exercise I often do is
to carry the bell around the circle of children and allow each one to gently
sound it, seeing if we can carry the sound right around the circle. This holds
the attention of the group really well.

. . . to Help Students with Their Emotions

Teachers are usually eager to cultivate greater focus in their students and calm in their classroom atmosphere, but it can be hard to achieve. Teachers describe vividly the extraordinary quality that the bell can impart to the classroom, once students are used to the sound. It often has an almost instant and even "magical" ability to induce an atmosphere conducive to communication and learning.

For some, such as Michael Schwammberger, an experienced educator working for many years in the Plum Village tradition in the UK and Spain, the sound has a "restful" quality.

> When you invite the bell and you are concentrated, coming back to your breath, you feel a certain quality of mindfulness . . . the children feel that. They can rest.

The bell can help people become centered, and make "time seem to stop" as Richard Brady, a retired math teacher and experienced Plum Village educator, suggests,

> I met Thay at Omega Institute in New York. There I was introduced to the custom of stopping at the sound of a bell and giving my full attention to the present moment. I came home with a small bell and brought it to my math classes. I sounded it at the beginning of class, and from time to time during the class period, to help the students stop and center themselves. Time seemed to stop during those brief moments. The students responded to the bell with respect.[1]

The bell can help a class "come back" to themselves. Meena Srinivasan, a longtime classroom teacher and mindfulness and social and emotional learning (SEL) program manager from the US, shares,

> I'll start by getting out my little bell, and I'll say to my students "Our bodies are here, but where are our minds? Our mind might still be at lunch; it might still be in math class. If so, when one hand represents our mind, and the other hand represents our body, when I invite the bell, and we bring awareness to our breathing, our mind and body come together. Let's take

a moment, invite the bell, bring our hands together, and come back to ourselves so we can be here." This is really helpful for me as a teacher.

John Bell makes a connection between the transformative quality of the sound of the bell and the teacher's familiar goal of encouraging students to "sound their best."

Now why I am talking about a bell? Well, it seems to me that as educators we are trying to create the right conditions in our classrooms and schools under which our students can "sound their best": to show up fully and touch their unique talents and innate joy of learning. Isn't this what we're about, really?

We can use the atmosphere created by the bell to cultivate particular states of mind. Coreen Morsink, who teaches elementary through high school classes in Greece, helps her students develop the ability to access happier thoughts through guiding them to link the sound of the bell with positive associations.

After singing a warm-up song I asked them to listen to the sound of the finger cymbals and think of a happy thought, or many happy thoughts. I wanted them to associate happiness with the sound of the bell. Most did this very quickly—it was a bit sad that some had trouble coming up with a happy thought. But after most of the children told the class their happy thought, the others found one too. The thoughts ranged from ice cream to spending time with Dad.

Teachers regularly find that the directness of using sound connects particularly strongly with students who are challenged or vulnerable in some way. Murielle Dionnet, a classroom and special education teacher in France, uses the range of sound in different ways to support younger children with learning and mental health difficulties, helping them to relax, calm down, and even, in one case, resolve conflict at home by simply remembering the sound.

The first practice I introduced to the children was mindful breathing: teaching them to breathe three times to relax and calm down. There was a "calmness minder" who was responsible for ringing the chime (after he or she had breathed mindfully three times) whenever the whenever the class got too noisy or too rough.

Each student could also come and sound the chime if he or she felt bad. One year I had in my class a little five-year-old boy who had just lost his dad. He used the chime often, making good use of this tool to help himself grieve and share his suffering with the group. This experience touched me deeply.

I remember a student who shared, "When I am angry with my sister, I go to my room and I ring the chime in my head."

I worked with other students who have mental disabilities. I applied the technique I use at home: I started using a clock that automatically rings every quarter hour. With this group, I gave thorough guidance to accompany the three breaths.

Breathing in, I know I breathe in

Breathing out, I know I breathe out

Breathing in, I calm down

Breathing out, I relax

Breathing in, I feel good

Breathing out, I smile

This practice helped a lot in class.

In a heart-warming and inspirational story, Shelley Murphy, a former elementary school teacher and now a teacher educator in Canada, describes how the bell helped one frantic young child in emotional turmoil calm his thoughts.

Raymond skips through the door of our classroom. He is talking from the moment he arrives, providing a running commentary on everything he sees. Raymond has a hard time "making the thoughts in my head stop," as he puts it. When we take our seats, his wide eyes fix on the Tibetan-like bells at the front of the class. I can almost see the thoughts begin to slow in his mind. When I first introduced the bells to our class, eight-year-old Raymond had a thousand comments and questions: "Where are they from? What are they made of? Can I ring them? Are they a musical instrument? I play the recorder . . . what do you play?" We are now months into the school year. Each day begins and ends with the chiming of the bells. I chime the bells a few times, and each student becomes increasingly more aware of his or her breathing. Raymond listens—and keeps listening until he can no longer hear the sound and vibration of the bells. His eyes are closed, his attention concentrated on his belly rising and falling and on his in-breath and out-breath. The thoughts that were monopolizing his attention appear to have receded to the periphery of his consciousness.

Raymond gradually became comfortable with his mindfulness practice. He looked forward to it and expected it to be part of his day. He learned that both he and I noticed his newfound ability to tap into deeper states of concentration. He was less restless and more easily able to deal with classroom stimulation and distraction. He was more at peace.[2]

. . . with Colleagues

Bells can also be used with our colleagues, to help create a calm mood and encourage authentic communication, as John Bell movingly describes.

> I often begin staff trainings for teachers by inviting the bell. I invite the bell three times. The participants slowly end their talking and the energy calms down. Then I say something like this: "Isn't this a beautiful sound? This is my meditation bell which I use every morning when I sit and meditate. It also travels with me. I've used it as a talking piece in circles where it is passed around. People have held it while pouring their hearts out."

Denys has used his bell extensively, both in meetings with colleagues and with the wider community. He finds it transforms not only the emotional warmth of the interaction, but also the very quality of the decisions made.

> Over time I introduced the bell to several friends and colleagues by inviting them to share my daily bell routine. This opened up opportunities to offer the gifts of calm and presence to colleagues. As we generated a collective energy of mindfulness, we had faith that we were also permeating our work environment with joy and compassion. It helped to have this kind of support

in the middle of a bad day, when despair over injustice or anger caused by messed up plans took over. Together, we practiced gratitude for our shared bell practice, and paused to remember that the sky or a flower could remind us of our true nature—the nature of wonder.

I have introduced bell practice at large community meetings too, where one hundred-plus people gather to plan or address controversy, with youth workers seeking better communications and in staff meetings of community-based organizations.

At public meetings, I asked people to set ground rules—respectful listening and speech, space for all voices—and introduced bell practice. People agreed to pause and breathe three times with silent awareness before continuing discussion. Even during heated discussions everyone respected the bell. Afterward, participants noticed a "buzz" of positive energy. Important decisions had been made while conflicts and anxieties were contained, rendering dialogue with the local city government more productive.

taking care to avoid religious connotations

Although the practices we are offering around the bell are secular, in some contexts any religious associations can be a barrier to people being able to relate to the human teachings of mindfulness. Using bells from a specific region, such as Japanese or Tibetan bowls, can sometimes produce this perception. Betsy Blake Arizu, a retired high school teacher and counselor we met earlier, gives the following practical advice.

I read an article about a school district in the Midwest of the United States that had implemented mindfulness practices throughout their district, and, unexpectedly, their school board announced that they could no longer do this. It wasn't clear what factors affected this decision. There were probably many, but someone speculated that it had something to do with the use of Tibetan bells in the classroom, and some imagined religious symbolism. Tibetan bells simply put forth a nice, long, resonant sound for mindful listening. Other bells can be used instead. I use a chime or a kind of bell that you might find in a school band or orchestra room.

Teachers have found imaginative ways around unwanted religious connotations. Some simply use bells with no such association at all. Coreen shares,

> I located a simple Greek *kymbala* (finger cymbals) to use as my mindfulness bell as I did not have a real crystal bell or any other suitable bell. This instrument worked fine.

Murielle who we met earlier uses different "bells" for different audiences, such as a music box, a ringing clock, and so on, choosing "neutral, pretty music that has no religious connotations for anyone." Jade Ong, a middle and high school teacher in Malaysia, uses the singing bell but avoids any religious feel by turning it into a game, issuing a "bell challenge."

> Working with multi-faith refugee students in a church-funded school, it was necessary to ensure that the training was not interpreted as having any religious context. Sitting all at one end of the room, I said, "Let's play the Bell Challenge!" "Yeah" was the enthusiastic consensus. Holding up a bell, I asked the group to keep silent. First I rang the bell. Then passed it around to encourage the students to feel, touch, and hear their own ringing. Then the bell came back to me. Each time it was rung I asked them to hold up a different finger. It seems so simple but worked marvelously to get all to listen quietly and rise up to the challenge. The next progression was to have volunteers come up to ring the bell. We went on to introduce mindful breathing. Learning from these games, the sessions now always start with complete silence, three rings of the bell, and mindful breathing.

Be still and know.
THICH NHAT HANH

three
sitting

in this chapter

- Explore the importance of sitting mindfully—to settle, calm, and relax our mind and body.

- Find step-by-step instructions and guidance for a sitting practice, with some suggestions for variations, to reach a comfortable and stable sitting position.

- Gather ideas on how to integrate sitting practice into our daily lives and into our teaching, with reflections, examples, and suggestions from practicing teachers.

sitting like a mountain

THICH NHAT HANH

Henri was a professor of mathematics in the French school of Toronto, who, after having spent three weeks in Plum Village, went back to his school and practiced mindfulness with his students. He walked slowly and mindfully into the class, and began to write on the blackboard mindfully. His students asked him, "Dear teacher, are you sick?" He said: "No, I am not sick. I'm just practicing mindful walking. I enjoy it. I feel a lot of peace. I am very much at peace because I have learned mindfulness. Would you like me to tell you what I did in Plum Village?" And they listened.

They agreed that every fifteen minutes, a boy would clap his hands—because they did not yet have a bell of mindfulness—and everyone, including the teacher, would practice mindful breathing and relax as they sat together. They practiced stopping what they were doing and coming back to themselves in that moment by bringing all their attention to their in-breath and out-breath. This helped them to improve their capacity to learn in the classroom.

In the beginning, it was like playing a game, but the more they did it, the more it became part of their everyday lives; the whole class profited greatly from the practice of mindfulness of breathing and sitting. Transformation and healing took place, and his class made a lot of progress, becoming a very joyful kind of family. Other classes at the school followed their example, and when Henri reached the age of retirement, the administration asked him to stay for a few more years. He could focus on bringing the practice of mindfulness into the school and improve the quality of teaching and learning in the school.

Henri's experience is possible, just by sitting and breathing, for a schoolteacher to help their students to suffer less and to be happy. You help them to generate a feeling of joy, and then later they will know how to create a feeling of joy by themselves.

There is a radio that is going on all the time in our mind called Radio NST: Non-Stop Thinking. While sitting, we turn off that radio and enjoy every breath more deeply. Healing and nourishment take place much more easily. If you are truly focused on your breath, even for just a moment, you find you will naturally stop thinking about the past or the future, about your projects or your worries, and develop your capacity to enjoy the wonders of life in the present moment with every breath. It becomes a habit, but it takes some training, like when you learn to play ping-pong or tennis. With practice, you get in the habit of enjoying your breathing while sitting.

During sitting meditation, then, we stop speaking and we calm our body and mind. We don't allow ourselves to be carried away by our thinking. Letting go of our thinking about the past or the future, coming back to the present moment, is very helpful. It is this thinking that removes you from the here and the now. If you are caught in your thinking all the time, you get tired and are not capable of being present.

The philosopher René Descartes said: "I think, therefore I am." But I don't agree: "I think, therefore I am not there—I am not really there to touch the wonders of life"; when I'm carried away by my thinking, I can't really be present. Sometimes thinking is productive, but sometimes it can take us away from the experience of being with who is there and what is happening in the here and now. You can naturally calm your thoughts if you focus your attention fully on your in-breath and your out-breath. You observe a kind of silence that is very eloquent and powerful, that allows you to be fully alive and present to enjoy every moment, every breath. This silence is not oppressive at all. It's very alive. When we stop our talking and calm our thinking and breathe, we become alive again, and aware of what is happening inside and around us. We can describe the silence as "thundering silence"— as powerful as thunder. When we all sit and breathe together like that we can generate a very powerful collective energy that will penetrate into everyone in the classroom, and help with healing and transformation.

The mind is like a river and thoughts are drops of water succeeding each other in a stream. To meditate is to sit beside the river of the mind and recognize every thought as it arises. You may like to practice with each one of these lines for two or three breaths while sitting:

Aware of my in-breath, I breathe in; aware of my out-breath, I breathe out.

Following my in-breath, I breathe in; following my out-breath, I breathe out.

Aware of my body, I breathe in; aware of my body I breathe out.

Calming my body, I breathe in; calming my body, I breathe out.

Generating joy, I breathe in; generating joy I breathe out.

Generating happiness, I breathe in; generating happiness I breathe out.

Aware of a painful feeling or emotion I breathe in;
aware of a painful feeling or emotion I breathe out.
Calming the painful feeling or emotion I breathe in;
calming the painful feeling or emotion I breathe out.

Suppose one thousand students are sitting still during a school assembly and practicing mindful breathing to calm their body and release tension with a guided meditation like this! The children in that group will feel a powerful energy that can help them to become calm and to feel happy. A child who finds himself or herself with a group of people in school who can generate the energy of love and understanding will have more chance to transform his or her suffering. A collective energy of peace, generated by mindfulness, is the answer.

....

sitting mindfully

Why practice sitting mindfully?

• To strengthen our ability to settle, calm, and relax mind and body.

• To bring the mind back to the body.

• To practice being alive in the present moment and enjoy "doing nothing."

• To build our awareness of thoughts, feelings, and bodily sensations.

• To increase a sense of connection and mutual support with others.

Sitting practice can bring great stability to the mind and the body. It gives us the opportunity to become more fully aware of what is happening inside and around us in the present moment.

Usually when we sit, while travelling to work or school or university, while at our desks, in meetings, or on the sofa, we are so driven by habit energies of "doing" that we feel we must be distracted, by work, TV, a computer, a book, or magazine. Sitting mindfully means we just sit. We stop what we are doing and bring our full attention to what is happening in the present moment, in our breath, mind, and body. Like a mountain during a storm, solid and stable, we sit and see how feelings and thoughts come and go. This is sitting just to sit—upright, with dignity, our minds fully awake.

We sit with the intention of being aware of what is happening in the present moment as best we can. Some days, especially when we start to practice, having the intention seems like all we can do, as we watch our mind swinging around like a monkey, here, there, and everywhere. Watching our monkey mind do this *is* to become aware of what is happening in the present moment: we become fully present with the dispersion. As John Bell, a mindfulness trainer from the US who we met earlier, suggests with some amusement, we can see that this is sometimes just the nature of the mind.

The mind! Its wild ups and downs, feeling good, feeling bad, ten thousand joys and ten thousand sorrows. We can't escape this experience. Meditation can teach us how to accept these changing states. The purpose of meditation is not to feel good, although we secretly hope that will be a result. It's to train ourselves to compassionately accept what is happening from moment to moment. Like the old spiritual says, "I'm sometimes up, and sometimes down, coming for to carry me home; but still my soul feels heavenly bound, coming for to carry me home."

During sitting meditation, we aim to let all things be equal—our passing thoughts, emotions, our bodily sensations, the sounds around us. We notice our emotions and thoughts as they come up, then gently release them, letting them go. There is no need to push them away, suppress them, or pretend they are not there. As best we can, we observe them all with a kind and accepting eye. We might picture ourselves like a well-rooted tree, allowing ourselves to be still and calm despite the storms that might arise within or around us.

The good news is that as we persist with our regular practice, over time we find that our mind will gradually become more settled, more accepting of what is, calmer, clearer, more spacious, and happier, and our heart softer and kinder—some days at least!

Our formal practice does not have to be based on sitting, and some people find they prefer walking or mindful movement, but it is worth experimenting with sitting practice to build up the ability to be still, calm, and stable. Even if it seems hard at first, practicing a short period of sitting can give us the stability of breath and body to investigate our thoughts and feelings. We can explore any sense of agitation or boredom that makes sitting still difficult. This can be illuminating, as whatever comes up in our practice often plays out in our daily life and relationships.

Learning to sit can bring stability to our eating, our work, and our ability to be there when we're talking with others. Any moment when we are sitting—when waiting, in a meeting, when commuting, even during a TV program or film—is an opportunity to become aware of our breath, mind, and body. Those around us do not even need to know what we are doing!

Sitting is one choice of practice, and may not be the best choice when we are upset, agitated, or sluggish. It is wise routinely to alternate sitting with more active forms of mindfulness such as mindful walking and movement. These may be more helpful at times when we need to get our body moving or dispel agitation.

. . . . .

There are further stories and reflections at the end of the chapter on how practicing teachers have integrated sitting into their own lives, the lives of their students, and into their classrooms, schools, and universities.

Sitting practice always goes together with mindful breathing, and sometimes with inviting the bell, so you may find the guidance and illustrations from chapters one and two useful.

core practice

....

short sitting practice

A practice summary is available in appendix A on page 294.

Materials and Preparation

- First, practice yourself so you have some personal experience to share with others. Arrange chairs, cushions, mats, etc., according to how you want people to sit (see guidance further on in the chapter on finding the best sitting position).

- Bell and inviter (optional but recommended).

The following practice takes about fifteen to twenty minutes.

You can stop at any point. It is better to do a little well than to rush through.

1. Finding Your Sitting Position

Settle yourself into a comfortable and stable sitting position.
    Sit up straight with dignity, tall but relaxed.
    Imagine you are sitting like a mountain, stable and solid, supported by the earth.
    Check that your head sits comfortably on your spine, tuck the chin slightly.
    Shut your eyes or rest them softly on a spot in front of you.
    Gently relax your face and jaw.

Go through the instructions slowly, with pauses at the end of each line, in time with the breath, and repeat any of them as you wish.

There are more detailed instructions for finding a comfortable position later in the chapter.

2. Contact

Be with how it feels to sit still, get a sense of contact with the earth—your feet in contact with the floor, your backside resting on your chair.
    Rest in your body, feeling a sense of the support beneath you.

If you or the students are on cushions on the floor, adapt the points of contact so that knees are supported and below the hips.

3. In, Out; Deep, Slow: Being with the Breath

Invite one sound of the bell to start the practice.
    Become aware of your in- and out-breath. Come back to the anchor of your breath.
    The phrases below are a guided meditation you may practice for yourself silently, or read aloud for others. After the first two lines are read, two keywords follow, each to be read with the in- and out-breath, respectively. Allow a few in- and out-breaths after each set of keywords.

    Breathing in, I know that I'm breathing in.
    Breathing out, I know that I'm breathing out.
    In, out.

Breathing in, I notice my in-breath has become deeper.

Breathing out, I notice my out-breath has become slower.

Deep, slow.

You could say here, or anywhere appropriate: "We notice when our mind drifts away. We move our attention back to our in- and out-breath to ground us in the here and now. We practice being kind to ourselves and not judging. We need not be frustrated if our mind is active; we just notice it, accepting it as it is."

There's no need to change anything; just be aware of your breath naturally becoming deeper and slower.

4. Calm, Ease; Smile, Release: In the Body

Allow our mind and body to feel calm and at ease.

Breathing in I feel calm.

Breathing out, I am at ease.

Calm, ease.

Breathing in, I smile to my whole body.

Breathing out, I release any tension in my body.

Smile, release.

5. Present Moment, Wonderful Moment

Once the students are used to the practice you might introduce "letting thoughts come and go" or "awareness of sound"—both described below—at this point.

Allow ourselves to become fully aware of the present moment and recognizing the conditions that make it a wonderful moment.

Rejoice—you are alive.

Breathing in, present moment,

Breathing out, wonderful moment.

Present moment, wonderful moment.

6. Simple Ending

With three mindful breaths, we bring our attention back to our sensation of contact between our body and the floor or the seat.

Without yet moving, we get ready in our mind and body for the practice to end.

Invite one full sound of the bell, to signal the end of the practice.

We take as long as we need to gently stretch, move slowly, open our eyes, smile, and breathe.

More Complex Endings

You may like to add one of these phrases to the end of your sitting practice as a final reflection.

Use just one per lesson/sitting session.

> **We realize we can just be present with whatever is within us: our pain, anger, and irritation, or our joy, love, and peace.**

> **We bring our full attention to all that is around us: sounds, smells, the sense of the room and of other people. Present moment, wonderful moment.**

> **When a storm of emotion passes through us we come back to the belly breathing, bringing our attention down from our head into our abdomen.**

We explore "taking care of our emotions" more fully in chapter seven.

> **We let our mind become spacious and our heart become soft and kind.**

> **Like a mountain we radiate peace and stability.**

—

variations and further elements to add to a basic sitting practice

- You and your students can sit longer with practice. It should always be enjoyable, not an endurance exercise, so always err on the side of shorter, simpler practice.
- You and your students can go deeper into the practice by revisiting any of the instructions above to support a longer sit. We suggest below two further practices, i) letting thoughts come and go, and ii) awareness of sound, which you might use when your students are used to the basic practice.
- You can try further images for finding a solid and stable sitting position. As well as a mountain, you could also suggest the trunk of a tree with deep roots in the ground, with its branches shaken by passing storms but its trunk standing strong (see chapter seven on emotions), or a solid rock in a fast-flowing river.

Practice: Letting Thoughts Come and Go

Move through this practice slowly.

Move through steps one to five of the basic practice above. Then add this variation:

> As you sit you will become aware of thoughts arising.
> When you notice that you have become caught up in
your thoughts, don't get frustrated. Noticing the thoughts

transforms the moment into a moment of mindfulness. Noticing your thinking *is* mindfulness of thinking.

You can use any of the other images suggested below.

Acknowledge your thoughts with a smile, and return to the awareness of your breath and body. You are a stable mountain; wind and weather play all around, but you are not shaken.

Use sparingly, only one for each practice.

Further Images for Letting Go of Thoughts and Feelings

As well as clouds moving across the sky, you could also suggest:

- traffic passing as you sit by the side of the road
- "thought buses" arriving and departing (possibly with the name of the thought or feeling on the front)
- a river flowing by as you watch from the bank
- a waterfall thundering down as you watch from behind
- characters who come and go across a stage or film (possibly carrying placards with the name of the thought or feeling).

When you and your students are used to this practice, you might invite them to notice any recurrent thoughts and feelings, for example, worry ("no one likes me"), planning ("I'm bored, what's for lunch?"), to gain awareness of their mental habits.

Move through this practice slowly.

Practice: Awareness of Sound as Sound

Move through steps one to five of the basic practice. Then add this variation:

Practicing this is especially useful if a distracting sound occurs during a sitting practice.

We are often distracted by sounds as we sit. It can be useful to find a way to be with sound as sound, with equanimity.

Become aware of sounds, in the room or outside, coming to your ears.

Focus on the quality of the sound—the pitch, high or low; the volume, loud or soft; the rhythm, fast or slow; and so on.

Notice and let go of any thoughts or feelings that arise in response to the sound.

Looking Deeply: Reflection Questions
for the Sitting Practice

Here are some questions for you, as the teacher, to reflect on yourself or to use with the students either during in-class sharing or by just letting the questions settle in the mind. Use them sparingly—it is not a checklist!

· How do I feel right now, in my mind, body, breath?

· How did the sitting practice feel? Was it the same experience throughout or did it change?

· Where was my mind today? Stressed, calm, distracted?

· Where was my body? How easy or difficult did my body find just sitting? Did I want to move a lot? If I did, did I manage to move mindfully?

· If I noticed my mind wandering, was I able to bring it back to my breath and the present moment?

Add other questions as appropriate. Keep them simple, open, nonjudgmental, encouraging, and accepting of all kinds of responses including "negative" ones and "I don't know." Gently but persistently keep bringing the sharing back to present, real-life experience.

teaching notes on

finding the best sitting position

You and your class might like to experiment with different ways to sit—on chairs or on the floor—so that you can determine what position best supports your sitting practice.

- Take plenty of time to find a position in which you are comfortable, so you can sit for a while without too much moving and distraction.

- Make sure your spine is straight and you sit in an upright but relaxed way, at ease, so that the sitting can be pleasant.

- Have your chin tucked in very lightly so your head is resting comfortably on your spine.

- Close your eyes or rest them softly on a point a few feet in front of you.

- If you are sitting on a chair, sit away from the back of the chair so as not to slouch, and have both feet planted firmly on the floor. Use cushions under your feet if the seat is a bit high.

- If you are sitting on a cushion or mat on the floor, try to have three points of contact with the ground, your bottom, and both of your knees. If this is not possible for you, consider putting extra cushions or supports under your knees.

Over time you or your class may like to learn to sit on the floor, cross-legged, on a cushion or a special meditation stool. Always make sure you are totally comfortable and do not try new positions for too long. Your knees need to be below your hips, so raise your buttocks on a cushion or two. Your knees should always be well supported. If you sit cross-legged on the floor and your knees are off the ground—as they likely will be when you start—use extra cushions to support them from underneath.

You will easily find instructions online for kneeling positions, for the cross-legged position, and for the half lotus and full lotus. Read all the instructions and warnings and go very gradually and carefully with an open and enquiring mind, taking care not to strain the body.

There are also meditation supplies that can help you, such as mats, stools, cushions, often called *zafus*; but any somewhat forgiving surface or firm cushion will do. Children are often happy enough on a wooden floor for a short period of time.

sitting mindfully in our lives and in our teaching

Sitting as Part of Our Own Mindfulness Practice

Establishing a regular daily sitting practice can provide a solid foundation for our practice of mindfulness. Learning to sit quietly can support us in offering mindfulness to those around us and the communities we serve, as the peace and stability it cultivates will naturally permeate our daily life.

At first, try to sit and focus on mindful breathing for just five to ten minutes every day, either in the morning or in the evening. Try to practice at the same time every day in a specific place—in a certain room or corner and on a certain cushion or chair. This will create a positive habit energy that supports the cultivation of calmness and concentration. It may be helpful to make notes after your practice of your experiences, writing down what thoughts and feelings arise for you in a "sitting notebook."

Sitting comfortably for longer periods takes a bit of training and practice. Our initial efforts to build a practice should be short and regular, with achievable goals. Fiona Cheong, a university teacher from the US who has worked in many parts of the world, shares the following words of advice.

> If we wish to awaken wisdom or compassion in the student, we must first set our own awakening in motion. The answer to my colleagues who ask, "How do you do it?" is simple. You can try to sit for a half hour every morning, and if that feels implausible, start with five minutes. I sit for twenty to thirty minutes, sometimes longer. I also practice mindful walking on the way to the classroom at a pace of three steps for each in- or out-breath, enjoying the contact between my feet and the earth. By the time I'm with my students, giving out the first instruction, I can hear how gentle my voice sounds. I can feel the smile on my face.

Sitting Mindfully before We Teach

You might like to sit mindfully if you get to class a few minutes early, to be ready for the lesson. It can help you have a clearer mind to run through your plans for the lesson, to bring your students and their needs and challenges to mind, and to ensure your authentic, grounded presence as you greet your students. For David Viafora, a mindfulness teacher and social worker in the US, sitting for a few minutes creates the space for some profound reflections on the ways in which his students can guide his teaching.

> I always try to take a few minutes before our session begins to breathe and reflect that these youth are not merely my students, but also my teachers.

In collaboration with years of personal practice experience, these fresh eyes and beginners' minds reveal anew how mindfulness can be most skillfully taught to truly benefit their unique lives, right here in this moment. If I pay attention well enough, the youth illuminate who I need to be very naturally in each moment to best serve them and allow an authentic relationship to bloom. In this relationship, mindfulness practice takes root very naturally for both of us—student and teacher alike.

Helping Students to Sit Mindfully

You can make sitting mindfully, combined with mindful breathing and/or listening to the bell, into a regular feature of your classroom. A few minutes spent sitting in this way is a refreshing way to begin and end a lesson. It can also help support you and the class before a challenging task as a transition between activities.

Derek Heffernan has found profound results from teaching what he calls "quiet time" to his students.

I am a high school teacher in Ontario, Canada. For the last three years, I have been using mindfulness in my classroom. I begin every class with one to five minutes of "quiet time." I use a bell to start the time and the students listen to the sound. I introduce this practice in the first week of class. Students sit quietly and breathe at the beginning of each class. The length of time varies from one to five minutes. I have found that students enjoy and look forward to the quiet time to start the class. If I forget to do it, they always remind me!

Students enjoy it for many reasons. It helps them transition from lunch to class so that they can focus better. I also know that students have taken this practice and used it at home to help themselves—for example, when they are feeling agitated or they can't sleep. I do this consistently through the whole semester (four months) that I teach the class. Every few weeks, I check in with the students to see if this practice has value for them and to see if we should continue it or not. This gives them ownership over the practice, and encourages participation among teenagers who need to have a sense of control over what they are doing.

Sitting mindfully is particularly valuable when a difficult incident occurs, or when people are experiencing strong emotions. It is important to have established the practice with your class so they are comfortable with it before applying it in a moment of difficulty. This special education teacher from Washington State in the US shares about her use of sitting when things "feel chaotic," a familiar feeling for many teachers.

> Sometimes I ask students to sit quietly with me for a few moments and concentrate on their breath or sounds. Especially when things feel chaotic I like to employ this practice. I find it helpful to describe simply how we can sit together at our desks, chairs, on the floor, etc., with hands, body, and voices quiet and relaxed. Often, I've seen students, whether troubled or not, take a few minutes and enjoy this simple pleasure that brings peace. Then, we start again.

Sitting can offer a space for students to touch stillness and feel comfortably centered, calm, and focused. It is important to remember that sitting is not always the right choice of practice, and that when people are agitated, moving practices are often more appropriate. We need to remember too that younger students usually cannot sit still for long, and that not every student will enjoy the practice every time. That is no problem, as Sister Tai Nghiem from Plum Village explains,

> At the end of the day's activities, we invite the teens to practice by sitting silently to enjoy the bell and their breathing for five minutes. Even if they don't like it at first, it's okay. With time they learn to enjoy it.

Sitting to Cultivate Connection

As you and your students get used to sitting, you can investigate more deeply the benefits of sitting with other people. You can reflect on how the feeling of mutual support, connection, caring, and peacefulness build a sense of collective energy. Suggesting images such as a flock of birds flying together or drops of water joining a river or ocean may be helpful. Sitting can also be used to help us cultivate feelings of being grounded and rooted to the earth, or being in touch with others, including those who are not physically present. Sitting can help us cultivate greater compassion and connectedness with the rest of life, with other living beings, and with the planet.

Connecting with nature may be particularly inspirational for this line of exploration, as Chelsea True, who teaches younger children in the US, suggests.

> I tell a story about a solid mountain to help us discover our body as a place of refuge. The mountain is home to many things: joyful horses in summer and plaintive songs of migrating geese in winter. Through it all, the mountain remains upright and tall, a home for all. I tell a story of Mindful Fox who listens all the way down to his heart and belly. I walk each child into the class one by one to their seat where they sit like mountains and enjoy breathing as each child arrives.

When the weather allows, literally sitting outside in nature, among its myriad sounds and smells, can be particularly delightful.

Peace is every step.
THICH NHAT HANH

four
walking

in this chapter

- Understand what it means to walk mindfully.

- Reflect on why we walk mindfully.

- Find step-by-step instructions and practical guidance for teaching and learning two core practices: i) walking a set path, such as a circle, and ii) a longer walk outside, with some suggestions for variations.

- Discover some practical ideas for ways in which we can integrate mindful walking into our daily life and into our teaching.

walking just to walk

THICH NHAT HANH

It is a joy to walk just for the sake of walking. With the practice of mindful walking we become fully present with our steps and our breath, our mind firmly established in the here and the now. Any moment throughout our day that we find ourselves walking becomes an opportunity to practice.

When we practice walking meditation, every step we take can generate the energy of peace, release tension in our body, and help us get in touch with the wonders of life that can nourish and heal us. If we have enough mindfulness and concentration, we can touch the earth deeply with every step. Walking to your school from the parking lot, you can enjoy every step.

By combining your breath and your steps you can deeply enjoy the practice of mindful walking. Breathing in, you may like to make two or three steps. Breathing out, you may like to make three or four steps. Pay attention to the contact between your foot and the ground. Don't let your mind stay up at the level of your head, but bring it down to the sole of your foot and touch the ground mindfully. Walk as if you are kissing the earth—Mother Earth—with your feet. You are mindful of Mother Earth, and that you are touching her with your foot. This can be very pleasant. You do not have to suffer or make any kind of special effort to be mindful of touching the earth. While you touch the ground with your foot as you breathe in, you can say, "I have arrived, I have arrived." I have arrived at the destination of life, because life is in the here and the now. The here and now are the only place and time where life is available.

We may be running our whole lives, sacrificing the present moment for the sake of the future. Living like this we are not capable of being happy right in the present moment. So mindful walking is a kind of revolution, a kind of resistance: you resist the running. You don't want to run anymore. You feel comfortable and at peace in the present moment, and that is why you can say to yourself, "I have arrived in the here and the now, where life is. I don't want to run anymore." Mindfulness gives us enough strength to resist the running.

For those of us who are used to the practice, we can arrive 100 percent in the here and the now. When you can arrive 100 percent in the here and the now, you feel peace and happiness right away. If you're new to the practice, you may like to try slow walking meditation. Breathing in, you make just one step, and you say, "I have arrived." Invest all your mind and body into the step and try to arrive 100 percent into the here and the now. If you have not arrived 100 percent, you might have arrived only 20, or 25 percent. In that case, do not make another step. Stand there, breathe out and breathe in again. Challenge yourself to arrive 100 percent in the here and the now. Then you smile the smile of victory, and you make another step, and say "I am home." "I have arrived, I am home." My home is right here in the present moment.

teaching notes on

mindful walking

Why walk mindfully?

- To reconnect our minds and bodies to the present moment as we walk.

- To enjoy slowing down and not rushing—practicing having "nowhere to go and nothing to do."

- To cultivate awareness of the body through movement.

- To become more aware of the links between emotion and movement.

- As an alternative to sitting, to develop focus, attention, and calm, to relieve stress and anxiety and let go of ruminative, repetitive thinking.

- To experience the wonders of life, connecting more deeply with ourselves, with those who are walking with us, and with the environment in which we walk.

Mindful walking is an invaluable basic practice for ourselves and for our students. With mindful walking, we can experience being fully present as something we can do during any activity, anywhere, at any time—right in the very midst of life. Adults often find that walking mindfully, letting go of their projects and worries, gives them permission to feel more carefree, connecting with the joy of dwelling happily in the present moment—something they may have experienced as a child. Moving practices, such as walking, can sometimes be more appropriate than sitting or lying down when our mind and body are busy or agitated.

    We walk with freedom and solidity, no longer in a hurry. We practice slowing down and not rushing, and touch the feeling of having nothing to do and nowhere to go. When we notice that our mind has got lost in thinking, which will naturally happen, we gently guide our attention back to our breath and our steps. As we practice, we may notice how we have become used to rushing and getting lost in our thinking, planning, daydreaming, ruminating, talking, or listening to music while on the move.

When we're first learning the practice of mindful walking, it's helpful to focus on our feet and to walk more slowly. Walking mindfully, however, is not something we must do in a super-slow, solemn, or artificial way. Walking naturally, at a gentle pace, can help our bodies remain relaxed.

We never force our breathing to change. We match our steps to accommodate our breath, just as it is in that moment. Walking should be enjoyable, not hard labor, with no need to change the breath—we are just aware of our steps and our breath. As we practice, we may find we can walk at the speed of a pleasant stroll and notice more of what is happening inside us and around us, staying mindful of our breath and our steps.

If we are lucky enough to be outside in nature we may like, from time to time, to stop, look around, and notice the beauty of life—the trees, the white clouds, the limitless sky. We can listen to the birds and feel the fresh breeze. Life is all around us, and we are alive!

Even if we have injuries or disabilities, we can walk in peace. Maybe we need help to walk—perhaps support from other people, or aids like a cane, a crutch, or a wheelchair. However we move through the world we can still be aware of the privilege we have to move as a free person. We may feel our breath relax and our body feel lighter as we practice.

. . . . .

There are further examples and reflections at the end of the chapter on how practicing teachers have integrated mindful walking into their own lives, the lives of their students, and into their classrooms, schools, and universities.

core practice

....

mindful walking in a circle

A practice summary is available in appendix A on page 296.

Notes on Choosing Where to Walk

When you are first learning to walk mindfully on your own you may like to choose a place that is quiet and secluded, where you can walk without feeling self-conscious or being disturbed. You can walk indoors, or outdoors, in a garden or quiet part of a park. You can choose a short loop or a path where you can walk slowly and in silence.

This practice is designed to help you learn to walk mindfully yourself, and be able to introduce a simple basic mindful walking practice to others.

When planning a walk for students, practice walking in that space yourself first. You may like to start in an indoor space, like a gym, hall, or a large classroom, walking around the edge of the room in a loop. But an enclosed outdoor space like a playground or schoolyard can also work well. Remember that enjoying the practice yourself is the best way to inspire the students to enjoy it.

Remember to take into account any difficulties some of your students may have with walking, and take care to include those with injuries and disabilities, or who need the aid of a cane, a wheelchair, or another kind of support.

1. Explain/Prepare the Students

- We walk in silence so we can focus on our walking without distraction.
- We stay together and follow the pace of the person in front of us.
- We practice walking without thinking of the past, the future, or our projects, bringing our attention back to our breath and our steps whenever we become aware that we've become lost in thinking.
- For a longer walk: we open ourselves to the wonders of life within us and around us—in the other people around us and in our surroundings as we walk.

Give clear instructions at the beginning: for example, letting students know if you will pause and continue or stop after one circuit.

2. Arrive

Begin by inviting one sound of the bell.

Three mindful breaths while listening to the bell can help everyone to get settled and focused.

You may like to sing a Plum Village practice song such as "I Have Arrived, I Am Home," or "Breathing In, Breathing Out" to bring focus and energy. This often works better with younger children and adults—teens can be self-conscious. You can find the lyrics and music to Plum Village songs at www.wakeupschools.org/songs.

3. Form a Circle

Everyone starts by forming a circle. Join hands if appropriate.

Drop hands and expand the circle outward so there is some space between everyone.

You can also sing a song that the class is familiar with if it is calming and relevant to the practice.

Everyone then lets their hands fall to their sides and turns to the left so that their right shoulders are toward the inside of the circle.

4. Standing Mindfully

Close your eyes or softly focus them with your gaze slightly downward— open them if you feel unbalanced.

Stand tall, in a relaxed way, and enjoy a few mindful breaths.

You may like to put your hands on your belly to feel the in-breath and the out-breath.

Become aware of the contact your feet make with the floor or the earth. Allow this to ground your body and mind.

At any point in the practice, remind yourself and your students to return to the constant anchor of the breath and to an awareness of the contact the feet make with the floor or the earth, to bring back wandering minds.

Become aware of all the tiny movements your feet are making, moment by moment, to keep you balanced and prevent you from falling over.

Let your attention come down from the level of your head into your belly, and allow all your thinking and worries to be released into the earth.

5. Walking Mindfully

Walk in a natural way, deliberate but not mechanical or forced.

After a few breaths, a sound of the bell is invited, and everyone begins to walk together clockwise along the circumference of the circle, following the person in front.

On the in-breath take a step with your left foot, on the out-breath step with your right foot.

Walk slowly together on the circuit, calmly and peacefully.

Concentrate completely on your breathing and the contact your feet make with the ground; walk as if you are kissing the earth with your steps.

When you arrive back where you started or when you hear the bell, stop, and continue breathing; notice how it feels to stand solidly on the earth.

6. Pause/End

If you are with a class, you can invite them mindfully to take their seats or sit on the floor

When they are settled, you might use the reflection questions below.

You and your class can finish after one circuit, or set off around the circle again.

Finish by turning to face each other and acknowledge each other by smiling or maybe even bowing to each other to express gratitude to the others for the collective energy that has supported us on the walk.

variations on walking practice

For these variations, practice slowly with full concentration and frequent pauses to become still and reflect.

- As you walk, move your attention gradually up your body—to ankles, knees, hips, arms—concentrating fully on this part of the body and how it is feeling as it moves.

- Change the speed of your walking—slower and faster than your normal walking meditation pace—and observe the impact on your mind and body.

- Recite the mindful walking verses below in time with your steps, either aloud or silently to yourself, for example say, "I have arrived" as you breathe in, and "I am home" as you breathe out.

> **I have arrived / I am home**
>
> **In the here / In the now**
>
> **I am solid / I am free**
>
> **In the ultimate I dwell**

Suggestions for using the verses:

On the in-breath, say the first part, e.g., "In the here," and on the out-breath say the last part, e.g., "In the now."

You may like to just repeat silently the key words: *arrived/ home, here/now, solid/free*, as each step touches the earth, arriving fully in the present moment. For example, say "arrived" on the in-breath, and "home" on the out-breath.

Remember the words are not something to repeat automatically, but an invitation to practice being fully present with each step.

You can focus on just one line at a time.

A Fun Practice: Walking As . . .

Many teachers like the idea of using their students' imagination to have some fun by making an active group game of "walking in different ways." The activity can create an energizing and joyful spirit of fun and laughter, while helping students to bond and trust. It enables students and teacher to be more in their body in the moment, and can be used to trigger reflection on how walking in these different ways affects mood, thoughts and feelings.

In this game, the teacher calls out a suggestion for how to walk. A few examples:

- Walking in different weather or situations, e.g., through rain or snow, on ice, on sand, through water, on hot coals.
- Walking as different kinds of people—jobs (e.g., business person, forest ranger, teacher), characters (e.g., astronaut, ballerina, zombie), or personalities (e.g., shy, confident), or ages (toddler, teenager, older person).
- Walking like different animals—monkey, elephant, mouse.
- Walking in different moods—in a rush, scared in the dark, happy in the park.

Everyone then walks in that way until the bell sounds. When the bell sounds everyone stops where they are and silently returns to their breathing. It is important to make this instruction clear before beginning, especially for younger students who can get quite excited when they try varying the tempo and manner of walking in this way. Toward the end, always calm things down by suggesting a slower way to walk—through honey, underwater—then inviting students to take one step per breath, or simply return to their natural mindful walking pace.

Once the students are used to the idea, invite new suggestions, using hands up or calling out, as appropriate.

core practice
....

longer mindful walk

A practice summary is available in appendix A on page 296.

Once you and the students are comfortable and at ease with a short predefined walking practice, you may like to go on a longer walking meditation together, with you, the teacher, leading at the front. Wait until you are confident that you and the students are ready so you can all enjoy the practice without anxiety.

Materials and Preparation

- Bell and inviter (optional but recommended).
- A teacher with experience of mindful walking.

Moving to a bigger space is lovely but the larger it is, the harder to keep focus, so build up to more challenging environments gradually.

Find a space where you can walk a route that is safe and the right length for the age of your students—this could be in the gym, school grounds, a quiet block of streets, a nearby park, or the countryside.

You may like to choose to make the first outside walk a short one in a very safe place, such as inside the school grounds.

Practice walking the full route at least once yourself before leading others. Think about details such as the opportunities, distractions, and obstacles along the way.

On an outside route, it is best to ask another adult to walk at the back to keep an eye out for safety and to be able to offer a quiet, supportive word to anyone who gets distracted.

Now—breathe, smile, and enjoy walking!

Some young people may be too uncomfortable to walk in a public place, e.g., some teenagers, or people with social anxiety.

1. Settle the Group

When everyone has gathered at the starting point of the walk, help the group to settle and focus by enjoying a few mindful breaths or a short bell of mindfulness practice together.

2. Explain the Activity

Remind the group of the techniques we've learned already in the shorter walk, which we can use to stay focused, e.g., breath, steps, verses—"arrived/home" (outlined in "variations" above).

Clarify the ground rules, e.g., follow the leader, stay behind the leader, keep together to maintain a collective energy, move like an organism, and stay in silence to be fully present for ourselves and for each other.

Demonstrate how to coordinate breath and steps, for example: two steps on the in-breath and three steps on the out-breath, or three on the in-breath and five on the out-breath, or even four on the in-breath and six on the out-breath.

Remind the students here is no need to force our steps to match our breath; we can just gently notice how many steps we need for the in-breath and how many we need for the out-breath. No matter how many steps per breath, we keep with the pace of the group to stay together.

Invite the group, and yourself, to become aware of any excitement or anxiety in mind and body about the first step we are all about to take, and relax with a smile.

Bear in mind that the more public it is the more other people may look and comment, and we need to be prepared. You may like to suggest that if someone we pass is staring or makes eye contact as we walk that we can simply offer a smile and then come back to our breathing.

If you plan to stop from time to time to enjoy the beauty of your surroundings, let the group know ahead of time. That way when pauses happen everyone is clear that the invitation is to stay in silence and breathe with the moment.

3. Begin Walking

Enjoy three full in- and out-breaths, using the bell if you wish. Invite the group to allow the sound of the bell to penetrate into the body as we stand solidly on the earth.

Songs can be found at
www.wakeupschools.org/songs.

If there is a Plum Village song, or another song the group is familiar with that is calming and relevant, you may like to sing it together before beginning your walk.

Then begin to walk—with ease and freedom. The group follows you.

4. Pause (Optional)

Remind everyone as the group sets off to be aware of the body and breath as we walk so we can get in touch with the wonder and joy of being alive.

If you see an inspiring place to stop, breathe and admire your surroundings—a tree, a river, or even just some bugs crawling on the sidewalk—you may like to stop walking for a moment and be present for that experience.

If there is a lawn or appropriate place for everyone to sit you can enjoy a short mid-walk sitting meditation outside. Invite them to keep the silence.

5. End

It is helpful to end the mindfulness walk where it began, giving everyone a sense of coming full circle.

After a sound of the bell you may like to invite the students to quietly share their experience in a pair or a group, e.g., the sounds, sights, smells, and thoughts and feelings of the present moment. You can use the reflection questions below to guide you.

Pace and structure the questions and invite the bell from time to time, so they have a chance to come back to their breathing.

If you are outside and there is an appropriate place to sit you may like to continue to enjoy the surroundings while you reflect.

Invite the group to maintain the energy of mindfulness as we move into our next activity (such as lesson, lunch, recess, home time).

looking deeply:
reflection questions on mindful walking

Here are some questions for you, the teacher, to reflect on for yourself or to use with the students either during in-class sharing or by just letting the questions settle in the mind. Use them sparingly—it is not a checklist!

• What did I notice when I walked—in myself, in my surroundings?

• How has the practice impacted me today? Did it change any of my thoughts and feelings, my body, my breath?

• Did walking like this feel different from how I normally walk? If so, how?

• How easy or difficult did I find the practice? Fun, boring, calming, challenging?

• How easy or comfortable was it to walk in silence? What did it add to the experience?

• How much did my mind wander? If I noticed my mind wander was I able to bring it back to my breath and/or steps?

• What was it like to walk with other people in this way?

Add other questions as appropriate. Keep them simple, open, nonjudgmental, encouraging, and accepting of all kinds of responses including "negative" ones and "I don't know." Gently bring the sharing back to present real-life experience.

mindful walking in our lives and in our teaching

Building Mindful Walking into Our Day

Mindful walking can be enjoyed anywhere and anytime and—a huge bonus for teachers—it can be built easily into a busy schedule, taking no more time than we already set aside for moving between places.

In the sitting chapter, we talked of the value of building up a regular, habitual practice. Mindful walking can be a cornerstone of our practice, alongside, or maybe instead of, sitting. To get the day off to a good start, it is helpful to create a routine of walking mindfully early in the day, on the way to school or university. As usual it is advisable to keep the focused practice short at first, choosing just part of the daily route to work, and setting an intention to walk it mindfully every day for a week. Your mindful walk can be along a specific block, or even just the walk from the car into the building. If you are on public transit, you can follow your breathing as you mindfully sit or stand on the bus or train.

Practice not to arrive at work in your mind before you arrive there in your body. By walking mindfully and being present you can have a bit more time for yourself before the work day begins.

> I sit in my car in the parking lot for five minutes practicing, paying attention to my breath and being present. Then, I walk to my classroom, all the while remembering to "walk as if your feet are kissing the earth." I remember that I will not be doing this forever and this brings a reminder of the here and now and of gratitude for simply walking.
> **INSTRUCTOR OF SOCIAL WORK, CANADA**

Meena Srinivasan, an experienced Plum Village educator, finds that mindful walking as she goes to her classroom at the start of her day helps establish a state of mind so she can arrive more fully present and ready to teach. Later in the day she again enjoys practicing mindfulness in little gaps of time.

> I try to walk from the parking lot to my classroom mindfully each morning using words like "joy," "happiness," "peace," or "love" with each step. When I do this, I can quickly shift my state of mind so I arrive at my classroom in a more receptive, positive mood. I also make sure to try to walk certain paths at my school mindfully, like the path from my classroom to the bathroom. Using these transitional times to nourish my peace of mind is a great way to take care of myself during the school day. Mindful walking is a great way to practice mindfulness on the days when you just don't have time to sit.

Walking Mindfully as We Teach

We can walk mindfully in the classroom too. Even a tiny moment of mindful walking can help us to remain more mindful and present for our students in the middle of a classroom activity. Sarah Woolman, an elementary and middle school teacher from the UK, practices mindful walking even when it is for just a few steps:

> I try to do this walking from the photocopier to the classroom, from my desk to the blackboard. Understanding that everything is in the moment and not in an aim or outcome has helped my teaching. Being present with what the children are experiencing and being open to change and responding to that enables the class to breathe, to be alive.

Over time, we can build the habit of mindful walking into any moment throughout our day.

Walking Mindfully When Others Are There

In a few schools, mindful walking has become an accepted part of the culture. In such spaces, we can openly "walk for others" as well as ourselves: the sense of inner calm that mindful walking generates can silently affect and remind others to be more mindful. Bea Harley, a member of a senior management team and a retired elementary school teacher from the UK reflects,

> We would each act as a "bell" for one another. To see a colleague walking up the stairs mindfully would remind us to breathe and take things more calmly.

Bea worked in a small elementary school where mindfulness practice is in the fabric of the school culture, but this is unusual. Tineke Spruytenburg, a special education teacher and mindfulness trainer from the Netherlands, works in more mainstream contexts. She suggests to her teacher students that one of the joys of mindful walking is that you can gain all the benefits without anyone even needing to know you are doing it!

When coaching teachers, I advise daily walking meditation when going to the washroom. I suggest they may not walk as fast as usual yet not so slowly that others will wonder what is going on. I propose they walk with their feet, not their head, and to take this kind of break when they feel that stress is on their shoulders. Nobody will question you about going to the toilet, so take advantage of this possibility even when you do not need to urinate. Take your time to mindfully walk to the washroom and once there really pay attention to what your body is doing, the movements you make while washing your hands, et cetera. You´ll be fresh when you return to your classroom.

Walking Mindfully Can Help with Stress

Mindful walking can be a great stress reliever. If you are heading for a stressful event or feeling agitated, you could try to walk there more mindfully at least part of the way. This may help relieve your mind from playing over a story or from worrying about where you are headed. You may like to explore any sense of difference from how you usually arrive in such circumstances. You can also try mindful walking when walking away from a difficult situation, noting how it may help you gradually to calm down, or just be with your agitation.

Sister Chan Duc, a senior Plum Village nun at the European Institute of Applied Buddhism, started her working life as a teacher in the UK. She reflects on the value of mindful walking in helping her to survive the challenges of working in a school in the center of a large city. She found mindful walking at the end of the day particularly useful in helping her to let go of difficult events and refocus on the pleasant, getting back in touch with the beauties of life through the simple sights she passed on her walk home.

When I was a teacher, I went to just one retreat and I learned about mindful walking. I knew that was the answer for me in my daily life. I decided to get up earlier and do part of the journey to school on foot, so I could really walk. And coming home I decided to do the whole journey on foot. It wasn't a long distance, but before I had gone by bus. That changed a lot for me. Doing walking meditation on the way to school made me so much more relaxed, prepared, and calm. And doing walking meditation on the way home allowed me to just let go of everything. In school there are always unpleasant things that happen during the day. There are pleasant things that can happen too, but at that time I was in a very difficult school with much violence—it wasn't very pleasant. I really needed to let go of everything. When I walked home each day, though it was in London, I could look in people's gardens and see the flowers. There were places where I could walk on the grass, and that was a wonderful opportunity for the unpleasant things that had happened during the day to be changed by my being in touch with what was wonderful in life.

Walking Mindfully Connects Us with the World Around

As we become more experienced, we can bring mindfulness to all kinds of walking—fast and slow, alone or in a busy street, in sun or rain, climbing stairs, and so on. We even might try mindful running, swimming, or cycling. We simply bring our attention to the sensations of our body, connecting our movement and breath, grounding our mind in the present moment.

Away from our jobs, mindful walking in our leisure time can help to clear the mind and connect us with the natural world. So, like Alison Mayo, a busy preschool teacher in the UK, you might take yourself for an intentional short mindful walk—no need for any other purpose—and enjoy some or all of it mindfully.

I now do walking meditation up a hill near my house most evenings, which I find clears my mind and also gives me some good exercise, fresh air, and connection with nature.

Mindful Walking Helps Manage Feelings and Builds a Calmer Atmosphere

Children and young people enjoy walking practice when it is taught in a light, fun way. Former elementary school teacher and UK outdoors educator Jess Plews reflects on how mindful walking helped a group of elementary school students notice and talk about their surroundings, including those students who were usually shy.

The mindful walking yesterday was beautiful. The students absolutely loved it, and they really focused. You could see that being shown how to notice things more was just allowing them to question everything around them. We had a few children who rarely speak, who are quite shy, but they were also motivated on that walk to point out things and ask questions about nature.

Self-regulation, which means the ability to manage your own feelings and behavior, and the closely connected skill of impulse control, are major challenges for many young people. Their restlessness can underlie many of the difficulties they have with learning, getting along with others and in managing their own lives. Teachers can find their students' impulsivity stressful and challenging, and are often delighted to find gentle and positive ways to help their students behave in a calmer way. Mindful walking can be an effective and kind method to achieve this.

Christine Petaccia, the occupational therapist we met in the chapter on the breath, shares an experience of how quickly mindful walking helped a class move into a state of calm, ready to learn.

One day I was called into a classroom to help the teacher use self-regulation techniques to calm the children down. I had just recently attended a group mindfulness session for the first time and had experienced walking medita-tion. So, I thought I would give it a try. I brought the entire class to my room and we worked on breathing and relaxation exercises, lying on our backs. Then I taught them walking meditation, and they walked back into to the classroom very calm and ready to learn. It was truly extraordinary how well it worked the very first time.

The sense of inner turmoil and distractibility in which many young people live often erupts in a frantic school atmosphere and high volume of routine noise, that are stressful for students and teachers alike. The sense of freneticism can be espe-cially apparent when students move around an enclosed building. Schools gener-ally attempt to tackle this with rules, sometimes with sanctions and punishments. Teaching students a routine of mindful walking, however, can offer a positive alter-native, helping students voluntarily maintain a restful sense of quiet and calm in the school building, as two teachers reflect:

At transitional times, things can get very frantic. The mindful walking up and down the stairs has transformed the energy exchange in between classrooms. We're practicing that, and it's becoming part of how we are.

—CAROLINE WOODS, ELEMENTARY SCHOOL TEACHER, UK

We used to line up quietly at the door, they'd go off to the cloakroom, and by the time they arrived there would be a lot of noise and scrambling about. We're now walking mindfully and peacefully to the cloakroom, there's quiet in the cloakroom, and they go peacefully outside. And as soon as they get outside, that's their chance to let off steam.

—SUSANNAH ROBSON, ELEMENTARY SCHOOL TEACHER, UK

Susannah's reminder that children need to "let off steam" is a valuable one—mindful walking should always be invitational, not imposed, and not used as a form of discipline to make children "walk nicely and quietly." Mindful walking needs to be just one part of an active school day in which children have plenty of safe opportunities to be lively, energetic, and make joyful noise.

Mindful Walking Builds Confidence

The mind-body connection is foundational to mindfulness. How we stand and move has a major effect on both our mood and on what we project on others. UK schoolteacher Mike Bell, experienced in applying the Plum Village tradition with his classes, used mindful walking to help children who felt bullied. He found that mindful walking allowed the students both to feel more solid in themselves, and also to embody confidence and non-reactivity.

Walking meditation has really worked with children who are being bullied. I point out that bullies are people who enjoy seeing somebody else upset, so the trick is to not give them any idea that you are upset. I have shown several pupils how to bring their attention down to the contact point between their feet and the ground and how to keep their focus there as they walk across the playground, not allowing any change in expression when somebody makes a taunting comment. I have observed a change in two or three pupils. One girl, who would stop behind to tell me how horrible people were, now stops and tells me something else![1]

Lively Ways to Teach Mindful Walking

What it means to walk mindfully can be conveyed using colorful words and images that speak vividly to the young. Chelsea True, from the US, uses the memorable image of "walking with fox feet" with her class of young children, an image they find so powerful that some take it home with them.

Using Thay's words along with playful imagery, I'll say, "Mindful Fox has soft, furry paws. When he walks, his furry fox paws kiss the earth with each step. Every step he takes, a flower grows. We can also walk like fox, with peace in every step."

Before we begin, we fold our hands at our tummies so they are still. As we begin walking, I'll introduce Thay's verse, "On this beautiful path, I walk in peace. Every step I take, a flower blooms." We sing this as a call-and-response as we make our way, with furry fox paws, kissing the earth with each step. Children as young as three can enjoy walking with fox feet.

One parent reports that her daughter Aubrey, age 5, now uses her fox feet to walk mindfully at home and that this imagery has become a part of their family's vocabulary. Gracyn, age ten, loved walking with fox feet so much that she found fox slippers to wear at home. When her family had to relocate for her father's job, she texted me a photo from the airport. She was wearing her fox slippers, walking mindfully into the next part of her life's journey.

Working with his cool teens at Plum Village, Mark Vette from New Zealand encouraged them to try mindful walking practice, calling it by whatever names they chose—with some amusing results when faced with the Zen Master himself!

When I worked in the Plum Village teens' program years ago, when we did a formal practice, we just did it. We made up our own names for it. One day Thay saw the group and complimented us for doing walking meditation.

An older boy turned to him and said, "We're not doing walking meditation, we're tai chi stepping," and happily, continued on.

In "variations" we described the "walking as a . . . " practice. Peggy Rowe Ward, an experienced teacher educator from the US, shares her experience of using this fun practice with both younger and older students.

Our young children are particularly fond of super heroes. Why not walk like Spiderman? We can use our Spidey-Senses. What about the Hulk—is he mindful? We mindfully walked like elephants, kangaroos, dogs, and chickens. We walked on different surfaces in our minds, like warm sand, one inch of water, two inches of water, honey, and warm wax.

When students were studying Egypt, we had a YouTube from *Saturday Night Live* with Steve Martin walking like an Egyptian. When the students were studying the ocean, we walked on the ocean floor. We walked like Mahatma Gandhi and Dr. Martin Luther King when this was the topic of study. Of course, this helps students to embody the lesson, and it creates happy teachers.

involving and empowering students

Mindfulness comes alive for students when they internalize it. Peggy shares some rich and inspirational ideas for student involvement in mindful walking.

Try partner practices. The children like getting to coach each other in trying new ways of walking. Being barefoot was an uncommon thing for many of our children from Asian countries, and some really loved it. All of the children enjoyed walking with a partner when one was blindfolded. We walked with books on our head, holding hands, and one person was the mindful walker and the other person was the mindless distractor.

Invite the students to demonstrate. Keep your eye out for the students who really love the practice and invite them to teach. Soon everyone will want to lead the practice. I learned a lot from the student interns. One of

the most moving classes that I experienced was led by Lukie, a kindergarten student who took the whole kindergarten class into a place of beauty
in motion. His face was so serene, each small foot mindfully placed on the
floor. All of the children stepped right into a field of peace.

Such engaging methods can keep the experience of mindful walking fun, alive, and
authentic, build student confidence and a sense of autonomy, and cultivate more
trusting relationships between the students and with you, the teacher.

Sensory Walking Practices

Mindful walking can help us appreciate and savor the world around us, through all
our senses. Anita Constantini, a retreat leader from Italy, shares some of her lively
sensory practices from a "Happiness Camp" summer family retreat in Italy, working
with children aged six to twelve and their parents.

> We walk barefoot in nature, waking up the sense organ of touch! How many
> impressions we miss wearing shoes! We put our eyes under our feet and
> let them guide us for at least twenty minutes. We notice the difference
> between stepping on sunlit surfaces and ones that are in shade, dryness or
> dampness, leaves, grass, and various textures. In time our feet adjust and
> our sensations change. When we put our shoes back on, we discuss the
> sensation of wearing our shoes again.

Bobbie Cleave and Gordon "Boz" Bosworth, former US forest rangers working
as environmental educators, use similar sensory methods to connect children and
young people more deeply with the earth and nature.

> Of course, mindful walking is a very powerful way to teach children to
> connect with the earth deeply. We have walked barefoot with classes, held
> hands, circled a tree, touched the bark, stood by water, looked closely at a
> leaf or mushroom. There are countless ways to deeply connect to nature in
> our quiet, slow, aware practices.

Mindful Walking Is for Older Students Too

Although it can be fun, mindful walking can also help us when we are engaged in serious tasks. Katrina Tsang, a professor of medicine from Hong Kong, summarizes her program of teaching mindful walking to her medical students. As she points out, they surely need the care, self-compassion and sense of peace it induces, both for their immediate well-being and to look after themselves in their future high-pressure careers.

For junior medical students, they generally enjoy mindful walking as well. Weather permitting, we walk outdoors, in places where they can get close to Mother Nature. We start with slow walking, then, after a period of practice, end with a fast walking with students going in random directions. They feel the difference in their level of concentration at different speeds and report that it's easier to stay with their steps while walking slower. I invite them to pick a path that they walk almost every day and designate that path for mindful walking. It could be a short path from their room to the bathroom or kitchen, or from their home to their bus or train stop. I suggest other opportunities for mindful walking in the future, e.g., when they're on-call in the hospital as interns and things are getting rather busy. They can come back to their peaceful steps, give their minds a rest from busyness and hurriedness when they are walking from one place to another inside the hospital.

It is very rewarding and heart-warming when the students share how peaceful they feel, how life is more wonderful, how they feel less stressful or angry, or other new insights they have about their mind or body that often lead to better understanding and care of themselves. I sincerely hope these students will remember that for health providers to care for others, we must know how to and take good care of ourselves first. When we have compassion and true love for ourselves, then we can have compassion and love for others.

Walking through the Neighborhood

A regular Plum Village practice is to walk as a large group through a community or neighborhood. The sight of people walking silently and joyfully together usually has a profound impact both on those who take part and those who witness it. The walk builds a sense of solidarity and peace—indeed, many times observers end up joining in. Victoria Mausisa, a retreat leader, describes one such walk involving university students on the campus in Santa Clara, California.

We led about thirty students from Santa Clara University, young men and women, slowly out of the classroom, through the hallway, through double doors and out to the courtyard—a pristine, landscaped area of grass, trees, and small bushes. The afternoon was warm, sunny, and bright. While other college students walked quickly through the courtyard, we walked slowly, mindfully. Our slow pace, walking in a line and then in a circle around a blossoming tree, was noticed by others. Many people smiled at us.

During this mindful offering, as we all stood in a circle around the large, blooming tree, my heart was touched by a tall, young man with both hands covering his heart, eyes closed. And then a few moments later, we were invited to all hold hands and all the students did so, standing quietly, holding hands, all in the circle.

Later, another student commented, "At first, it felt awkward . . . walking slowly, having others see me . . . but then as I kept walking, I got into it and stopped thinking about others." Another student said, "I never walked that slowly before . . . I had never really noticed a tree that closely before . . . but I really could see it as we walked and when we stopped."

Such a wondrous gift! To walk together, to feel the warmth of the sun, to breathe with the tree in front of us, and to explore our interbeing nature with the sun, the trees, the grass, the air, the college students!

I must take care of my body and treat it with respect, as a musician does his instrument.
THICH NHAT HANH

five
the body

in this chapter

- Explore the importance of awareness of body and breath, movement and relaxation—for ourselves and our students.

- Study step-by-step instructions and practical guidance for three core Plum Village practices: i) awareness of the body, ii) the ten mindful movements, and iii) deep relaxation.

- Reflect on ways in which we can integrate working with the body into our daily lives and into our teaching in schools, universities, and classrooms, illustrated with examples and suggestions from practicing teachers.

body and mind united

THICH NHAT HANH

When you spend two hours with your computer you may forget entirely that you have a body. And when your mind is not with your body, you cannot be truly alive; you are lost in your work, in your worry, your fear, and your projects. By breathing in mindfully and bringing the mind home to the body, we become fully alive. When we bring our mind home to our body, our mind becomes *one* with our body. Our body becomes a mindful body, and our mind becomes an embodied mind. This state of oneness of body and mind allows us to get back in touch with the wonders of life, and our body is the first wonder of life that we encounter. Our body contains the Earth, the sun, the stars, and the whole cosmos, including all our ancestors.

You cannot be a happy teacher if you do not know how to release the tension in your body. Suppose as a teacher you have a lot of tension and pain in your body. The practice of total relaxation can help you to release the tension, and thus reduce the amount of pain in your body, including chronic pain, because pain is always a function of tension. That is why a good teacher should know the art of relaxation. When you know how to relax your body, then you know how to restore a feeling of peace to your body, and not only do you benefit right away, but your colleagues and students also benefit.

You may like to practice using the phrase, "Breathing in, I know I have a body, and my body is a wonder of life." This is a very concrete way to enjoy having a body.

While breathing in, if we notice there is tension in our body, then while breathing out we can allow the tension to be released from our body. That is one of the most frequently practiced exercises of mindful breathing. "Breathing in I am aware of my body and the tension in my body, breathing out I release the tension in my body." You can practice this in your car, on the train, or in the classroom. You may like to start by relaxing the muscles in your face. There are about three hundred small muscles in our face, and when they are tense we don't look very beautiful at all! If we breathe in and smile gently, then with the out-breath, we can release the tension in these three hundred muscles. We can learn to relax these muscles very quickly, with just two or three breaths.

Wherever you are, you can practice mindful breathing to be aware of your body and to release the tension in your body. Sitting on the bus, you can practice breathing and release tension. Walking to the classroom or walking to a meeting, we can allow the tension to be released with each step. We walk like a free person, enjoying every step we make. We are not in a hurry anymore. In that way, we release tension.

When we walk from the parking lot to our office or our classroom, why not practice to release tension in our body? We can arrange things so that we can walk as a free person, releasing tension with each step. That is the style of walking we adopt in Plum Village whenever we need to go from one place to another.

The practice of total relaxation can be applied in any kind of position—sitting, lying down, walking, or standing. We can always enjoy the practice of mindful breathing and release the tension in our body. It can become a habit—the habit of relaxation, the habit of peace. If we learn the practice of relaxation well, we can transmit it to our students, because they also have a lot of tension in their bodies. There are schoolteachers who begin the class by breathing in and out mindfully with their students. It only takes a few minutes. They do their best to be fully present and to release the tension in their bodies—this facilitates the teaching as well as the learning.

teaching notes on

the body practices

Much of our unhappiness comes from dividing the mind and body in an unnecessary and unrealistic way. We can neglect our bodies, abuse them, or even lose all sense of them and live "from the neck up." We often do not listen to what our bodies are telling us about ourselves, our minds, our bodies, and what is happening to us. We forget to care for our body in many ways, such as by eating unhealthily, using harmful substances, or by not exercising.

Schools and universities try to help students look after themselves, but in practice they tend be rather sedentary places. As students get older, students and teachers alike are asked to focus increasingly on the academic curriculum and on the mind, and the body gets forgotten. As teachers and students we can lose touch with our bodies as we go through the day, living in our heads, full of thoughts, plans, and worries. We breathe, eat, and drink without noticing; our bodies are full of tension that we don't even recognize. This distancing of ourselves from the physical reality of our existence can create sickness in the mind and body.

As we practice mindfulness, we get in closer touch with body and mind, and gently integrate them. This integration helps us take better care of ourselves, allowing for an increased sense of wholeness and well-being. We become more aware of bodily sensations, getting to know ourselves and our feelings, becoming able to respond to important messages our body may be giving us about our moods, our feelings, our intuitions, and our state of health. Through gently exercising our whole body, we show it care and gratitude, increasing our fitness, strength, stamina, and flexibility, while bringing a sense of peace and calm to our minds. Teaching ourselves how to relax deeply helps us to recuperate and heal both the mind and body, reducing mental health problems, such as stress, anger, depression, and anxiety.

The three practices we describe in this chapter, "Awareness of the Breath in the Body," "Mindful Movements," and "Deep Relaxation," are simple structured ways to help ourselves and our students come back to the body, so that the body becomes the seat of our mindfulness practice and our wise friend.

. . . . .

At the end of the chapter, we hear reflections and examples from practicing teachers on integrating body-based practices into their lives and classrooms.

In the following practices it's assumed that teacher and students are familiar with the foundations of breathing, inviting the bell, and sitting.

teaching notes on

....

awareness of body and breath

Why develop awareness of body and breath?

- To develop a sense of the mind and body connection.

- To increase the ability to be aware, focus, and pay attention to what is happening here and now—in the breath, body, and mind.

- To become aware of the breath as a bridge between body and mind.

- To decrease stress and increase positive feelings, such as calm, relaxation, and happiness.

We can bring our attention back to our body at any time, no matter what we're doing. At first, though, it can be helpful to practice stopping whatever work or action we're engaged in to more easily get back in touch with our body. The bell can be a useful reminder.

Once we stop, we practice mindful breathing. We become aware that we are breathing, and then we follow our in-breath and out-breath all the way through. Just following three full in- and out-breaths can bring calm, peace, and harmony to the breath, the body and the emotions, and have an impact on our physical and mental state, especially when we are reacting to a difficult situation.

We continue mindful breathing while we gradually embrace our whole body with our awareness. Then as the practice unfolds, we release tension in the body (this is explored in more detail in Deep Relaxation later in this chapter). The whole body becomes the object of our mindfulness.

A practice summary is available in appendix A on page 298.

core practice

....

awareness of the body and the breath

Materials and Preparation

- A teacher experienced in this practice.
- Chairs, cushions, mats, etc., arranged according to how you want people to sit or lie down.
- Bell and inviter (optional but recommended).

You or your class can carry out this practice in any position—lying down, sitting, or standing. This version assumes you are sitting.

If you do it several times it is interesting to invite yourself and your students to explore the difference it makes to be in various positions—to mind, body, feelings, sensations, experience.

Start: Getting Settled

Invite yourself and your class to sit and become settled (now familiar from the sitting meditation—grounded, stable, aware of contact points between the body and the chair, floor, or cushion).

1. Bell

In what follows, take it slowly, with pauses in between the instructions, giving people plenty of time to breathe, and allowing them to drop deeper into the practice.

Invite the bell for one full sound to begin. Then draw on the following script, breathing in and out each time with the words as you go.

2. Awareness of Breathing and Following the Breath

> Breathing in, I know that I am breathing in.
> Breathing out, I know that I am breathing out.

> Breathing in, I follow the whole length of my in-breath, from the beginning to the end.
> Breathing out, I follow the whole length of my out-breath, from beginning to end.

3. Aware of the Body

> Breathing in, I am aware that I have a body.
> Breathing out, I know my body is there.

> Breathing in, I am aware of my whole body.
> Breathing out, I smile to my whole body.

4. Calming and Releasing Tension in the Body

Breathing in, I am aware of my body.
Breathing out, I calm my body.

Breathing in, I relax my body.
Breathing out, I release any tension in my body.

5. End

One full sound of the bell, breathing in and out mindfully,
to finish.

teaching notes on

ten mindful movements

Why practice mindful movements?

· To develop the sense of the mind and body connection.

· To increase the ability to be aware, focus, and pay attention to what is happening here and now—in the breath, body, and mind—through experiencing the body in movement.

· To decrease stress and anxiety.

· To increase positive feelings, such as calm, relaxation, and happiness.

Mindful movements are any movements that are carried out mindfully, synchronized with our breathing. The movements should be easy, enjoyable, and practiced in a relaxed way; there's no straining to gain or achieve anything. This may be very different from the way we usually approach exercise, which is often a competitive activity involving stress, effort, and specific goals. Mindful movement is a simple opportunity for us to unite our mind and body in a relaxed and calming way.

The following instructions contain suggestions for a basic practice of about ten minutes with "ten mindful movements" that stretch various parts of the body. These movements invite us to be mindful of our body and help us find a sense of balance and flexibility in our body and mind. As teachers, we need to adapt the movements in this practice to suit the age, mood, space, and physical ability levels of our group. We can use whatever movements we wish, encouraging students to carry them out with full awareness of their breath, their body, and the movement. For safety, we take care not to overdo it, and remember that mindfulness of the body is what we are practicing, not energetic exercise.

core practice
....
ten mindful movements

A practice summary is available in appendix A on page 299.

Materials and Preparation

- A teacher practiced in mindful movements.

- A space large enough for everyone to be able to stretch their arms out all around them (if you do not have this much space you may want to follow a slightly modified set of movements that work within the confines of your room).

In what follows remind the group to do only what is comfortable and not to strain the body. Smile and have fun together!

Start

Invite the students to stand comfortably with both feet firmly on the ground, a shoulder width apart. Knees are soft, slightly bent, and not locked; shoulders are loose. Keep the body upright and relaxed. Give enough space to allow everyone to move their arms freely without bumping into one another.

Invite them to become aware of each in-breath and out-breath, allowing their breath to come down into their bellies and exhaling completely on the out-breath. They may put their hands on their belly if they wish.

Invite the students to become aware of the contact of the soles of their feet with the earth. Imagine an invisible thread is attached to the top of the head that pulls up toward the sky. Everyone may like to relax and enjoy standing like this for a moment.

You can explore more on mindful standing at this point if you wish— see the suggestions in the early stages of mindful walking.

1. Raising the Arms

Starting position: Standing centered, back straight, arms at your sides.

After each movement, you can invite the group to stand quietly and become aware of their breathing. Or if time is short and/or boredom sets in, you can just move straight through.

In-breath: Raise both arms in front of you until they're at shoulder level, parallel to the ground, palms downward.

Out-breath: Lower the arms down again to your sides.

Repeat two or three more times.

2. Stretching the Arms (Touch the Sky)

Starting position: Standing centered, back straight, arms at your sides.

In-breath: In one continuous movement, raise both arms straight above your head, palms facing inward, face looking up.

Out-breath: Bring your arms slowly down again to your sides.

Repeat two or three more times.

3. Opening the Arms (Flower Blooming)

Starting position: Standing centered, back straight, bend your arms so that you touch the tops of your shoulders with your fingertips.

In-breath: Extend arms to each side, palms up, arms horizontal at shoulder level.

Out-breath: Slowly bend your arms in again to touch your shoulders with your fingertips.

Repeat two or three more times.

4. Circling the Arms

Starting position: Standing centered, back straight, arms at your sides.

In-breath: Bring your arms in front of you, palms together, raise them up and separate them as they stretch over your head.

Out-breath: Continue circling your arms behind you, down, and forward, bring your palms back together in front of you.

Repeat two or three times, then reverse the direction and repeat the movement three or four times.

5. Circling at the Waist

Starting position: Standing centered, hands on your hips, legs straight, but not locked.

In-breath: Bend forward at the waist, back straight, and begin to make a circle with your upper body.

Out-breath: When your upper body is leaning back half-way through the circle, keep turning and complete the circle. End with your head in front of you while you're still bent at the waist.

Circle around two or three more times, then repeat the movement in the opposite direction, repeating it three or four times.

6. Stretching the Body

Starting position: Continue from the end position of Exercise 5, body bent at the waist, back straight, your arms reaching towards the ground.

In-breath: Bend your knees slightly and, keeping your back straight, raise your upper body and arms, bringing your arms above your head, palms facing in. Your heels are firmly planted as you stretch all the way up to touch the sky.

Out-breath: Bend at the waist as you bring your upper body and arms down to touch the earth. Release your neck.

Repeat the cycle: Breathe in and keep your back straight as you come all the way up to touch the sky. Then continue the movement two or three times.

7. Squats (like a Frog!)

Starting position: Standing centered, hands on your hips, your feet in a V-shape with heels together. (For a more challenging movement, those who wish to can try standing on their toes the whole time.)

In-breath: Rise onto your toes, keeping your heels together.

Out-breath: Stay standing on your toes, keeping your back straight, and lower your whole body by bending your knees. Keeping your upper body upright, and your back straight, go down as low as you comfortably can, maintaining your balance.

Repeat the cycle: Breathe in and come all the way up, straightening your legs, still standing on your toes, and repeat the movement five or six times.

8. Stretching the Legs

Starting position: Standing centered, hands on your hips, begin by putting all your weight on your left foot.

In-breath: Lift and bend your right knee and keep your toes pointed to the ground (raise your knee only as far as you can while feeling comfortable and balanced).

Out-breath: Stretch your right leg out straight in front of you, keeping your foot pointed forward.

In-breath: Bend your knee again and point your foot downward.

Out-breath: Lower your foot back down to the ground.

Repeat the cycle: Continue another two or three times, then put your weight on your right foot to repeat the series of movements with the left leg three or four times.

For the next two movements, which involve balancing on one leg, it may be helpful to invite everyone in the group to focus their gaze on a spot on the floor about three feet in front of them to help them to balance, or to put one hand on the wall or chair back for support if they feel wobbly.

9. Circling the Legs

Starting position: Standing centered, hands on hips, begin by putting all your weight on your left foot.

In-breath: Lift your right leg straight out in front of you and circle it to the side, keeping your leg straight.

Out-breath: Circle your leg to the back and then bring it slightly forward so it touches the back of your left leg, without touching the ground, ready to circle back to the front.

In-breath: Straighten your leg out behind you and circle it back, keeping your leg straight.

Out-breath: Circle your leg to the front, then bring it together with your left foot, so you're standing on your two feet.

Repeat the cycle: Make two or three more circles with the right leg. Switch legs and repeat with the left leg three or four times.

10. Side Lunge with Arm Stretch

Starting position: Standing centered, back straight, feet together and parallel, hands on your hips. Next, make an L-shape with your feet by keeping your left foot where it is and stepping two feet to the side with your right foot and pointing it out ninety degrees. Put your left hand on your left hip and keep your right arm at your side.

In-breath: Bend your right knee, bringing your weight over your right foot. Keeping your right arm straight lift it out and up to the side, in one continuous movement, sweeping it up to the sky. Turn your head to look up at your raised hand, your chest open and your right arm roughly parallel with your left leg.

Out-breath: Straighten your knee and bring your arm gently back down to your side.

Repeat the cycle: Stretch your arm up two or three more times in this direction. Switch legs and repeat the movement to the left side three or four times.

End

Stand firmly with your two feet parallel and shoulder width apart. You may want to invite a sound of the bell and close your eyes to enjoy your breathing. Feel your body relax. Quietly thank each other with a smile, or a bow if appropriate.

—

variations for mindful movements

- You and your students can adapt or create your own set of mindful movements—as an alternative, for fun, to fit a smaller or bigger space, or to accommodate students' ages, abilities, and disabilities.

- You can take opportunities to make any stretches you already do (such as in a yoga class, or as exercise warm ups) into mindful exercises—which means with full awareness of the movement, body, mind, and breath.

You can use the reflection questions listed later in the chapter for all the body practices here.

deep relaxation

Why practice deep relaxation?

· To increase our ability to reduce tension and relax body and mind.

· To develop our sense of mind and body connection.

· To increase our ability to be aware, focus, and pay attention to what is happening here and now—in the breath, body, and mind—through experiencing the body in relaxation.

· To decrease our levels of stress and anxiety.

· To increase positive feelings, such as calm, gratitude, acceptance, and happiness.

Stress and tension are a problem for many of us: even young children are becoming increasingly affected by stress. Schools can be driven and unsettling places, offering little time to rest and recover. Deep relaxation offers us a concrete practice to reunite our body and mind. By focusing our mind on our body, we give ourselves the opportunity for our body to release tension, rest, heal, and be restored.

the relaxation process

Relaxation is a simple process. First we practice letting go of all thoughts, worries, and anxieties, bringing our attention to our breath and to the contact our body makes with the floor. Then we bring our attention to different parts of our body, focusing our attention on each part one at a time. As our awareness reaches each part:

· We breathe in and out, aware of that part of the body.

- We become aware of any sensation in that part right now, giving it our full attention.

- We invite that part of our body to relax, releasing any tension we find there.

- We smile to that part of our body, sending it our love, tenderness, care, and gratitude for the work it does for us.

- When our mind wanders, we simply note the wandering, and bring our mind back to the part of the body we are focusing on, or to our breathing.

As we bring our attention to different parts of the body, from time to time we can bring our attention back to our breathing.

know your students and adapt as needed

You will need to know your class as individuals and be aware of any physical problems they may have (such as pain, injury, or disability). Adapt your instructions accordingly and/or talk to the individual students on how to handle the practice when it reaches the relevant part of the body. Students who are unable or unwilling to lie down can carry out the practice seated. If students are sitting in a chair for the practice it may be useful to have them put their heads down on their desk so they are not enticed to look around the room.

A practice summary is available in appendix A on page 302.

core practice

deep relaxation

Materials and Preparation

- A teacher experienced in total deep relaxation.
- Mats, blankets.
- Bell and inviter (optional but recommended).
- Music or musical instrument (optional).
- Clean floor, with mats and/or blankets for warmth and comfort (students may be invited to bring some in).
- Students invited to wear clothing they are comfortable to lie down in.
- A warm room (either the normal classroom or, ideally, a larger space like a hall or gym).
- Some version of a polite "do not disturb" notice on the door.

Deep relaxation can be any length. The following is a version that takes about twenty minutes. There are other options in the "variations" below.

When first teaching it to yourself, you might like to record and play the instructions below, or have someone read them to you. You can also find links to guided relaxations online in "What Next."

1. Getting Settled

Invite the group to lie down on their backs.

Allow time for the class to settle.

Gently invite them to get comfortable, with their legs stretched out, and their arms by their sides or with their hands on their bellies.

Invite them to close their eyes if they wish.

Just allow any initial silliness and giggling to depart.

Sit where you can see every student clearly, and keep your eyes open and be aware of what is happening throughout the practice.

There are teacher's notes below with more detailed guidance on inviting young people to lie down calmly and safely.

2. Bell

Invite three sounds of the bell, with three in- and out-breaths between each bell, to begin the session.

3. The Practice

Slowly move through the practice below.

Read the following text to the students. Allow the space of at least one full in- and out-breath between the sentences.

Close your eyes and allow your arms to rest gently on either side of your body, letting your legs relax and turn outward. Allow your **whole body** to start to relax and let go.

As you breathe in and out, become aware of the floor beneath you and of **the contact of your body** with the floor, noticing all the places where you are in contact such as heels, the back of your legs, back, shoulders.

With each out breath allow your **body to sink** deeper and deeper into the floor, letting go of tension, worries, thoughts, and ideas.

Become aware of your **belly rising** and falling as you breathe in and out. Rising, falling, rising, falling. You can place a hand there if you wish.

Breathing in, bring your full awareness to your **eyes**. Breathing out, allow your eyes to relax. Allow your eyes to sink back into your head, letting go of the tension in all the tiny muscles around your eyes. Your eyes allow you to see many different shapes and colors. Smile to your eyes and allow them to rest, sending gratitude to your eyes for giving you the gift of sight.

Breathing in, move your awareness down to your **mouth**. Breathing out, allow your mouth to relax, releasing any tension around your mouth. Let a gentle smile bloom on your lips. We use our mouth so much—to talk, breathe, eat. You may send gratitude to your mouth that works so hard for you.

Breathing in, bring your awareness down to your **shoulders.** Breathing out, allow your shoulders to relax. Let them sink into the floor. Our shoulders often get tense. Let all that tension flow into the floor. You carry so much on your shoulders. Now let them relax as you care for them.

Breathing in, be aware of your **arms**. Breathing out, relax your arms. Let your arms sink into the floor, your upper arms, your elbows, your lower arms, your wrists, your hands, your fingers, all the tiny bones and muscles. You can gently wiggle your fingers a little if you need to, to help the muscles relax.

Breathing in, bring your awareness to your **heart**. Breathing out, allow your heart to relax. Your heart beats for you night and day. Embrace your heart with tenderness, taking care of your heart.

Breathing in, bring your awareness to your **belly**. Noticing your belly rising as you breathe in, and falling as you breath out. In and out. Deep and slow. Belly rising, belly falling.

Breathing in, bring your awareness to your **hips**. Breathing out, allow your hips to relax.

Now begin to move your awareness down your **legs** releasing all tension in your legs as you move your attention down your thighs, your knees, your calves, your ankles, your **feet**, your toes. You may want to move your toes a little to help all the tiny muscles in your **toes** relax. Send love and care to your toes.

Come back to your in- and out-breath. Breathing in, breathing out. Your **whole body** feels light like a water lily floating on the water. You have nowhere to go to, nothing to do. You are as free as a cloud floating in the sky.

4. Music/Singing (Optional)

Play some relaxing music.

If appropriate, with younger children perhaps, you could sing some songs to allow time for people simply to rest in the practice and in their bodies.

It is great if you feel you can sing, not use a recording. It is not important to have a beautiful voice, but rather to be aware of the tone so that it is appropriate to the situation of collective rest and relaxation.

5. Getting Ready to End

Bring your awareness back to your breathing, to your abdomen rising and falling.

To avoid startling students, you may want to gently warn the class that the sound of the bell is coming as an ending to the practice.

6. Bell

Use a half sound as usual to wake up the bell. Invite one sound of the bell to signify the end of the session.

7. Ending the Practice

Take this slowly.

Invite students to move a little, wiggle toes and fingers. Then invite them to open their eyes and roll onto their side, and stretch gently before slowly sitting up.

8. Bridge to Next Activity

If you want to reflect on the practice—and you may not feel you need to—you can use the reflection questions below. Use them while the students are still sitting on the floor so as not to break the mood, or maybe when they have returned quietly to their chairs and/or desks.

Give instructions for what follows, such as getting up, returning to desks, packing up, leaving the end of the lesson, etc.

Encourage them to move slowly and mindfully, and take the spirit of relaxation and calm into the next part of their day.

—

variations on teaching deep relaxation

- You can vary the order and move through the parts of the body in any sequence that flows.

- Deep relaxation can be any length according to how much time you have, as long as forty or as short as five minutes.

- To make it longer, add in different parts of the body, and/or go into more detail, bringing a deeper awareness to each part. You can allow a little more time between each line, unless the students get fidgety.

- For a shorter practice, focus on the whole body lying on the floor, the sense of contact, getting in touch with the breath, and using the out-breath to let go of tension and sink into the floor.

- Bring to mind any place in the body that is sick or in pain. Take this time to be aware of it and send it love. Breathing in, allow this area to rest. Breathing out, smile to it with tenderness and affection. Be aware of the other parts of the body that are strong and healthy and allow this strength to be sent to the weak area, soothing it.

- Relaxation does not have to be carried out lying down, although this is a good position in which to learn the practice. You can try it sitting or even standing.

- Try total relaxation in nature. When the weather is good and the ground dry enough, go outside where the sensations, smells, and sounds can support a sense of tranquility, contact with the earth, and interconnectedness.

- You can also use imagery to help students focus while they bring awareness to different parts of the body, using an image such as a small rain cloud, waterfall of light, or a laser beam. We imagine it, then move it gently across the body, with the water, light, or laser representing the energy of our mindful awareness so that wherever it reaches becomes relaxed and calm.

lying down in the classroom

Young people can find lying down in a classroom environment odd and somewhat exciting at first. This is fine and fun, but to ensure as much calm as possible it is good to plan the practicalities of lying down thoroughly and rehearse instructions beforehand, especially if you are trying to do this in a confined space like a classroom. For example:

- Be clear and explicit about how the students will move from what they're doing to lying down.

- Make sure the floor is clean and the students have something soft like a blanket or mat to lie on.

- Plan and be clear about where they will lie down. In a normal classroom this will take some forethought to work around desks.

- Have them lie down feet-to-feet and head-to-head, to keep smelly feet away from others' heads.

- Quietly ensure that students who should not lie next to one another—perhaps because of animosity or a tendency to distract—are not together.

- Consider safety hazards. For example, make sure students are not lying near a door, and if you put the chairs on top of the desks to make more space, upend the chairs so their legs aren't pointing downward.

- Make sure all students feel safe and dignified in terms of clothing—maybe separate boys and girls if they are preteens or teens.

- Make students aware that no part of their body should be touching anyone else and that if they need to adjust their position during the practice it is fine to do so, but they need to not bother their neighbors.

- Share with the students beforehand that some may fall asleep or even snore— and that this is fine, natural, and not a problem. You can invite them to consider the snoring of their classmates as a different kind of mindfulness bell. But expect giggles when snoring does happen. There is no need to be concerned, just continue to guide the relaxation with calm and concentration. Giggling will subside.

looking deeply: reflection questions for all the body practices

Here are some questions for you, the teacher, to reflect on or to use with the students either during in-class sharing or by just letting the questions settle in the mind. Use them sparingly—it is not a checklist!

- How do I feel right now? (Can be asked at any point in the practice.)

- What was the effect of the practice on my mind, body, breath? (You can make the question specific to something that happened in the practice.)

- How easy or difficult did I find the practice? Fun, boring, calming, challenging?

- How much did my mind wander? If I noticed my mind wander, was I able to bring it back to my breath and my body?

- Did I notice any specific parts of my body that held a lot of tension?

Add other questions as appropriate. Keep them simple, open, nonjudgmental, encouraging, and accepting of all kinds of responses including "negative" ones and "I don't know." Gently keep the sharing based on present real life experience.

awareness of the body, and body practices, in our lives and our teaching

Body and Breath

> I feel very strongly that we need to teach students to move their bod-
> ies and pair their breath with the movement to have that real body-mind
> connection, and so they learn that we are all one unit, not a separate mind
> and body . . . and to teach that our thoughts are just that—thoughts. They
> are not us!
>
> **—MARIANN TAIGMAN, OCCUPATIONAL THERAPIST, US**

Mindfulness can help us experience mind and body as two faces of one reality, with no separation. Dzung X. Vo, the pediatrician teaching mindfulness to teens in British Columbia who we met earlier, is a keen advocate of teaching the mind/body connection. He found that teaching body and breath awareness was transformative for one of his adolescent patients' health problems.

> Many of the youth I work with have difficulty attending school due to health
> challenges. For example, one teenager in our group was missing a lot of
> school due to stomachaches. During the group, she developed an insight
> into how her stomachaches were related to stress and anxiety (mind-body
> connection), and also to confidence in being able to cope using mindful-
> ness. She shared, "I started to have a stomachache in class. But this time,
> instead of leaving school and going home, I decided to step out of the class
> and do a breathing meditation. I just focused on my breath. . . . I noticed
> how stressed I was, but kept breathing. . . . After a while of doing this, I was
> able to feel better and to go back to class." After that experience, she didn't
> miss any more school for the rest of the time she was in our group, which
> was a huge and life-changing transformation for her!

Moving Mindfully

Moving mindfully helps us stay centered and in the moment. We can bring mindful awareness to an increasing range of everyday movements, starting in the morning with picking up a toothbrush or breakfast plate, and putting on our coat. As with mindful walking, the joy of mindful movement is that it can be done as part of our everyday life and so need not take more time. It is best not to attempt too much at once when practicing this at first. Aim to experiment and play with different times and types of movement, gradually increasing the amount of time spent in mindful awareness, taking care to keep the practice a joy, not a chore.

Showing kindness to ourselves through paying attention to our body and our movement is not just for ourselves, it helps us in our relationships and interactions with others. How we breathe, walk, move, sit, stand, and hold our body reflects our states of mind. When we move with ease, others around us will also feel more light and relaxed in our presence. Once we have mastered the art of mindful movement in our personal life, we can bring it to our presence in school. As we enter class, as we sit or stand, as we approach a student, we can keep some of our attention on the movement itself (as well as its purpose), on how it feels from within and on how it impacts our mind, body, and breath.

University teacher and mindfulness trainer Lyndsay Lunan from the UK found moving more mindfully herself in the classroom to be transformative in her relationships with her students, while also, incidentally, piquing their interest in mindfulness.

It's my feeling that mindful walking and movement is one of the most crucial transmissions from the teacher to the student. It makes the teacher feel more grounded and calm, and this way of being reaches the class. In fact, this was my own first experience of bringing mindfulness into the classroom. I'd just returned from a retreat at Plum Village and was so inspired by the way Thay cleans the whiteboard, with such gentle attentiveness to each stroke. And I thought about how often I clean the whiteboard after a class with arms full of rushed and jagged energy. So, I decided to make cleaning the whiteboard my mindfulness bell. After each lesson, I would clean the "whiteboard of my mind" by bringing my breath into each slow stroke of the duster and enjoy that simple activity. My social science class had begun to notice that I walked around the class quite slowly and one week a few of them stopped to watch me at the end of class. They wanted to know what I was doing and why I moved so slowly and smiled a lot! And this led to a very lovely conversation about what mindfulness is, which concluded with them asking me if I would teach them. This taught me a big lesson about how to bring mindfulness to students, not by teaching it, but by being it.

When working with students, any set of movements can be carried out mindfully, with full awareness of the connection of the breath and body to the movement. Again, keep it fun and enjoyable, and practice in a relaxed way, not straining to achieve anything. Ruth Bentley, a mindfulness educator in France, provides a substantial example of all stages of a lesson that integrates mindful movement, music, and deep sharing of the emotions, as taught to her elementary school class.

> I guide them through a set of mindful movements where we bring our breath into alignment with our stretching, flowing bodies. Sometimes we do this in silence, sometimes I play calming music. I particularly like Mozart as a way of bringing both Eastern and Western cultures together, rather like aligning both sides of the brain.
>
> Now we ease more into a dance of awareness. I select a range of tracks to which the children move instinctively, observing how their bodies blend with the music. After a brief time with one track, I fade out the track as the children gradually come to stillness, standing straight but relaxed. At this point I ask them to close their eyes as I sound the bell. Then we focus on our breath and also our physical feelings. Sometimes I talk them through the different parts of their body, bit by bit. Sometimes I just say "notice how you feel." Other times I might say "notice any tingling," or "notice any aches and pains." I might also go on to ask them how they are feeling emotionally, to follow on from their physical feelings. And sometimes I don't say anything. It varies according to my present-moment observations of both my own feelings and those of the children. After some moments of silent reflection, I sound the bell again and gently fade in the next track, and encourage the children to start dancing again. I repeat these steps for as long as I feel is beneficial to the students.
>
> With the final bell, I ask the students to come back to sitting and to reflect on their physical and emotional states. Just like at the start of the session, sometimes we keep our observations to ourselves, sometimes we share them with a partner, or maybe with the whole group. When a negative emotion is shared, we might discuss how all emotions are valid and not to be rejected or judged, but rather accepted and acknowledged with kind observation. Over time, this can encourage a deep sharing of emotions without shame.

Mindfulness can enhance any contemplative class movement session such as yoga, tai chi, and dance—as yoga teacher and former dean at a US university, Gail Williams O'Brien, outlines.

> I have incorporated mindfulness and Thay's teachings into yoga classes for the past six years at a nonprofit for teens who are homeless or having problems at home. I find that breathing with slow movements (suited to the students' physical abilities) helps calm them so that they can rest at the end of the practice, during which I often chant songs from Thay's tradition such as "Breathing In, Breathing Out," and "When I Rise." We then sit up and do a loving-kindness meditation as we hug ourselves. Although I am not in a classroom setting, I think a few mindful movements with breath could be helpful before students do meditation, or mindfulness practice.

For those who engage in sport it is interesting to explore the impact of bringing the energy of mindfulness to the activity—being in the moment and in the body, rather than the mind, aware of body and breath, cultivating a sense of relaxation and effortless ease.

Tineke Spruytenburg, a special education teacher in the Netherlands who we met earlier, describes an experience of integrating mindfulness into soccer, or football is it is called in Europe, which radically shifted the very essence of the game!

> During the annual Dutch retreat in Germany last year, we were aware of the children's need to play football in the park. The older children—eight to twelve years old—were invited to fill in the blanks in their program with any activity they could think of. There was just one rule: whatever they would suggest, we would ask them to come up with a mindful variety of the activity. We knew football was what they wished for most, so we asked them how they would play football mindfully.
>
> Each goal is answered with a bell of mindfulness. When the weather is good, players lay down on the ground to listen to the bell and practice belly breathing three times. When someone is hurt somehow, the game is stopped and children around take care of the child in pain. Playing this way, the teams often forget to count the goals and everyone is a winner!

Deep Relaxation

Relaxation can be an antidote to a stressful school day, as Sarah Woolman, an elementary and middle school teacher in the UK, outlines:

> We can say, "Relax," but it is a very difficult thing to do. Reading the deep relaxation meditation to children or teenagers allows them to experience relaxation in their busy, stressful school day. It helps them feel peace and quiet when they are used to the opposite. It gives them a point of comparison.

As with mindful movement, relaxation can be applied at any time in our everyday life, perhaps before getting up in the morning or going to sleep at night, or half way through the day, or when getting home from work or school. For people with sleeping problems, relaxation can be particularly helpful—just follow your breathing as you lie on your back on the bed. Even if you don't sleep, the practice nourishes you and allows you to rest.

You can relax while engaged in other mindfulness practices, such as mindful walking or mindful eating. As with all mindfulness practice, it is good to establish a regular routine for deep relaxation, and to encourage your students to do the same.

Deep relaxation is one of the most requested practices for children, teens, and adult students. As the experience of Bea Harley, a UK elementary teacher we met earlier, shows us, young people very much enjoy relaxation, and can get very "into it" if it is done regularly.

> Deep relaxation is done throughout the school with all ages, and I had the privilege of often leading the oldest group (ages nine to eleven). At times the children would ask if they could bring in their "onesies," and would settle themselves under blankets looking forward to taking time out of a busy day to just relax.

Bea encourages her students to write their own relaxation scripts and reflects, "I am always touched by the breadth of their imaginations and their ability to capture the sense of going deep within themselves." She gives an inspirational example of class guidance, written by one of her young pupils, with a compelling narrative and vivid imagery: as she comments, the child shows deep understanding that the source of peace and relaxation is within ourselves, no matter what is going on in the world outside.

> Are you comfortable? Well, if you are, good. Now we can begin. Imagine you are lying on a rug . . . a very fluffy, very warm rug. But your stay on your very fluffy, very warm rug is not long because now you can feel the floor sink beneath you, and you just keep slowly falling down and down. But you stop, and when the darkness clears you realize you're on a cloud, floating in the air, and in the background—just ever so faintly—is the noise of a busy city below you. But you choose not to hear it. It's just you and your cloud up in the sky and it's peaceful and quiet. You sit there for a while, just peaceful and quiet.

Bea comments that she loved this child's realization that through this practice they had a choice not to be distracted by the noise (as we so often are) but to remain in the peaceful, quiet place they had found within themselves.

Knowing how to relax in the face of pressure helps the mind and body to continue to work in harmony so we can do our best. This can be particularly helpful for students when facing exams and sports competitions. Mike Bell, a classroom teacher from the UK, describes teaching relaxation in his article "The Wisdom of Ordinary Children." He offered it to his students as a tool to use before their exams, which produced some entertainingly robust responses to the taunts of other students.

> On the day of their exams, I was waiting with my pupils outside the examination hall when two of them asked if they could do the relaxation practice again. (I had told them it would help them with their exam.) A group of five or six started breathing meditation. One of their friends came over. "What you lot doin'?" he asked in a jeering voice. One of my pupils immediately replied, "Meditating. Sir taught us . . . and it's gonna make us better in our exam, so you can shu' up!"[1]

This is maybe not entirely "loving speech," but as teachers we take one step at a time!

Drink your cloud.

THICH NHAT HANH

six
eating

in this chapter

- Reflect on what it means to eat mindfully—slow down, savor, and contemplate where our food comes from—and the impact that how and what we consume has on ourselves and our surroundings.

- Find step-by-step instructions and practical guidance for three core practices for teacher and students, i) mindful eating of a tangerine, ii) eating a mindful snack, iii) eating a whole meal mindfully.

- Read thoughts and suggestions from practicing teachers on ways we can integrate mindful eating into our daily lives and into our teaching in classrooms, schools, and universities.

the cosmos in a carrot

THICH NHAT HANH

Eating can be a deep meditation. Thanks to mindfulness and concentration, every minute of eating breakfast, lunch, or dinner, or even just a snack, can become a minute of joy and happiness.

In the practice of mindful eating we allow our talking and thinking to stop, because thinking always takes us away from the here and the now. We just enjoy being together with others and with the meal. Everyone eating with us can participate and contribute to the collective energy of mindfulness and joy.

During the time of practicing mindful eating we focus our attention on only two things. First of all, we're aware of the food that we serve ourselves to eat. We breathe in and out and become aware of the vegetables, of the rice, or whatever we are eating. When I pick up a piece of carrot, I do it mindfully and I take one second to look at the carrot. Just one second is enough to see that there is sunshine in the carrot, there is the rain in the carrot, and there is the good earth in the carrot. Time, space, the farmer, the truck driver—they are all present in the carrot. The piece of carrot carries within itself the whole cosmos. In this way, one second of looking mindfully can put you in touch with the whole cosmos.

Next, put the carrot into your mouth mindfully. Do not put anything else into your mouth, like your worries or your projects. Just the piece of carrot. The stars, the sun, Mother Earth, and the cosmos have all come to you in the form of a carrot, for your nourishment. That is love. When you chew, you chew only the carrot and not your projects, your anger, or your fear. Chewing these things is not good for our health. So, we can enjoy eating each morsel of our meal with a clear mind in that way, with thanks, joy, and gratitude in our heart.

The second object of our mindfulness is the presence of other practitioners around us. We can eat mindfully together with our colleagues, in the classroom with our students, or at home with our family. When we eat together like this, we generate the energy of mindfulness and joy so that we will be nourished not only by the food, but also by the collective energy of brotherhood, sisterhood, peace, and joy. Eating like this can be very joyful, even though we do it in silence. This kind of silence while eating is very eloquent: it speaks a lot about togetherness, brotherhood, and sisterhood. Eating like that can be nourishing for the body and for the spirit at the same time.

Your health depends very much on what you eat. Let us eat in such a way that can preserve compassion in our heart, that helps living beings to suffer less, and that helps to protect our precious planet.

a food contemplation

We can read these verses at any time to ourselves and to our students when we are about to begin eating.

> This food is the gift of the whole universe: the earth, the sky, the rain, and the sun.

> We thank all the people who have brought this food to us—the farmers, the people who work in the shops, and the cooks.

> We only put on our plate as much food as we can eat.

> We chew the food slowly so that we can enjoy it.

> We eat in a way that nurtures our compassion, protects other species and the environment, and heals and preserves our precious planet.

> This food gives us energy to practice being more loving and understanding.

> We eat this food to be healthy and happy and to love each other as a family.

> —THE PLUM VILLAGE "FIVE CONTEMPLATIONS BEFORE EATING,"
> ADAPTED FOR CHILDREN AND YOUNG PEOPLE

The original version of the "Five Contemplations before Eating" for teens and adults can be found at the end in appendix A.

teaching notes on

mindful eating

Why practice mindful eating?

- To become more mindful of the process of eating—slowing down, savoring and enjoying, and eating a sensible quantity of food chosen mindfully with thought and care.

- To develop awareness of our own habit energies around food, eating, and consumption (which may well apply to more than just how we eat—there are many forms of consumption).

- To develop a sense of gratitude through awareness of the connection between the food on our plate and the processes and people that brought it to us.

Mindful eating can transform the everyday activity of eating, a basic human need that we normally tend to do on "autopilot," into a wonderful opportunity to bring mindfulness into our own lives and the lives of our students in a simple way, on a regular basis. In this way, eating becomes a source of deep pleasure and connection with others.

Learning to eat mindfully has a wide range of benefits, helping us develop our mindfulness and compassion, enjoy our food, improve our own physical and mental health, and feel more in control of our lives. We can use the experience of mindful eating to reflect on the common feeling of being constantly driven and busy. Teachers are particularly notorious for working long hours and not taking time to look after ourselves properly. This often includes working through breaks—for example, doing lesson prep or administration while eating. It is not a great model for our students. This can lead to choosing processed, packaged, and unhealthy food, eaten in a rush and "on the go." We often feel we must combine eating with some other activity, like answering emails or talking to colleagues or peers. We may even feel awkward if we eat alone without distraction.

Through mindful eating we get increasingly in touch with our thoughts, emotions, and body sensations around food. This helps us to distinguish when we need to eat from when our impulses and choices are driven by the automatic pilot of habit and emotion. It may be that we are trying to fill an inner void that has nothing to do with hunger. Once we are more aware, we're then more able to seek other more productive ways to help ourselves, and our students, manage our stress and unhappiness. We free ourselves to make healthier diet and nutrition choices. This freedom can help avoid obesity and eating disorders such as anorexia, bulimia and orthorexia, that are becoming sadly common, especially in the young.

We can mindfully eat a mouthful of food, a snack, or a whole meal. We start by preparing the food carefully, slowly, and with mindfulness. We have the simple intention to be truly present throughout the process with our whole mind, body, and senses. As we eat and serve ourselves, we are aware of any other people who are eating with us, as well as our own needs, and so we choose with care, taking only the amount of food that we need. If we are eating with others we acknowledge the people eating with us with a smile, a head nod, or even a little bow. If we choose to eat for a while in silence, we will find we are more able to focus on our eating. We consciously see, smell, chew, taste, and enjoy every morsel of our food. We notice when our mind wanders, smile kindly to ourselves, and then go back to eating with attention. When we are chewing, we can put our fork or eating utensil down, not preparing our next bite until we are fully finished with the one in our mouth. As we contemplate the food, we realize that many elements, such as the rain, sunshine, earth, air, and love, have all come together to bring this food to us. In fact, through this food we see that the entire universe is supporting our existence. When we finish, we take a few moments to notice that we have finished, the food is gone, and that we now feel satisfied. We can contemplate how fortunate we are to have had this nourishing food to eat, supporting us on the path of love, understanding, and concern for others. We realize how lucky we are to eat every day, and how we tend to take our regular meals for granted, forgetting what a gift this would be for many in the world who go hungry.

As we leave the table, we may again acknowledge with a friendly smile, or bow, the people with whom we have shared this food.

mindful eating—in a nutshell

- Preparation (of the food, mindfully)
- Arriving (in the present moment, e.g., breath, bell)
- Looking deeply (interbeing, gratitude)
- Intention (to eat mindfully)
- Choosing
- Seeing (textures, color, shape)
- Smelling
- Placing (in the mouth)
- Savoring (chewing, tasting, swallowing)
- Fullness (how the food feels in the belly, satiation)

take care of the students

When we practice mindful eating, we need to take care of ourselves and of our students, as food and eating often bring up emotions—sometimes strong ones. We keep the practice light, pleasant, and fun. We keep any periods of silence short to start with and then maybe allow quiet chat. We go slowly, keep the experience brief to start, watch out for students in difficulty, and perhaps have a helper ready to take care of them. When we encourage students to reflect, we take even more care than usual to accept all kinds of responses. Throughout all the practices, we stay alert to any difficult feelings arising—in ourselves and in our students—and take care of them kindly.

Before learning mindful eating practices, you may find it useful to first do the breathing practices, so you and your class know how to return to the safety of the breath.

At the end of this chapter, we explore mindful eating with the help of practicing teachers who talk about why and how they use it themselves and with their students.

A practice summary is available in appendix A on page 304.

This can be a sticky exercise!

Fresh fruit is a good choice, but if you think that it will make too much mess, or your class is very fruit averse, you may like to use a raisin or small piece of hard shelled chocolate instead. You will need at least three per student.

It is good to pick something that will be easy, appropriate for your environment, and enjoyable for a first experience.

Keep the introduction minimal, especially the first time—let the practice itself do most of the work.

Some of the students will probably eat it immediately anyway—just go with it.

As the tangerines are given out, invite the students, and yourself, to stay with the breath and be aware of any reactions, e.g., impatience, wish to hurry it up, dislike of fruit, wish to eat it, and so on.

core practice

tangerine meditation

These instructions are to guide you, the teacher, in the practice, and form the basis for a script to follow in teaching others. Adapt the words as you need to.

Materials and Preparation

- A teacher experienced in eating meditation.
- One tangerine for each student and one for the teacher
- Access to running water and soap to wash hands, or sanitizer and paper towels to clean hands, before and after.
- Bell and inviter (optional but recommended).

1. Prepare

In what follows, take your time at each stage, being aware of the impulse to hurry along, in yourself and your students. Quietly, with the breath, allow the impulse to pass.

2. Introduce the Practice

The first time they do this, students will assume they are getting the tangerine to eat straight away, so prepare them so they don't feel foolish. First, invite them to enjoy their breathing and to be aware of their body. Tell them that we will soon begin eating the tangerine all together.

Tell them we will do the activity without talking so they can focus, and that you will be guiding everyone through a series of reflections.

3. Be with the Breath

Invite one sound of the bell to begin, giving everyone an opportunity to breathe in and out mindfully three times.

4. Pick up/Hand Out Tangerine

Give a tangerine to each member of the class, or you can invite some students to pass them out.

Pick up your tangerine, and invite each student to hold their tangerine gently in the palm of their hand.

5. Contemplate the Food

Read aloud to the class the first two lines of the "Food Contemplation" (full version below):

> **This tangerine is a gift of the whole universe:**
> **the earth, the sky, the rain, and the sun.**
> **We thank the people who have brought this tangerine to us,**
> **especially the farmers and the people at the market.**

Take a moment to imagine and visualize all the things that happened, and the people who helped, to bring this fruit into your hand, such as:

- Where it grew and how
- What caused it to grow and ripen (the earth, sun and rain and so on)
- The various people involved (who grew it, tended it, picked it, packed it, transported it, sold it, delivered it, and so on)

6. Look Deeply

Look closely at this tangerine as if you had never seen one before—and indeed you have never seen this particular one. Notice the color, texture, shape, pits, navel, or how the light reflects off it. Roll it around in your hand to look at it thoroughly. Notice any difference between one side and another.

Be aware of any reaction in your body, e.g., anticipation, salivation, aversion.

7. Smell

Hold the tangerine to your nose and smell the fragrance. Notice where exactly you sense this—nostrils, palate, throat?

Closing your eyes can help focus on the scent.

8. Touch and Peel

Gently peel the tangerine, or half of it.
　　Notice how this feels to the touch.
　　Really look at the peel, e.g., the difference between the two sides—fluffy on one side and pitted or smooth on the other, the color, the smell of the aroma that's released.
　　Gently separate one segment.

Some younger children or even older students may have never learned to peel a piece of fruit and may need a little quiet help or a clear demonstration from the teacher.

To include the sense of sound, you may even like to have them peel it a bit while holding it close their ear, so they can hear the rind being torn.

9. Place in the Mouth—Then Eat

Gently place the segment in your mouth, on your tongue. Try not to chew and swallow just yet.

Notice how your mouth responds—increased salivation, urge to chew.

Gently roll the segment around your mouth—noticing the texture and taste.

Gently bite into the segment—you may be aware of the sudden burst of flavor. Notice where exactly in your mouth you experience that, and your response.

Slowly and mindfully chew the segment.

Be aware of the impulse to swallow. Chew the segment well, resisting the urge to swallow for a little while to see how it feels.

When the segment is fully chewed, swallow.

Be aware of the whole feeling of swallowing in the back of your mouth, throat, and stomach.

10. After Eating the First Segment

Notice any impulse to reach for a second segment straight away.

Sit and breathe, experiencing the aftermath of the taste in the mouth, and any sensations elsewhere in the body and mind.

11. End

Not all your students may like tangerines. If this is so, perhaps invite anyone who wishes to reflect with gratitude for not ever having to do this again!

You may like to think what to do with the peel, and talk about recycling, composting, or maybe making flowers or hearts from it.

Eat the rest of the tangerine if you wish. Eat as mindfully as you wish.

Sit quietly, in touch with your breath, and reflect on the experience. If you enjoyed it, be thankful for all the conditions that made this tangerine, and the taste in your mouth, possible.

—

variations on simple eating practice

- Mindfully eat any small item of food—a raisin is the classic choice as it is easy to eat, makes no mess, and is flavorful. Try also a small square of chocolate, small tub of ice cream, a nut, a segment or whole piece of fresh fruit.

- You may like to experiment with eating one piece of food normally and a second mindfully, noticing any difference.

- Eat one or more mouthfuls of a snack or normal meal mindfully.

- The section at the end on "integrating mindful eating" contains real examples from practicing teachers of many types of mindful eating.

core practice
....
eating a snack mindfully

Materials and Preparation

You will need: an assortment of healthy snacks in bowls or on plates (fresh or dried fruit, pretzels, crackers, or cookies—whole grain, low sugar); optional: healthy drinks (fresh juice or water), trays, napkins, cups (preferably reusable so students can wash them at the end), bell and inviter. You may like to involve some students in getting these ready for the group.

We recommend that you and your students experience the tangerine practice before eating a larger meal in mindfulness

You need to know about any food allergies in your students, e.g., nuts, gluten, dairy. Generally, err on the safe side and avoid serving foods that are potentially dangerous.

1. Introduce

Invite the group to become quiet and focused.

Remind the group about their experience of mindful eating a small piece of food—the process of contemplating, looking, smelling, tasting, and so on.

Emphasize the collective energy of mindful eating we will be generating today.

Remind everyone that this practice will be done in silence and that everyone should wait to eat until all are served.

A "picnic" atmosphere is nice, e.g., sitting on the floor, in a group or circle, outside if you can, but the normal classroom and desks will do.

2. The Eating Practice

Place the snack, napkins, and the drinks on trays. Introduce the practice by saying something such as:

> We have the chance now to practice a mindful snack meditation. As you pass the tray around, please hold the tray so the person next to you can serve themselves. If someone is holding the tray for you, smile, take a napkin and a snack, or a drink, and then hold the tray for the next person. Make sure you look at the other person when serving or being served. Please wait to begin eating and drinking until everyone has their snack and we have invited one sound of the bell. We will eat in silence to really taste and appreciate the food.

It is helpful if you as the teacher also participate so you can model sitting solidly like a mountain and eating your food mindfully.

Ask a student to invite the bell once everyone is served.

If you wish, read aloud the "food contemplation" from the guidance at the start of the chapter.

Or you can say something simpler such as:

Let's all begin together and enjoy mindfully eating and drinking our snacks in silence. Take your time to eat mindfully—to really see, smell, taste, and chew the food and think about where it came from.

Enjoy eating your snack!

If appropriate, you can pass around the snacks again for those who want seconds.

3. End

Invite one sound of the bell to signal the end of the silent period of eating.

Sit quietly, in touch with your breath, and reflect on the experience. If you enjoyed it, thank all that made this possible.

core practice

....

eating a whole meal mindfully

Once the mindful eating practice is established, you may like to become more ambitious and set up some mindful meals. Take it slowly as you expand the practice and learn as you go. You could try a mindful meal with a class, with a whole group of same-year students, with a group of teachers, and when you are practiced in it, with the whole school community, and then including parents. The instructions are as for the practice above, plus the following details for working with a larger group.

- People are invited to stand quietly in line to serve themselves food, selecting it with care, and taking only as much as they need. If people are bringing their own food, they can be invited to enter the room silently and place their food in front of them, waiting for everyone to take a seat before beginning.

- Before eating begins, participants might like to listen to a reading of the "food contemplation" (above), inviting them to reflect with gratitude on the many people and processes that have brought the food to their plate, and reflecting on the need to consider the impact their consumption has on the rest of the world.

- Before beginning to eat, participants acknowledge their companions at the table or around them on the floor. This can be done with a smile, nod, or bow before and after the meal.

- You can begin eating with a sound of the bell, or by just the reading of the contemplations. Everyone is invited to eat their food at their own pace, anchoring themselves in their breath and in the present moment.

- If you sound the bell during the meal, participants stop and return their attention to their breath before continuing to eat. These moments of stopping remind participants to be aware of their active mind and to bring their focus back to the present moment by becoming aware of their breath.

- Decide ahead of time if the full meal or only part of the meal will be taken in companionable silence to enable people to focus fully on eating mindfully.

looking deeply: reflection questions for mindful eating

You may feel the practice is enough in itself, but asking the following questions may help you and/or your students to reflect further. Use them sparingly—they are not a checklist.

- What was my experience—in mind and body—at different points in the mindful eating process? Give prompts—thoughts, anticipations, feelings? Pleasant, unpleasant, neutral?

- Was it different from how I usually eat? In what ways? Prompts—do I usually eat with the TV on, using the phone, doing homework/lesson preparation?

- How did I find being invited to contemplate where the food has come from, and to feel gratitude and connection? Prompts—was it easy, difficult, enjoyable, deepening, calming, difficult, or irritating, etc.? Where in my body do I feel this? What were my thoughts and reflections?

- How was it to eat in silence?

- How was eating with other people?

Add other questions as you wish. Keep them simple, open, nonjudgmental and encouraging. Accept all kinds of responses including "negative" ones, and keep the focus on life experience.

mindful eating in our lives and our teaching

Learning to Eat More Mindfully

At first it is best to keep the experience of mindful eating short and vivid so we can focus on the experience. We can use all kinds of food, but many teachers prefer to use fruit, with its fresh, healthy, and distinct flavors.

Kaira Jewel Lingo, a longtime teacher in the Plum Village tradition, reflects on her class's experience tasting a banana as if for the first time.

We sat down on the grass for "banana meditation." Each child got a piece of banana still in the peel. They held the fruit in their hand and just looked at it; how many colors could they see? What did it feel like in their hand? Cool? Wet? Soft? How would you describe the smell? Slowly they peeled the skin and tried to listen to the sound, noticing the way the peeled skin left grooves along the side of the banana. They then took a very small bite and just let it rest on their tongue without chewing it. They noticed the temperature of the banana and the saliva in their mouths. Leisurely they began to chew the small piece, noticing the taste, where the flavor was strongest on their tongues, how they chewed with their teeth and used their tongues to swallow. We needed a good five minutes for just one small bite!

In our reflections afterward, one boy shared with amazement that he realized he had never really tasted a banana before doing this exercise! His teacher told me later that he was so impressed by this exercise that he introduced it to his family. His mother reported to the teacher that now their family practices "fruit meditation" regularly!

Lauri Bower, a mindfulness teacher working with young children in the UK, uses the mindful eating of a raisin as the first practice to introduce mindfulness to the class. She notes that starting to teach mindfulness in this way helps her avoid from the outset the stereotyped image that mindfulness is just about sitting with your eyes closed.

I have recently been introducing mindfulness to a UK primary (first) school where my daughter teaches, throughout Key Stage 2, which is ages seven to eleven. We begin with mindful eating, by paying attention to one raisin and using all our senses (including listening!) to explore it. This can be a great way of introducing the concept of mindfulness, as it doesn't appear to be a meditation. It can also be a way of exploring what their understanding of meditation is, which can be quite limited and usually involves hands in a particular position, sitting cross-legged, and so on. I'm happy to dispel the myth that this is all meditation is about.

We can use many different items of food, including those to which young people may be reliably attracted, such as cookies or chocolate, helping the students to savor the intense flavors and develop a greater respect, and even reverence, for the food they eat. Carme Calvo Berbel, a professional development trainer in Spain, recounts:

> To build concentration in my courses and discover how different a daily experience can feel, we eat a cookie and practice being present with the five senses (sight, smell, touch, hearing, taste). We capture a lot of information about all the processes that enable us to eat and enjoy the cookie. Thanks to this reflection, we experience wonder, gratitude, and relaxation.

Eating Whole Meals Mindfully

Once the basics are established, we can eat whole meals mindfully. In an elementary school in the UK, mindful eating has become an enjoyable routine for the very young children in the nursery class. Their teacher, Alison Mayo, notes that it is starting to influence their families' eating habits too.

> Eating mindfully together, as part of the class "family," now forms an important part of our nursery routine every morning. Eating and drinking healthy foods nourishes our bodies and minds, but it can also be a healing, nurturing experience on many levels: personal, social, and spiritual. . . . We sometimes share food that the children have cooked themselves, and also occasionally include foods from other cultures, or things the children may not have tried before. After about one minute we sound the bell again, and continue to eat, and enjoy time to chat together as a group.
>
> I have been struck by how quickly the children (three- and four-year-olds) pick up this practice, with new children who join the group learning by copying the older ones. They seem to really enjoy it, and are starting to reflect about their food, unprompted by me. "I wonder where oat cakes come from . . . " one child said last week. Mindful snack is now a highlight of our daily routine, and some children have introduced their families to doing something similar at home.

Chelsea True, an educator in the US, describes an after-school program in which families are invited to bring healthy food to a mindful eating picnic.

In our after-school program, we share a period of mindful eating in class. Whenever possible, we sit under the apple trees in the gardens. Observing subtle changes in the trees throughout the seasons becomes a part of our practice. Families bring organic, whole foods—as what we put into our bowls matters as much as how we consume it.

To begin, breathe in and out together for one sound of the bell. When we can no longer hear the bell, we recite "The Harvest" by Alice Corbin Henderson. At the end of this poem, I say, "Enjoy the sunbeams in your food!" We usually do not eat in complete silence. Instead, we bring greater care and attention to our snack.

Often, I'll ask a child to pause just as they're about to put a bite into their mouth and notice what happens in their body. Maggie, age nine, reported feeling empowered. She had a strong impulse to put the bite in her mouth—and mindfulness gave her the choice of what to do in that moment. Other children have reported noticing their mouths watering, tummies grumbling, and hunger increasing. In this way, eating mindfully helps us cultivate greater awareness of our bodies and impulses.

She notes too how the impact of this experience extends to the classroom.

Mindful eating has a strong impact on the students and the classroom environment. Liam, age five, noticed that the strawberries appear more bright red when we eat mindfully. The whole classroom often feels more vibrant and awake. A sense of community grows from the collective energy of mindfulness. A sense of ease arises while we eat together—often allowing us to transition into a new activity or lesson with increased attention and harmony within the group.

Natural Opportunities for Mindful Eating

There are countless natural opportunities to encourage mindful eating, such as when someone brings in a birthday cake to share, when the class eats during their break or lunch together, or when the class goes on an outing and eats together. One teacher observes,

> When it is a child's birthday they will often bring in cake for us to enjoy. We will always eat this through the process of mindful eating and the children love to talk about all the flavors and potential ingredients that could have been involved in making it.
>
> Nowadays I notice my children at snack time will just pause a moment, as they open a packet, and sniff what's inside.

It is helpful to allow the students' reaction to suggest how often we do this, keeping the practice positive, fun, and inviting. We can quietly acknowledge and encourage any students who decide to eat their snacks or meals more mindfully. Most of all we can remember to walk the talk ourselves, eating mindfully in our daily life so that when we eat in front of the class, we naturally model mindful eating.

Enjoying a Sense of Peace While Eating

Hearing that mindful eating sometimes includes some periods of silence can sound oppressive if you haven't experienced it. So long as we keep the periods of silence short at first, or maybe with younger children encourage very quiet talk, in practice adults and children very much enjoy the peaceful break—as Grace Bruneel, a volunteer in a Catholic school in Hong Kong, describes.

> We have introduced a practice called "Quiet Meal, Happy Meal." The usual scene in the canteen was noisy, with lots of screams, running around, and playing around. The teachers would describe crossing the canteen during lunch to be like crossing the Red Sea! Now each class first lines up outside the canteen, and, when everyone is ready, a teacher or a student invites the bell. Then they enter the canteen. When all classes are there, Father Vicente Sanchez, or the School Principal, or the Spiritual Education Coordinator, invites the bell and says a prayer. Then everybody starts their meal. Classical music is played in the background and students are encouraged to eat mindfully. If they talk, they are encouraged to speak softly. . . . This change was really welcomed by the teachers and surprisingly even by the students, who also complained about the noise level and their suffering ears!

Building a Sense of Interbeing through Mindful Eating

When we take time to eat together mindfully we can feel a greater sense of connection with those around us. As we are invited to contemplate where our food has come from, we can cultivate a deeper sense of gratitude, connection, compassion, and understanding with those who produced the food, with those with whom we eat, and for those in the world who do not have enough.

Gratitude and appreciation can spread to the cooks, as Shantum Seth, a senior Plum Village teacher working in India, notices.

> During a school-wide retreat at the Welham Boys' School, we implemented five minutes of silence at the beginning of lunch to encourage eating meditation. A school cook shared that in that silence he heard the students' appreciation for his hard work—for the first time ever.

Medical school professor Katrina Tsang in Hong Kong uses mindful eating as a starting practice with her medical students, finding that it immediately triggers a sense of deep connection.

> Raisin meditation is how I usually introduce mindful awareness to beginners. Students experience slowing down to notice the joys and miracles of life and of being alive. Some report that the raisin is more vivid and flavorful, and that they find the practice enjoyable and pleasant. Many are paying attention to their minds intentionally for the first time and they notice the wandering nature of it, and learn from the group that this in fact is the universal nature of the mind, and they realize that other medical students are also finding it difficult just as they are. The guided raisin meditation includes the journey of the raisin, highlighting the non-raisin elements in the raisin, the interbeing with other people, animals, plants, and minerals, and the transformation a raisin goes through from grape to raisin to nutrients. In the group sharing afterward, we discuss mind-body connection (how the mouth starts to salivate before the raisin even gets inside the mouth)—the importance and power of the mind, something often neglected in most medical curricula. We discuss the importance of learning and knowing how to be

present in the present, to show up to life, to truly be there for the patients we care for.

After mindful eating of a raisin, we transition over to a brief awareness of breath practice, and then practice mindful lunch together. I invite them to eat mindfully together as a group, or on their own at home, for their entire meal or for the first fifteen to twenty minutes of their meal. It brings me a smile to see students really slow down and get intensely curious about the various vegan snacks, savoring the snacks moment by moment.

Working with a very different type of student, marginalized young people "thrown away" by society, a volunteer working in a large city in the US uses an imaginative variation on mindfully eating an orange. The young people are invited to first hold up and identify "their" orange, which they then put back into the pile so that they can try to find it again. The practice/game helps these rejected young people both feel unique and experience the "interconnectedness of life."

In this inner city where I dwell, so many children I encountered after school hours are "thrown away," and they said so with their words, as well as of course demonstrating this truth with their actions. I want to impact on this reality with my work when I implement mindfulness techniques for the children. One example was the way I demonstrated "mindfulness of seeing." I would bring a bag of oranges. Everyone present took an orange. They were asked to observe it closely and then place their orange in the middle of the table. The next action required them to retrieve their particular orange. Without exception, they claimed this would never work, and then without exception they found "their" orange. At this moment, we would shout out elements showing the interconnectedness of life as manifested in the orange. We named the sky, rain, workers, a market, truck, etc.

Mindful eating can help us become more aware of the impact of what we eat on our physical and mental health. After experiencing the practice, people are often more likely to seek healthy alternatives, helping with the struggle many of us have to avoid being overweight in a world with heavy commercial pressure and overabundance. The practice can encourage us to reduce overeating and waste for ourselves, our students, our families, and our communities by taking only what we need and eating slowly enough for us to become aware when we are full.

As educators with responsibility for making policy and shaping the school and university environment, mindful eating can help us become more motivated to try to ensure the school and the university have policies and practices around food and nutrition that promote the health and well-being of all who work and learn there.

Peace in ourselves, peace in the world.
THICH NHAT HANH

seven
taking care of
our emotions

in this chapter

- Find ways to develop the capacity to recognize and take care of our emotions more effectively, cultivating greater joy and happiness, and transforming our experience of difficulties and suffering.

- Receive step-by-step instructions and practical guidance for three core Plum Village practices: i) getting in touch with our emotions through our breath and body, ii) the "tree in a storm" practice to help us relate more effectively to difficult feelings such as anger, and iii) pebble meditation to cultivate feelings of freshness, presence, solidity, calm, and freedom.

- Reflect on some ways in which teachers are helping themselves and their students relate to their emotions more effectively, cultivating joy and transforming suffering and difficulties—in schools, classrooms, universities, and in daily life.

no mud, no lotus

THICH NHAT HANH

I believe that happy teachers will change the world.

When you are not happy, you cannot help other people to be happy. To love is to offer happiness. The practice of mindfulness can help us to have more happiness, more love, so that we can offer others our happiness and our love. If a teacher has a lot of happiness and a lot of love in her, she can surely make her students happy.

The practice of mindfulness is an art. We train ourselves to be able to generate a feeling of joy and happiness at any time, no matter what the situation. We learn to see that mindfulness is a *source* of happiness, because it helps us to be in touch with the many wonders of life inside and around us. With mindfulness, we also learn to handle and take care of painful feelings and strong emotions. But we must first learn to generate a feeling of joy and happiness to be strong enough to handle the suffering inside.

If we want to learn the art of suffering, we must first learn the art of happiness. Inside us, there is a belief that we do not have enough conditions of happiness. We tend to run into the future to look for more conditions of happiness. We think, if only we had this or that, *then* we would be happy. But as practitioners, we want to train ourselves to be able to generate a feeling of joy or happiness at any moment. How is this done? If we master the practice of mindful breathing, it becomes very easy, because when we breathe in and out mindfully, we bring our mind back to our body, and release the tension in our body. We find ourselves established in the here and the now, and we are able to recognize the many conditions of joy and happiness that are available—we make the discovery that right in the here and now, there are more than enough conditions available for us to be joyful and happy.

There is a little difference between joy and happiness. In joy, there is still some excitement. But in happiness you are calmer. Imagine a very thirsty man walking in the desert who suddenly sees an oasis, with trees encircling a pond. That is joy. He has not drunk the water yet—he is still thirsty—but he is joyful, because he need only walk a few more minutes to arrive at the pond. There is some excitement and hope in him. But when that man arrives at the pond, kneels, cups his hands, and drinks the water, he feels the happiness of drinking water, quenching his thirst. That is happiness—very fulfilling.

Suppose we practice meditation with the thought, "Breathing in, I notice that my eyes are still in good condition." To have eyes in good condition is wonderful—you need only to open them, and there's a paradise of forms and colors always available to you. All you need to do to enjoy the paradise and the sunshine, is to open your eyes. Imagine what it would be like not to be able to see the sunshine, to live always in the dark. Mindfulness helps you to see that there is sunshine, there are rolling hills, there are birds, there are trees, and there is this beautiful planet. With mindfulness, you remember that you have a body, and your feet are strong enough for you to run and to walk. Realizing this brings happiness right away, like the man drinking the water.

When we learn to generate a feeling of happiness, we can create happiness not only for ourselves, but also for other people. Our mindfulness of happiness is a reminder to the people around us, and this kind of mindfulness can be contagious. We remind them that they are in a wonderful world, that the wonders of life are available to them, and that makes them happy. We light up the lamp of happiness in them. As a teacher, you can perform that miracle in just a few seconds, and you can make the students in your class happy.

It is very important that we do not try to run away from our painful feelings. Most people in our society, including teachers and young people, try to run away from painful feelings by covering them up with something else. We are prepared to do almost anything to avoid being confronted with the suffering inside us—we listen to music, we look for something to eat in the fridge, we go online or turn on the TV, and modern society provides us with many forms of consumption to help us try to cover up our suffering. By consuming like this, we allow the suffering inside to grow and grow.

It is only by looking deeply into the nature of our suffering that we will be able to see the way out. If we try to run away from our suffering, we have no chance. We can learn a lot from our suffering. There is a beautiful flower called a lotus that grows from the mud in the bottom of the pond and blooms on the surface. When we look into a lotus flower, we see the mud. So, happiness is a kind of lotus. Without the element of suffering, you cannot make happiness. This is one of the deepest teachings of mindfulness: this is because that is. Because the mud is, that is why the lotus can be.

That is why we must train ourselves to handle our suffering, rather than to avoid it. How can we do this? The first thing we need to do is to practice mindful breathing or mindful walking to generate the energy of mindfulness. Suffering and pain are a kind of energy that is not pleasant, which is why we do not want to be with them and we try to run away. Our practice is to do the opposite.

We are made up of body, feelings, perceptions, mental formations, and consciousness. We are vast. There are at least two layers of consciousness: the upper layer called "mind consciousness," and the lower layer called "store consciousness."

Store Consciousness

Our fear, anger, and despair are there in the bottom of our consciousness in the form of seeds. So long as the seed of anger is asleep, we are okay; we can laugh and have a good time. But if someone comes and says or does something that touches that seed of anger, it will come up as a source of energy. Down in store consciousness it is called a seed, but when it comes up to the level of mind consciousness it becomes a kind of energy called a "mental formation"—in this case it is the mental formation called anger.

Taking care of our strong emotions—our difficult mental formations—with mindfulness has five steps:

1. The first step is to **recognize** that an emotion is present. When joy is there, we know that joy is present. When anger is there, we recognize the fact that anger is present. It helps to call the emotion by its name. If we don't recognize what emotion(s) is present within us, it is very difficult to take care of it.

2. The second step is to **accept** that the emotion is really there. It is okay to have anger; in fact, as a human being it is completely normal. If we don't accept that an unpleasant emotion is there, we are likely to continue thinking in such a way that we feed that emotion. So we should not try to suppress or cover up the painful feeling. Mindfulness does the work of recognizing and accepting—not suppressing, not fighting. This is nonviolence, because the pain is you; it's not your enemy. And mindfulness is you. And mindfulness is helping to transform the pain. The same is true for pleasant feelings like happiness. We need to give ourselves permission to be happy, and to continue to nourish our happiness so that it stays for a long time.

3. The third step is to **embrace** the emotion with mindfulness, like a mother embracing her crying baby. When the baby cries, the mother picks up and holds the baby tenderly. She doesn't yet know the cause of the baby's suffering, but the fact that she's holding the baby makes the baby suffer less. In the beginning, we may not know where our suffering has come from, but because we're able to recognize, accept, and embrace it tenderly, we suffer less already.

4. The fourth step is to **look deeply** into the emotion. The light of our mindfulness helps us to see clearly the roots of our difficult emotions, and how these roots have been nourished by our thinking and perceptions. Seeing the emotion clearly in this way is essential to transforming the compost of difficult emotions into the flowers of joy, peace, and happiness.

5. The fifth step is to get the **insight** that we are more than just an emotion. Even in the midst of a strong emotion, we can see that the emotion is impermanent and ever-changing. We see that the territory of our being is large and one emotion is just a very tiny thing. With this insight, we know that transformation is possible.

With the practice of deep belly breathing, we can survive an emotional storm very easily, but we should not wait until strong emotions come up to begin the practice. We should begin right now. If we practice just five or ten minutes every day, we will naturally remember to come back to our breathing the next time a strong emotion arises, and we can survive the storm more easily. When we have mastered this practice, we can transmit it to our students. In class, many children have strong emotions and do not know how handle them. As teachers, we should help them— we help them to prepare themselves for when strong emotions come. If a child has a crisis in class, you can help him or her to practice deep belly breathing, and one day, they will be able to practice by themselves. You can save their life by helping them to prepare now.

teaching notes on

....

taking care of our emotions

As is evident by the words "Happy Teachers" in the title of this book, the Plum Village approach is centrally concerned with the importance of taking care of our emotions. All the practices can contribute to helping us become happier, be in touch with our feelings in mind, body, and breath, recognize and embrace our difficult feelings, and cultivate in ourselves and our students positive emotional states such as calm, clarity, stability, trust, compassion, and gratitude. These skills help us build a happy community in which people relate effectively to one another.

As we and our students practice mindfulness, we get to know ourselves and the workings of our mind and body more directly. We become more skilled in observing our own feelings and the judgments, perceptions, and habitual patterns that underlie them, and we note the impact on our breath and body. We gain more freedom to use our breath and our body to quiet our mind, and gradually replace our unhelpful mental habits and perceptions with ones that are more accurate and work better, for ourselves and for those around us. We become more responsive and less reactive. We become more present for others, without as much judgment and mental clutter, and we communicate with others more openly and freely. We find more effective ways to soothe and calm ourselves, and help ourselves and others feel happier.

Time spent helping ourselves and our students to relate more effectively to our emotions is not a distraction from what some would see is the "core business" of teaching and learning; it is in fact the vital foundation. Stress, anger, anxiety, and other difficult mental states block effective thinking, teaching, and learning. Positive mind states such as calm, joy, engagement, "flow," and feeling safe enable our minds and bodies to operate at an optimal level, in our work and in our learning, and enable us to "be the best we can be."

Opportunities for taking care of our emotions arise constantly: the teaching and learning day is a stream of potential practice. We can monitor ourselves and our ever-fluctuating reactions to our everyday tasks; we can help students learn and get involved whether they are getting on or dropping out; we can face a rewarding or a difficult class, and an angry or appreciative parent. We can remember to praise ourselves and our students when we stay calm, solid, and relate to our feelings well. When we are not as successful as we would like to be, we can let it go, with a friendly smile to ourselves, and simply start again.

This chapter contains three specific practices, which focus directly on taking care of our emotions. The first two teach us to use our body and our breath to get in touch with how we are feeling in the present moment, to find a calm center within, and generate the positive energy of mindfulness to help us embrace difficult feelings, such as anger and sadness, with kindness and acceptance. The iconic "pebble meditation," invented by Thich Nhat Hanh, and popular with children and adults the world over, provides a concrete way to get in touch with the helpful and nourishing qualities inside ourselves, to appreciate the happiness already within and around us and to further cultivate a stable base to take care of our more difficult feelings and strong emotions.

This is strong and deep work, which you and your students may find moving and possibly challenging, so go slowly and take care.

. . . . .

At the end of the chapter we hear from practicing teachers who explore some of the myriad ways in which we can help ourselves and our students take care of our emotions, embrace our suffering and difficulties, and cultivate positive states of mind.

....

using our breath to get in touch with our emotions

Why study this practice?

- To calm and relax the body and mind.

- To get in touch with the breath in the belly, the sense of having a "friend" who is always there to help us bring our mind back to our body, to be with our emotions, and to return to the present moment.

- To increase the ability to recognize how we are feeling—in body and mind.

- To become aware of and cultivate embodied feelings of peace, joy, and happiness.

- To become aware of our more painful feelings, and learn how to take care of and embrace them with kindly acceptance.

core practice

....

using our breath to get in touch with our emotions

A practice summary is available in appendix A on page 306.

What follows is a powerful practice intended to cover several sessions to allow you and the students to build your skills. Take the process slowly. It is best to focus first on cultivating calm, after which you can practice moving on to feelings of joy and happiness. Once this is established, you can then move on to being with painful feelings.

Materials and Preparation

- A teacher experienced in the practice—so practice a good deal yourself before you teach this to others.

- Mats or chairs, depending on how you want people to sit or lie down.

- Bell and inviter (optional but recommended).

This practice assumes that you and your students are familiar with the foundations of breath, bell, and sitting practice. You may also like to practice "coming back to the body" practices first.

In what follows, use the words to guide you in what you say to yourself and to the students. When teaching yourself you may like to record it or have someone read it to you.

1. Prepare the Group

Find a comfortable, relaxed, and stable sitting position, with eyes closed or partially open.

Lie down, if you prefer and if there is space.

2. Invite the Bell and Begin

Invite one sound of the bell to begin the practice.

Take the practice and the words slowly and allow plenty of time between instructions for you and your students to feel the breath, to get in touch with the experience of body and mind, and for the breath gradually to calm down and lengthen.

This is the full practice. You can stop at any point.

3. Notice You Are Breathing

Take a few moments to gradually become aware of the fact that you are breathing.

There is no need to change anything, just be aware of, notice, and recognize the breath, just as it is.

4. Feel the Breath in the Belly

Put your hands on your belly and become aware of it rising with the in-breath and falling with the out-breath.

Just notice the sensation of the in-breath and the out-breath, feeling the hands and belly move.

Notice the length of the breath, and the pauses in between.

Take some time for this stage.

5. Using the Breath to Calm Mind and Body

Gradually become aware of what is happening for you in your mind and body right now—your state of mind, your mood, your feelings, any areas of tension in the body or discomfort in the mind.

Whatever is there for you right now, recognize it, and maybe call it by its name.

Then use the breath to gradually release any tension and embrace any difficulties, as best you can, and see if you can gently be aware of increasing a feeling of calm and ease in your mind and body.

Naming the emotion—anger, sadness, boredom, or joy—can help in understanding it.

> **Breathing in, I calm my mind.**
>
> **Breathing out, I calm my feelings, my emotions.**

You can stop here if you wish. If so you may like to invite the bell.

6. Feeling Joy and Happiness

Enjoy the feeling of the breath quietly entering and leaving the body.

Gradually become aware of any parts of your body that feel okay now.

Use the breath to focus on them and enjoy that feeling.

Become aware of any conditions for happiness or joy you may have inside you, even if they are very small. Breathe with those feelings.

> **Breathing in, I feel the joy of having two eyes.**
>
> **Breathing out, I smile to the joy in myself.**
>
> **Breathing in, I feel the happiness of sitting here peacefully.**
>
> **Breathing out, I smile to the feelings of happiness in myself.**

You can stop here if you wish. If so invite one sound of the bell.

7. Being with Painful Feelings

Become aware of any difficult or painful feelings in your mind or body.

If you have no painful feelings right now, that is great. You may still find it helpful to name a painful feeling you have quite often (e.g., sadness, worry, anger) and practice being with the words now to help you later.

> **Breathing in, I am aware of a painful feeling.**
>
> **Breathing out, I calm my painful feeling.**

If you have a painful feeling right now, you might like to explore whether you can get clearer about what the painful feeling is, and even name it. Maybe you have a small or larger tension or pain in your body or mind. Maybe there is a feeling of restlessness, worry, fear, or anxiety, maybe sadness about something or someone you lost, or anger with someone or something—maybe yourself—or maybe jealousy.

Identify where you experience it in your body, how your body responds to it, what kind of thoughts are going around your head.

> Breathing in, I know that (name feeling *x*, e.g., anger, fear, jealousy, restlessness) is in me.
>
> Breathing out I embrace my (*x*) feeling.
>
> Hello there, my feeling.
>
> Your name is (*x*).
>
> I know you.
>
> I will take good care of you.

You can stop here if you wish. If so invite one sound of the bell.

Example: Being with Anger

Maybe you feel anger, or at least some irritation at the moment, or perhaps you don't right now. Now, or the next time you feel anger, here is something you can do.

> Breathing in, I know that anger is in me.
>
> Breathing out, I know I am still angry.
>
> Breathing in, I know mindfulness is there.
>
> Breathing out, mindfulness is embracing the anger.
>
> Hello there, my feeling.
>
> Your name is anger.
>
> I know you.
>
> I am here for you.
>
> I am taking good care of you.

8. Bell and Ending

Invite one sound of the bell to close the practice, allowing the students time to take three mindful breaths before they gently open their eyes and stretch.

teaching notes on

....

tree in a storm

Why practice like a tree in a storm?

• To get in touch with the breath in the belly in the present moment.

• To calm and relax body and mind.

• To increase a sense of stability and safety.

This variation uses the image of a tree in a storm to help you and your students experience the sense of having a strong and stable "trunk" on which you can rely while emotions rage in your "branches." It may be best to practice it after you and your students have become used to belly breathing and getting in touch with the emotions. It can also be used as a basic practice instead of the one above, especially for younger children.

It is best practiced first when things seem calm—with you and your class. It may be helpful to have a short discussion first with your class about what difficult emotions they have and what those emotions feel like. Be ready to hold the space for strong emotions as they then may arise. It can be helpful to focus on just one emotion, like anger. This way there is a specific felt experience to draw on in the practice. Once the students are used to the process, it will be easier to help them practice when strong emotions have arisen.

core practice
....

tree in a storm

Materials and Preparation

- You need to be experienced in the practice yourself before you teach it to others.
- Mats or chairs depending on how you want people to sit or lie down.
- Bell and inviter (optional but recommended).

You can do this practice sitting or lying down.

1. Bell

Invite one sound of the bell to signal the beginning of the practice.

2. Notice Your Breathing

Become aware of the in- and out-breath. No need to change the breath; just be aware of it.

3. Belly Breathing

Start with belly breathing—see above—and cover all stages up to and including "using the breath to calm mind and body."

4. Aware of Painful Feelings

Become aware of any difficult or painful feelings in your mind or body.

   If you have none right now, that is fine. By learning this practice when you are calm, you will be better prepared next time a strong emotion comes.

Remember, there's no need to rush through what follows, take it steady and at a pace that feels appropriate.

5. The Tree

Imagine now that you are a tree.
   Your belly is like the trunk of the tree.
   The strong feeling—anger or hurt or sadness—is like a storm making the high branches of your tree sway backward and forward in the wind.
   Now come back down to the trunk of the tree, to your belly.
   It feels stable and safe down at the trunk of your tree.

There is no need to think about what happened just now.

Just be aware of your breathing, your belly rising and falling.

Breathing in, I calm this strong feeling,

Breathing out, I can even smile to this strong feeling.

Stay breathing in and out.

We stay with the trunk of our tree.

There is still a storm going on. There is still emotion in us.

But we are breathing, in and out, deep and slow, belly rising, belly falling.

Down at the trunk of our tree we can breathe and feel safe.

Soon the storm will pass.

6. Bell and Ending

Invite one sound of the bell and allow for three mindful breaths to close the practice.

....

pebble meditation

Why practice Pebble Meditation?

- To provide a concrete way to get in touch with the helpful and nourishing qualities inside ourselves—of freshness, solidity, calm, and freedom.

- To help us appreciate the happiness that is already within us and all around us.

- To provide a stable base to take care of our more difficult feelings and strong emotions.

- To calm and relax our body and mind.

introduction to the practice

THICH NHAT HANH

Some years ago, in a retreat for children I invented a practice called Pebble Meditation, so the children could learn to cultivate the four qualities that we all need to be happy. To do the meditation we start with four pebbles, each one representing an image and a quality.

The instructions for the practice are on the next page.

The first quality is **freshness**. We should do something to preserve our freshness and beauty. As humans, we are born as a **flower** in the garden of humanity, but if we don't know how to live mindfully we will lose our freshness, and we will not have much to offer to the people we love. The practices of mindful breathing, mindful walking, deep relaxation, and smiling can help you to restore your freshness, for yourself and for whoever encounters you.

The second pebble represents **solidity**. The image is a **mountain**. In the sitting position, you feel solid. Without solidity, you cannot be a happy person. You should cultivate stability and solidity for yourself and for those who rely on you.

You and everyone around you will profit from it. You can't ask someone to give you stability; you must cultivate it yourself.

The third quality is **calm**. The image is that of **still water**. When water is still it can reflect the sky, the clouds, and the mountains faithfully. When your mind is calm, you see things as they are; you don't distort anything. Calm is a condition for happiness. If you are not calm, you suffer and those around you also suffer. If you are calm, you are happy, and your friends profit from your peacefulness. We generate calm by breathing, walking, and sitting in mindfulness.

The last quality is **freedom**. A person who is not free is not a happy person. Freedom here is not political freedom. The image is that of **space**. Freedom here is freedom from craving, anger, hate, despair, and ambition. All these afflictions keep you from being free, and the happiness of a person relies very much on his or her freedom. If you have many worries, anxieties, projects, and fears in your heart, you are not free, and you cannot be a happy person. The practice of this last pebble is to empty yourself of these kinds of afflictions so you can find a lot of space within your heart.

core practice

pebble meditation

A practice summary is available in appendix A on page 310.

Preparation

You need to be experienced in the practice before you teach it to others. Invite your class to sit in a circle, on cushions or chairs, or at tables or desks.

You may like to sing the song "Breathing In, Breathing Out" as a way to introduce the practice. Find the lyrics and music at www.wakeupschools.org/songs.

Materials

- Four pebbles for each person, in a basket or bowl to pass around.
- Bell and inviter (optional but recommended).

1. Start

Give out the pebbles, or invite the students to take four of them from a basket or bowl as it is passed around.

Invite the students to put the pebbles beside them on the left.

Alternatively, you may like to introduce the practice to them first before they choose their pebbles, so that they can later pick for themselves the pebbles that they feel represent for them a flower, mountain, still water, and space.

2. Bell

Invite three sounds of the bell to begin the practice.

Use the following script to guide the students, and/or yourself, through the practice.

3. First Pebble: Flower

Pick up one pebble and place it in the palm of your hand. Look at it closely as if you have never seen a pebble before.

This pebble represents a flower. It is the fresh, beautiful, pleasant, and loveable human being in you. All of us can be a fresh flower, full of energy and life, and when we are like that we have a lot to offer to ourselves and other people.

Place your other hand over the pebble, holding it gently at your belly, and close your eyes.

Read aloud:

> Breathing in, I see myself as a flower.
> Breathing out, I feel fresh.
> Flower, fresh.

Invite one sound of the bell.

Follow three in- and out-breaths all the way through while saying to yourself silently:

Flower (as you breathe in).

Fresh (as you breathe out).

No need to rush through, take it steady and at a pace that feels appropriate.

After three breaths, look at your pebble, smile to it and put it down beside you on the right.

4. Second Pebble: Mountain

Now pick up the second pebble and place it in the palm of your hand. Look at it closely with fresh eyes. This pebble represents a mountain. We can all be a mountain, solid, safe, and secure in ourselves and with other people. We are stable enough to cope with whatever happens to us.

Place your other hand over the pebble, holding it gently at your belly, and close your eyes.

Read aloud:

Breathing in, I see myself as a mountain.

Breathing out, I feel solid.

Mountain, solid.

Invite one sound of the bell.

Follow three in- and out-breaths while saying to yourself silently:

Mountain (as you breathe in).

Solid (as you breathe out).

After three breaths, look at the pebble, smile to it, and put it down on your right.

5. Third Pebble: Still Water

Now pick up the third pebble and place it in the palm of your hand. Look at it closely with fresh eyes. This pebble represents still water, like a calm lake. Still water reflects everything around it—sky, clouds, trees—just as they are, without changing and distorting them. We can all be like still water, calm, clear, reflecting the truth. When we are like this, we see how things actually are.

Place your other hand over the pebble, holding it gently at your belly, and close your eyes.

Read aloud:

> **Breathing in, I see myself as still water.**
> **Breathing out, I am calm. I reflect things as they truly are.**
> **Still water, calm.**

Invite one sound of the bell.

Follow three in- and out-breaths while saying to yourself silently:

> **Still water.**
> **Calm.**

After three breaths, look at your pebble, smile to it, and put it down beside you on the right.

6. Fourth Pebble: Space

Now pick up the fourth pebble and place it in the palm of your hand. Look at it closely with fresh eyes. This pebble represents the space and freedom in you. When we help ourselves to feel more spacious and free, inside and outside of ourselves, we can be kinder and more generous toward ourselves and other people.

Place your other hand over the pebble, holding it gently at your belly, and close your eyes.

Read aloud:

> **Breathing in, I see myself as space.**
> **Breathing out, I feel free.**
> **Space, free.**

Invite one sound of the bell.

Follow three in- and out-breaths while saying to yourself silently:

> **Space.**
> **Free.**

After three breaths, look at the pebble, smile to it, and put it down on your right.

7. Bell

Invite one sound of the bell to close the practice.

Here, you may use the reflection questions listed below if you wish.

8. Ending

You can offer to collect the pebbles, but it is better if you can allow the students to keep them, so they have them to practice with any time they want.

—

variations on pebble meditation

- This practice can be taught gradually, spread out over several sessions, contemplating a different quality each day.

- Discuss and/or draw on paper the different qualities, to help students focus deeply.

Instructions on how to make a pebble bag may be found in the book *Planting Seeds*. See section "What Next?"

- Make a pebble bag. Some younger students might like to keep their pebbles in a bag they can decorate. Julie, an elementary school teacher in the UK, says that when the students make the pebble bag themselves, "It gives them a sense of ownership and control over their practice. It feels like it is theirs, rather than something that is imposed upon them."

- Keep a pebble in your pocket. You, the teacher, might like to use the practice yourself by carrying around one pebble, to stand for all four, to remind you of the different qualities you want to bring to your teaching and your life. It may be helpful to just quietly bring your hand to your pebble from time to time. For example, when you feel scattered or when things are difficult, the pebble can bring you back to the four qualities that will help you meet the challenge. You can put the four pebbles somewhere you sit regularly, such as your desk or worktable to remind you to return to these qualities in you.

looking deeply: reflection questions on being with our emotions

Here are some questions for you, the teacher, to reflect on or to use with the students either during in-class sharing or by just letting the questions settle in the mind. Use them sparingly—it is not a checklist!

- How do I feel right now? (Can be asked at any point in the practice.)

- What was the effect of the practice on my mind, body, breath? (You can make the question specific to the practice.)

- How easy or difficult did I find the practice? (Fun, boring, calming, challenging?)

- Can I imagine using the pebbles and the practice to help me take care of my emotions in my daily life? Shall I keep my pebbles? Can I think of times when they might be useful and how I might use them?

Add other questions as appropriate. Keep them simple, open, nonjudgmental, encouraging, and accepting of all kinds of responses including "negative" ones and "I don't know." Gently bring the sharing back to present real life experience.

taking care of our emotions in our lives and in our teaching

Taking Care of Our Own Emotions

One of the first gifts that mindfulness rapidly brings is a shift in perspective—we simply start to see things rather differently. This gift is particularly apparent in the ability of mindfulness to help us transform strong emotions.

Our immediate thoughts and actions when we are in the grip of difficult emotions are rarely wise and helpful, a fact most of us tend to realize too late in the process. So, we end up saying and doing things we later regret. Taking time to practice mindfulness when we experience a strong emotion can help us respond rather than react, and give ourselves the space to start to let go of what is clouding our view. Michael Bready, who has developed and now leads a mindfulness program for young people in the UK, finds that when he is in a worried state, the most basic mindfulness practices bring a tranquility and clarity of mind that transforms his perspective.

> I find the simplest practices can often bring great benefit to me. Sometimes when I worry too much about work, simply spending forty minutes resting my mind with my breath, brings a sense of ease, calm, and relief and a very different perspective, allowing me to reengage with life with more clarity and self-compassion.

Maggie Chau, teaching in a university in Hong Kong, has learned that not reacting immediately enhances her ability to respond in a more considered way, with greater compassion and wisdom.

> Being aware of my reactions in everyday life through the practice of mindfulness, I become truly more mindful of my emotions and thoughts. As a result, I can either respond with more compassion and wisdom or at least— if I am unable to "not react" right away—with this awareness, I can improve over time.

This sentiment is echoed by this special education teacher, for whom mindfulness helps "hold" the painful and the difficult for a time until greater calmness can move in.

> Over the years the practice has brought me great relief from painful situations, without ignoring the depth of the problem or situation. Over time, I have learned to slow down, hold a difficulty for a time, and respond when calm, rather than with a strong emotion (anger, fear, denial, etc.).

Teachers are often so busy striving to meet challenges and to fix things for others that we can forget to pause to focus on what is pleasant. In this way we are not fully present when we or those around us experience positive emotions such as joy, fun, excitement, and the feeling of being loved and cared for. Humans tend to focus on the difficult and take the neutral and the pleasant for granted. We can even feel self-indulgent or unworthy if we are aware of enjoying ourselves too much, or feel that we are tempting fate. Mindfulness can help us take time for ourselves, to appreciate the positive, enjoy the moment, and feel grateful for what we have. Mariann Taigman, an occupational therapist whom we met in earlier chapters, cultivates happiness for herself and her students by focusing on "precious moments" and using "positive reminders."

> I created a "Precious Moments" journal for myself the year I had surgery, with the goal to write one precious thing that happened to me each day, no matter how challenging the day had been. That was eight years ago and I still write in my journal every day, generally listing four to eight precious moments daily :-). I have given this idea to a number of children with positive results, and I generally buy them a journal with a cute picture on the front. For my upcoming presentation for a conference at which I've been asked to speak, I plan to put positive reminders (e.g., "Enjoy every moment," "Breathe, you are alive!") around the room, as I loved this aspect of Thay's retreats—the monastics even put reminders to be mindful on the inside of the restroom doors!

Relating Effectively to Our Emotions Helps Us Be with Others

Being able to relate to our own emotions more effectively can transform how we are with others. It can reduce the mental clutter that can get in the way of us being fully present which, as we will see in the next chapter on "being together," is the foundation of all loving and authentic relationships. Coreen Morsink from Greece reflects on this quality.

> I am able to focus on the person I'm teaching or on the class without extra emotions or outside thoughts getting in the way.

Alan Brown, a high school dean and teacher in New York City, manages to "control my own nervous system" so he can be present for those around him.

Only when I have taken care of myself am I able to show up for those around me—students and colleagues. As an administrator, I have many difficult conversations each week. The ability to hold space for others, to listen deeply and truly hear them and their experience, is invaluable. Stopping to take a breath and control my own nervous system, as well as practicing loving kindness and compassion when others are out of control, makes a difference in how situations resolve themselves.

Goyo Hidalgo Ruiz, a teacher of teens in Spain, feels "everything is easier" for himself and for others around him since he has learned to relate effectively to his emotions, reducing their intensity, and moving his mind toward the positive.

Now everything is easier. Fewer thoughts and emotions with a lesser intensity. What I think affects me less. My emotions are less negative. I notice the emotions and thoughts that help me, as opposed to those that make me sink into depression. I used to be a rather sad and sometimes angry person. This has changed. I still have moments of sadness, but once I detect it, I can embrace my sadness mindfully and create an increasingly freer space inside. Now I also get angry less. Sometimes when my students are on the verge of a nervous breakdown, I do not react with anger as before. I try to focus on my breath before anger springs up.

Songs can help us relate more effectively to the emotions through their direct appeal, embodiment, and repetition. Matt Spence, a high school teacher and coach in North Carolina, found solace in song, discovering that a Plum Village song about happiness he had learned on retreat was there ready and waiting to soothe his anxiety.

Last December, I attended a professional development conference in California, and the timing of this was unfortunate: I was away from my classes as my students were writing their exam essays, I was laying out the student newspaper that was due to be published, and I was writing a proposal for a new, progressive course. On top of that, I was away from my family, which is always hard for me. One night, I went for a walk and found myself gradually taking slower and slower steps. My breathing slowed and deepened, and I began to feel lighter at my core. To my surprise, I found that I was quietly humming a song I'd learned at Blue Cliff, a Plum Village retreat center: "Happiness is here and now. . . ." I started to sing the song aloud. I repeated it over and over again, and each time I felt just a little bit happier. By the time I returned to my hotel, my smile was back, and I felt free and happy.

Helping Students Be with Their Emotions

Betsy Rose is a talented singer, songwriter, and peace activist-educator who is often invited to work directly with children in schools. Here she describes how she teaches children to feel the energy of their strong emotions through their participation in a song. (You can find the recordings of this song and see it and others in action under Betsy's entry in "What Next" on page 325.)

I use a song called "When I Feel Mad." (Sung to the tune of "The Wheels on the Bus.") This is a fun and active song for the very young (three to seven or so) that invites them to feel with their bodies the energy of strong emotions—anger, fear, excitement, sadness—and to feel the peaceful transition back to a place of balance and safety through movement and song.

Strong emotions can sweep through us like a storm, and this can be frightening to young people who live so fully in their bodies, where emotions happen. A song and a regular predictable movement pattern provide a container of rhythm, rhyme, repetition, and thus a sense of safety, as they help regulate the body and nervous system. Children delight in acting out emotions in exaggerated ways, then finding solid ground through the breath and arm motions, and then comfort in the hug. Singing is a great way to move a group from one activity to another through singing the instruction!

In chapter ten on mindfulness in classrooms, we explore the role of creativity and of song in more detail.

Gloria Shepard and Richard Brady both teach mathematics, and both reflect on using mindfulness to help students with the anxiety many can feel around this subject. Gloria says,

When I was a classroom teacher (most recently third and fourth grade), I often used a moment of mindfulness during the transition to math work because many students found that stressful. We worked together over the course of the year to notice physical and emotional reactions to particular subjects and classroom responsibilities and to use a breath, a movement, or even just internal acknowledgment of the experience to release stress, worry, or other challenges.

Richard Brady offers guided meditations before tests.

Since math tests were a source of stress for so many students, I started to offer guided meditations before each test and quiz. First I asked students to get in touch with their emotions—excitement, nervousness, even fear—and then to observe these emotions without getting carried away by them. Next, I asked them to visualize a time when they had felt good about some mathematical accomplishment, perhaps learning to count or solve a particularly challenging algebra problem. After a couple of minutes, students were ready to begin work with a positive focus.[1]

We can help our students manage their emotions even when we are not able to teach about this issue directly. Dutch special education teacher Tineke Spruytenburg, working in a situation where she is not able to teach mindfulness explicitly to her students, teaches emotional skills "without words" by simply embodying the emotional stability she wants to transmit.

At work I cannot introduce the teaching explicitly, so I never talk out loud about Thay's teachings to the children. I use my breath to calm emotions and I transmit the practice of mindful speech and mindful listening without comments. Children recognize perfectly when I am stable and solid inside. I teach belly breathing whenever there is an opportunity—for example, when a child is engaged in a discussion or a fight with another child, or when a child is in pain, emotionally or physically. I teach Thay's teachings without words.

Murielle Dionnet, a special education teacher from France whom we met earlier, practices breathing with strong feelings in her class of young children.

> When a child in the classroom had too much suffering, I practiced "hugging meditation" with him or her, embracing this strong feeling, just breathing in and out with him or her and saying: "Let's breathe together," until whatever it was subsided.

Healing Difficult Feelings with Mindfulness

Relating effectively to difficult emotions can be an interesting challenge right across the school and university day. Gift Tavedikul, the assistant director of the American School of Bangkok, Thailand, tells a moving story of a team of basketball players who used their mindfulness to manage the strong emotions which arose both in competitive "success" and, more significantly, in "failure," learning to acknowledge their sad feelings authentically and use them to heal the difficulty rather than to be devastated by it.

> In 2014, I was working with our high school basketball team to incorporate mindfulness for the first time. I sat with our players and asked, "what would you like to achieve to make you a better player?" A few teenagers said they wanted to learn how to control their emotions, especially when the competition was fierce. Others said they wanted to be able to focus and feel calm when shooting. When I told the players I had a technique to help all of them, several kids stood up like they were ready to hit the court. "No, sit down," I said. "We're going to practice breathing." I received a few skeptical expressions, but once the players settled back down, we practiced mindful breathing together. This was the beginning of many sessions when I taught the players to focus on aligning their breathing with their mind, body, and spirit.
>
> Our basketball team progressed wonderfully and was peaking just as we started playing in a tournament in Hong Kong. I had great hopes for our squad, but then the unthinkable happened. Two of our starting players were injured so we couldn't rotate players, and after five straight games

in forty-eight hours, our players were exhausted. Feeling dejected, we sat down for a talk to gather ourselves, but there was only silence. As we looked at one another, our chests moved up and down, and it was right then that the players' eyes lit up and we fell into a session of mindful breathing. When we finished, we talked about how hard we had worked, how we had grown as a team, and how our setbacks from the start of the tournament should not discourage us.

The following day, we had to win all three games to have a chance at winning the championship. Our team wore our American School of Bangkok jerseys proudly as we battled in the first game. The lead went back and forth, and with five seconds left, the score was tied. Then the unthinkable happened again. The opposing team made a miraculous shot and threw in the winning basket at the buzzer. We returned to our locker room with eyes full of tears, knowing that the championship was out of our hands.

Without hesitation, I gathered our team and led them outside the stadium. We found a quiet spot with a beautiful view of the sea and mountains. A soft cool breeze blew across our faces and we quickly learned that mindfulness was a great tool, not only for winning, but for healing. We looked at each other's faces, calmly breathed together, and I spoke about what was most important. "We have each other," I said. Small smiles slowly replaced our sad faces and we had truly become one spirit on our journey together.

Working with the Emotions of Our Colleagues

Teacher and administrator Meena Srinivasan, an experienced Plum Village practitioner, helps school leaders work with their strong emotions, which she feels has been "transformative" in engendering greater self-compassion and resilience.

In our work with school leaders, a major focus has been around strengthening one's own inner resources and cultivating resilience to more skillfully navigate the challenges that come with leading a school in a district that has great inequities. Specifically, teaching leaders how to work with strong emotions has been transformative. Through sharing Thay's teachings on how we are both the crying baby and the mother that can soothe the baby, and how we all have the capacity to embrace ourselves with love and friendliness, many leaders have begun to practice self-compassion throughout the school day.

I know you are there and I am very happy.
THICH NHAT HANH

eight
being together

in this chapter

- Explore ways in which we can be more present for others, developing the relationship skills of sharing our thoughts and feelings openly, deep listening, loving speech, and reconciling conflicts—with kindness, empathy, understanding, and compassion.

- Receive step-by-step instructions and practical guidance for two core Plum Village practices, i) sharing in a circle, with deep listening and loving speech, and ii) beginning anew (applying deep listening and loving speech to our relationships, restoring communication and reconciling conflicts).

- Reflect on ways in which we can relate to others more mindfully, authentically and deeply, and help our students develop these qualities in their relationships—illustrated with examples and suggestions from practicing teachers.

Note on language: If the words we use in this chapter are not appropriate for you or your students, substitute whatever words work for you.

- For "mother" or "father," you may prefer to use "parents" or "guardians."

- For "family," you may prefer to use "loved ones," "friends," or "people you live with."

- For "love" and "compassion," you may prefer to say "caring," "kindness," "empathy," or "respect."

deep listening and loving speech

THICH NHAT HANH

Learning to be together, fully present with other people, is in itself a mindfulness practice. We develop love and compassion toward ourselves and others, and understand more fully our deep connection to one another. The greatest gift any of us can offer others is our own practice of mindfulness. Through helping us to develop the capacity to dwell happily in the present moment, the practice of mindfulness enables us to be truly there for ourselves and others, with the awakened presence that is the foundation of our relationships.

Love is the capacity to take care, to protect, and to nourish. If you are not capable of generating that kind of energy toward yourself, it is very difficult to take care of another person. We need to learn to love ourselves, to be fully present and at peace with ourselves. So, our mindfulness always begins with ourselves as teachers and students. When we practice like this, our very smile and our conscious breathing contribute to creating a calm, caring, and solid community.

To love fully, we should try to understand the other person. Observation alone is not enough to see them fully as they are and to understand their suffering. We must become one with the subject of our observation and recognize their physiological and psychological suffering. We get in touch with their body, feelings, and mental formations, and we see that their suffering and our suffering are not separate. Compassion means literally, "to suffer with or together"; it is the human quality of understanding the suffering of others coupled with the motivation to relieve their suffering. When we listen deeply to the other person and we are in contact with their suffering, compassion is born in us.

If we know how to use loving speech, and if we can talk lovingly and compassionately to another person, that person will open her heart and tell us all about the suffering and difficulties she has. If you know how to listen with compassion, then you can restore communication and bring about reconciliation and healing. In the case of teachers, this practice may be done with the people in our family first. When we have succeeded with the members of our family we can then bring the practice to our school. With this practice, we can restore communication with our colleagues and reconcile with them.

To listen deeply, we maintain compassion alive in our heart, and because compassion protects us, we can listen without interrupting. While telling you things, the other person may be bitter or angry. What the other person says may be full of harsh words and wrong perceptions. What you hear might touch off the seed of anger and irritation in you, and cause you to lose your capacity to listen. But if you bring your attention back to your mindful breathing, letting go of your reaction, and keep compassion alive within you, you are protected. Breathing in and out, you remind yourself that you are listening to the other person with only one purpose: to help him empty his heart and suffer less. Even if he says things that are wrong you do not interrupt him and correct him, because if you did you would transform the session into a debate, ruining the session. After a few days, you may offer him or her some information to help them to correct their perceptions, but not now. Now is only for listening. If you can breathe in and out and maintain that awareness alive, you are protected by compassion and you can listen deeply without judging or reacting. That will be very healing for the other person. That person may be our partner, or our father or mother, or whoever lives with us in the same house. When we have restored communication and reconciled with them, we are stronger. Then we can bring the practice to our school. This practice of deep listening can transform our relationships, both at home and at work.

The students in our time suffer greatly, and because they suffer we, the teachers, also suffer. Some come from broken families where nobody has understood them or even listened to them. When they suffer, we also suffer, and we lose a lot of energy. With the experience of mindfulness practice, the teacher can recognize the suffering right away in the student.

There may be a young person who is difficult to deal with, who has a lot of violence, fear, and anger in him, and we can see that he does not know how to handle it. Since the teacher has learned the practice of looking deeply, she can see that this child comes from a difficult family. If he had come from a family where the father and mother are happy and loving, he would not be like this. He is a victim of the kind of suffering that has been handed down to him by his father and mother. When we encounter a young person like that—stubborn, violent, and angry—we are not angry at him anymore. We know such a young person is a victim of his environment and of what has been transmitted to him by his parents. In this way, the teacher feels compassion arising in her when looking at him, and she does not suffer out of anger.

Instead of trying to punish him, the elements of understanding and compassion arise in her and she has the intention to do something to help that young person to suffer less. Since she has been able to understand her own suffering and to generate the energy of compassion for herself, she is in turn capable of seeing the suffering in the other person and can generate understanding and compassion for that person.

Let's imagine teachers and students sitting together, talking to each other about the happiness they experience and the suffering they have gone through. We need to *listen* to understand each other. After we have mutual understanding we won't blame each other or make difficulties for each other anymore, and we can go along more easily and quickly on the path of teaching and learning. Teachers may tell the students: "I know you have suffered. I know you may have difficulties in your family," and so on. "If you don't make much progress in your studies, it is due to these difficulties. So please, tell me, tell us." The whole class can sit and listen with compassion. Doing this together will transform the students, because other students may have the same kind of suffering. If you notice that a boy or a girl suffers and seems to be very upset in the class and you see that her mind is not really there, you can address her and ask what is wrong. She may say, "My mother was hospitalized this morning, and I don't know if she can survive or not." With that kind of feeling, how can she possibly learn? You cannot impose your will on her. So, the teacher can address the whole class and say, "We have a student whose mother is hospitalized and she worries deeply about that. Shall we, the whole class, practice breathing together, mindfully? We will send this energy of mindfulness and compassion to her mother." Using that kind of collective energy of mindfulness generated by the breathing of the teacher and the other students, you can help calm that student down so that she may be able to follow the class. This is what we as teachers can do with the students. Listen to each other and understand each other's suffering so that together we can calm down our feelings and emotions. In this way we promote mutual understanding, and we don't make each other suffer anymore.

When these young people have overcome their difficulties and understood the suffering of their parents, they can go back and help their parents. We have organized retreats of mindfulness for young people in Europe, North America, and Asia where many young people experienced transformation and healing. When they went home afterward, they were able to restore communication with their parents, and many of them have been able to invite their parents to join them in the practice. Teachers can do the same. We can help students to suffer less, to understand how to suffer less, and the student can then go home and help his parents to suffer less also.

There should be time for teachers to sit down with the students to listen to each other. Good communication and the work of teaching and learning will become much easier. That is why using loving speech and inviting the other person to speak out so they may suffer less is one of the best things a teacher can learn. What the young person has not received from his father or mother he can get from his teacher. With the practice, the teacher can transform his class into a real family where there is communication and love.

teaching notes on

....

being together

Why do this practice?

· To help us learn to talk about our thoughts and feelings more openly and authentically.

· To develop the skill of deep listening—which helps us focus, wait our turn to speak, benefit from each other's insights and experiences, see beyond our limited perspectives, understand others, and to feel greater kindness, compassion, and empathy.

· To develop the skill of loving speech, which helps us learn to speak mindfully about our experiences, joys, difficulties, and questions with an openness that's balanced with care and consideration for the feelings of others.

· To help us to feel seen, heard, understood, valued, and that we belong.

· To build a sense of connection with ourselves and with others, and to realize our experience is not unique.

Most teachers understand how vital having a sense of connection is to our experience of education, and they aspire to develop caring and authentic relationships themselves and between their students. They know that good relationships are the foundation, not only of personal happiness and well-being, but also of a well-run school where people teach and learn effectively, and thrive. Feeling safe and cared for, and feeling a sense of connection with your classmates, friendship group, school or university, and family are the prerequisites for being ready to teach, ready to learn, and really to enjoy your school day.

However, as we also know well, relating to others is often not easy. Human beings struggle to form meaningful attachments, to develop a social sense, to move beyond our own self-centeredness and misguided perceptions, and to understand

and care about others deeply. Becoming more familiar with the workings of our minds through the practice of mindfulness, we see that we all tend to spend so much time in our heads—rehearsing opinions, planning for the future, or reviewing the past—that we can forget to pay attention to the people around us in the present moment.

Relating to others would appear to be getting ever more difficult in the complex and pressurized world we are creating for ourselves. Loneliness and isolation are the modern epidemic, ironically made more acute by the apparent "connectedness" of our digital screen-based age. Mental health issues such as anxiety and depression are spiraling for both young people and adults. Families are fragmenting. Humans have always been liable to use aggression as a misplaced solution to all kinds of conflicts, globally, locally, and domestically, but now, even if we live in peaceable surroundings, violent images are constantly fed into our homes by the media in a way that young people find chronically worrying. In our homes, we are at constant risk of being distracted by the twenty-four-hour world of social media, the Internet, and virtual connections, plagued by advertising that attempts to create insecurity and a sense of personal inadequacy and comparing of our lives, usually unfavorably, with the lives of others.

Schools are not always good at helping build a sense of safety, calm, present-centeredness, and friendship. Many schools are busy and pressured environments, where both teachers and students are constantly being asked to orient to the future, to press on to the next hurdle to help students succeed in an increasingly competitive and materialistic society. In classrooms, schoolyards, and on the Internet, taunting and bullying are often an undercurrent, sometimes erupting in major ways that are at best stressful and at worst seriously undermining of mental health and well-being.

As Thich Nhat Hanh suggests, our schools and universities need to help reverse this trend, and place themselves at the heart of the effort to find ways to build loving kindness and to help human beings cooperate and care for one another. All the practices outlined in this book form a vital foundation for helping us understand our own minds, motives, thoughts, feelings, and bodily reactions, and for cultivating a sense of calmness and space that can help us relate to others authentically and harmoniously.

This chapter builds on that foundation with two formal practices: "Circle Sharing with Deep Listening and Loving Speech," and "Beginning Anew," the first stage of which, called "flower watering," or positive appreciation, can be taught on its own or as the prerequisite for the other three stages: expressing regret, healing a hurt, and asking for support. These practices intend explicitly to help us relate to others more effectively, to help us develop the ability to be more present, caring, and compassionate and to resolve hurts and difficulties. They are not about mechanically applying a simple instant formula to fix a problem; they are a way of creating the conditions for people to be listened to deeply and appreciated, which can itself be restorative.

At first these formal practices may seem a little artificial or over-structured. It is important to give them a chance; they are a scaffolding to help us build our ability to listen deeply and share from the heart with loving speech. Over time, the habits these practices cultivate in us become more natural, and we find that we do not always need all the scaffolding and structure. When we are learning, however, or when emotions are very strong, these structures will give us the support we need to share and listen with kindness and compassion.

. . . . .

At the end of the chapter we hear some reflections from practicing teachers on the value of relationships, being together in skillful ways, and the specific practices of sharing in a circle, deep listening and loving speech, and Beginning Anew.

A practice summary is available in appendix A on page 312.

core practice

....

sharing in a circle with deep listening and loving speech

What follows is a basic method for sharing thoughts and feelings. Try it out several times first yourself with a group of friends or colleagues before sharing with your students.

Preparation and Materials

- Chairs in a circle.
- Bell and inviter (optional but recommended).

1. Bowing In

When sharing in a circle we need to find a way for people to indicate they wish to speak. The traditional Plum Village method to help people share is called "bowing in"—when someone joins their palms to indicate they wish to speak. In response, everyone else joins their palms "bowing in" to acknowledge the person who is going to speak. A popular alternative method with fewer traditional connotations is to use a "talking piece" such as a feather, shell, stick, or stone to be passed around; the person who holds it has the right to speak without interruption.

    The speaker then talks without interruption, until they show they have finished by, again, putting their palms together and bowing.

    The others in the circle put their palms together and bow to show they have understood that the speaker has now finished.

    After a moment, someone else can indicate they wish to speak.

If "bowing in" is not appropriate, you can use some other gesture which is acceptable to the group—but we don't recommend raising a hand as it has traditional connotations of competition and intellectual discussion.

There may sometimes be quite long pauses between sharing. This is fine. See it as an opportunity for us all to come back to our breathing.

2. Prepare the Room and the Group

Gather into a circle, sitting on chairs or on the floor.

    Make sure everyone is comfortable and can see one another.

3. Explaining the Basic Process of Sharing

Explain that we are going to practice a way of sharing our thoughts and feelings.

Explain that we are going to listen mindfully, without judging or reacting, and with an open heart.

Explain how the sharing will work, e.g., bowing in or talking piece.

Participation is voluntary, anyone can "pass" and just listen.

4. Further Ground Rules on Deep Listening and Loving Speech

The speaker practices **loving speech**, in other words, speaking mindfully from the heart, direct from their personal experience, not blaming or judging, just describing.

As the other person talks, we try to practice **deep listening**, doing the best we can to simply listen without judgment, and without planning what we are going to say next or getting lost in our thinking, feelings, and perceptions about what is being said.

We respond to what others share **without giving advice or offering an opinion.** If someone shares something that inspires us, we may like to continue on that topic, but we keep what we say grounded in our own personal experience, not in ideas or theories, and we don't offer advice.

We agree that whatever is said will be **confidential,** that what is said in the circle stays there, so we can feel safe when we share, that our story will not be told to other people outside of the circle.

If we want to talk to somebody about their sharing outside the lesson, we ask them first if that is okay. If the answer is no, we respect their wish.

5. Start: Breath and Bell

Invite three sounds of the bell to begin, with three mindful breaths in between each bell.

Keep the initial explanations as brief as possible to begin with so you can get started, and return to some of the finer details later when the group is more skilled in the process. Begin with safe topics, and as you introduce those that are more sensitive, add in more of the ground rules.

Make clear that you have a special role as the facilitator/leader. You will be keeping it safe for everyone by guiding the sharing, e.g., in starting and finishing, indicating who will speak if there are many offers, gently stopping someone who is going on too long.

Again, don't let all the details hold you up at the start. Explain the finer details once the basic process is established in students' minds.

Invite the students to only speak about what they feel safe talking about in this group. Explain that if they want to share further but do not feel safe to do so, to quietly sit with their feelings and talk to you, the teacher, afterward.

6. Group Sharing

Introduce a topic and invite the group to share their thoughts and feelings about it.

Some suggestions for first topics when working with children:

- One good thing about the place (school, university, town, village) where we all live and learn
- Something that made me laugh or smile this week
- What kind of animal I am most like or would most like to be
- My current "internal weather" (sunny, cloudy, rainy, etc.)

From time to time, depending on the length of the sharing, you may invite a sound of the bell so that everyone in the circle has a chance to breathe mindfully together.

Allow some silence, but if it turns into a long silence during which no one shares, you may like to pose a question or a further topic to stimulate sharing.

7. End

When everyone has shared, or when time is up, bring the discussion to a close.

Invite three sounds of the bell to close, with three mindful breaths between each sound.

You may like to share a brief heartfelt reflection from your point of view as the group facilitator, before you invite the bell to finish, to bring together the thoughts, feelings, and questions that have been shared.

As the group prepares to leave, invite the group to respect the spirit of this practice, which is to care for other people.

Remind them that when they leave the classroom, whatever has been shared remains confidential. Take care not to gossip, tease, or bully afterward. If someone has said something in the circle, they may not wish to talk about it later outside the circle.

—

variations on sharing in a circle

As the group becomes more experienced, and the level of trust increases, personal and emotive topics can gradually be raised. Some "medium intensity" topics that teachers have used effectively have included:

- What makes a good friend or colleague?
- How do we show we care about someone?
- Something that made me laugh, cry, get mad, get scared, feel really happy.
- How has my practice of mindful breathing, walking, eating, etc., been over the past twenty-four hours?

Take it slowly, gradually deepening the topics for discussion as the class gets used to the practice and builds trust. Do not encourage students to open up in the group if you feel it will make them too vulnerable to bullying by others. Keep a balance between more serious and lighter and fun topics. Gradually students can offer their own topics for discussion. Use circle sharing sparingly at first, until the group is used to it, to ensure they do not get bored.

Sharing in a circle with deep listening can be used in many ways—to have fun, share feelings, talk about events, plan, and solve problems. As a classroom method, it can be used to teach any topic or subject.

Over time, as we sit together, look at each other, and share together in this respectful way, we build a sense of family, of brotherhood and sisterhood, in the class.

looking deeply: reflection questions for sharing with deep listening and loving speech

You may feel the practice is enough in itself. If you want to explore it further, these questions may help you. They are for you the teacher to reflect on or to use with the students—in class sharing or just by letting the questions settle in the mind.

- What was the effect of the practice on my mind, body, breath? (You can make the question more specific to what happened during the practice.)

- How do I feel right now? Where is my mind, body, breath? (This can be asked at any point in the practice, using the bell if you wish.)

- How did it feel to practice loving speech? Did it feel different from how I normally speak? Did it feel authentic or forced?

- How did it feel to practice deep listening myself? Was it hard not to turn off, to judge, or comment?

- How was it to be listened to by the group?

Add other questions as appropriate. Keep them linked to real life experience: simple, open, non-judgmental, encouraging. Accept all kinds of responses including "negative" ones like "boring," "annoying," "I feel angry"—without reacting or trying to "fix it" yourself when a participant does not like the practice.

....

beginning anew

Why practice "Beginning Anew"?

- To practice further the skills of authentic communication: deep listening and loving speech.

- To build a sense of connection—with ourselves, with other people, in the classroom, school or university, community, and family.

- To create safer and more harmonious environments and communities—in classrooms, staffrooms, and families.

- To learn ways to show our appreciation of one another, to express regrets and hurts, and to ask for support.

- To learn a structured way to resolve difficulties and conflicts.

We are all familiar with the experience of conflict and difficulty with others; it is part of our everyday experience, built into any human society. Children experience countless small and larger conflicts, in their peer groups, classrooms, playgrounds, homes, and communities. Hurts, difficulties, and conflicts are normal, and they can be resolved if we have skill and goodwill. Many schools and universities are undertaking positive, proactive work in this area as part of their efforts in relation to social and emotional learning, anti-bullying, tackling stigma, violence prevention, conflict resolution, reconciliation, and restorative justice.

Beginning Anew can form a useful part of this effort. It is a structured way to help people deal with conflicts that have already arisen and prevent conflict from arising in the future. We can use it either when something specific has happened or when longer-term difficulties such as anger, resentment, or bullying are marring the relationship. The intention is to prevent feelings of hurt from building up over time, so that the situation becomes safer for everyone—in the family, the group, the class, and the whole school or university.

We can come to see difficulties positively—as opportunities to help us to grow and deepen our sense of connection—if we handle them skillfully, with open-mindedness, empathy, and kindness.

Beginning Anew can be used by both teachers and students, in a group setting or one-on-one. The version written here includes up to four steps.

notes on timing and planning to help the process work well

- Pick a time when everyone feels calm and ready to listen. When something specific has happened and people are still angry or upset, a sitting or walking meditation may be more useful.

- Participation should be voluntary and agreed upon by all participants.

- Make sure that each person proceeds in order through the steps of Beginning Anew during their sharing, as the steps need to follow one after another: flower watering, followed by expressing a regret, followed by expressing a hurt. The steps help to structure the sharing so that the person listening will be better prepared to receive what is being said.

Decide beforehand how you will allow people to speak in turn. You can use the suggestions in "Sharing in a Circle" above to decide how people might show they want to speak, e.g., "bowing in" or using a talking stick.

- Always encourage the group to include plenty of step one when they share—that is, flower watering, positive appreciation of others. That will often go a long way to resolving difficulties and may sometimes be all that is needed. It is a lovely, restorative practice.

- Take your time in moving through the process. There's no rush and not everyone needs to go through all the steps of Beginning Anew right away.

- It is best to allow people to indicate on their own when they wish to speak, rather than choosing people you feel are ready to share. Alternatively, during flower watering, you can go around the circle and have each student "water the flower" of the person sitting next to them—always with the option to "pass" and perhaps speak later.

- Set a tone of ease and lightness. If people are tense or feel threatened they are unlikely to share.

the four steps of the full practice of beginning anew

These are notes for the stages of the practice to help you understand it yourself and explain the practice to the group. You will find instructions on how to actually run the practice further on.

step one: flower watering (showing appreciation)

Flowers need water to stay fresh, and we begin our sharing by finding some "refreshing" things to say and hear about one another.

Here or later you might pursue the garden watering metaphor and say we are gently nurturing seeds in the other person such as kindness, openness, and gentleness so they can sprout and grow, and we are letting seeds like anger, jealousy, and mistrust stay where they are in the ground.

The practice sets a tone of ease and lightness, and can bring a lot of joy.

You might say, to reassure the group: "What you say about the other person does not have to be a big thing, if we look deeply we can always find something to appreciate about another human being." (You might model it with one or two students.) They may be general qualities ("you're funny/kind/good at math/I like your smile/your shoes are really cool"), although it is usually more helpful to say something more concrete, about something specific that happened ("I liked it when you shared your sandwich with me last week").

You can stop at the end of this step if you wish.

step two: expressing regrets (taking responsibility)

In the second part of our sharing, we express regrets about our own mistakes, weaknesses, and/or unskillful actions. Sister Chan Khong of Plum Village explains why we "express regret": "When you truly apologize for something you regret, any hurt the person felt may be completed dissipated by your apology. Expressing regret on your own initiative, before the other person has even let you know that he or she is hurt, is a very effective way to refresh your relationship. Even if you are apologizing for only a part of the situation, if your regret is genuine, the other person will hear and appreciate it."[1]

> We are not perfect in every way; everyone has things they can work on. This is the moment to recognize those things we have thought, said, or done in the past few days, weeks, or months that we think may have hurt others, and make the commitment to try to do better.

You can stop here at the end of this step if you wish.

step three: expressing a hurt

In this step, we express a hurt we feel someone has caused us.

This is a sensitive area, and this step is best skipped in a group setting where people are not experienced. In this case it is better carried out one-on-one, along with a solid and experienced person, who both people trust and respect, present to support and help them by inviting the bell and facilitating. If the group is experienced and cohesive, there can be benefit in doing it collectively.

- If we are the one speaking, we start by saying: "I feel hurt because I perceived you said or did this or that."

- Explain that when we speak, we focus on *our own* feelings and perceptions, and what support we would like to have. We do not blame others; we just describe what we perceive others have done and what effect those perceptions had on us. This allows for the very likely possibility that our perceptions are not 100 percent correct.

- If we are the one listening, we try to listen with calm and understanding, with a willingness to help the suffering of the other person, and not to judge or argue.

- Even if we hear something that we feel is not true, we practice to continue to listen deeply without interrupting. This may not be easy, and if we become upset we quietly practice to recognize, embrace, and calm our own feelings by breathing with them. We will have time to respond later with our own perception of the situation when we are calm; it may even be a few days later if our emotions are strong in the moment. Later on, when we are ready to respond, we first water the other person's flowers and express our own regrets.

> As the teacher facilitating this, keep in mind that sharing our feelings is always personal and, when emotions are strong, disharmony can arise. Be aware of how participants are feeling, and know that it is okay to stop the Beginning Anew practice and just invite everyone to listen to the bell and breathe.

- Now is the time for listening. Our main purpose in listening is to develop compassion in our heart for the other person. If we interrupt, we may cause the other person to become angry, and the session may likely turn into a debate. In a debate, we become defensive, and transformation of the difficult feelings or emotions—and therefore resolution of the conflict—becomes very unlikely.

> Asking for support is not to complain or blame others. Choosing to frame what might otherwise be complaints as "asking for support" can help participants to clarify how they are feeling—they see for themselves that they need the help of the group and ask for it—and this makes it easier for those who are listening to feel less defensive and more positive about how they might offer support.

- If we feel like we need to follow up on a hurt that was expressed to the group, we can ask for a one-on-one Beginning Anew session. This could be facilitated by the teacher if it is between two students, or another colleague if it is between two teachers.

step four: asking for support

Here we express how we would like support for a difficult situation (e.g., "My cousin died recently and that has made me quite sad; I don't understand why he died; I would like to ask for support now," or "I would like support to stop getting angry so easily").

Asking for support can happen at any point in Beginning Anew; you need not follow the order of flowering watering, expressing regrets, and expressing a hurt as above.

A practice summary is available in appendix A on page 314.

core practice

beginning anew

Materials and Preparation

- A teacher well prepared in the practice, i.e., someone who has first practiced this at home or with friends.

- Chairs or mats on the floor in a circle.

- Small vase with a few flowers, or a beautiful potted plant (recommended). Put the vase or plant in the middle of the circle.

- Bell and inviter (optional but recommended).

1. Introducing the Practice to the Group

You can stop at any point, and remember that expressing a hurt may be best carried out one-on-one.

Begin by sitting in a circle. Invite three sounds of the bell, allowing for three mindful breaths in between each sound.

Remind the group of what they already know about how to share in a circle using deep listening and loving speech, e.g., one person shares at a time, no interrupting, "pass" if you wish, and so on.

It is essential to review the processes of deep listening and loving speech if there is even just one new person in the group. However much you try to structure things, sharings can be unpredictable, including expressing hurts. People will say what they will. As leader, just remain calm, kind, and positive by following your breathing and ask yourself: How can I respond in a way that causes less harm for everyone involved? By doing this, you usually find a way. Use the bell at appropriate moments, and guide the group back toward talking about their feelings rather than blaming others.

Explain clearly only the steps that you plan to practice in this session, so everyone understands the order and nature of each of the steps. For example, if you are only practicing flower watering in this session, you need only cover step one in the introduction. It is essential, however, if you are practicing expressing a hurt, that the participants know to follow the order, and to start with flower watering and move on to expressing a regret themselves, before expressing a hurt.

2. Start the Sharing

Invite one more sound of the bell, and enjoy three mindful breaths.

If it is the first time for many in the group, you may want to **model the first sharing yourself**, so the participants understand how to proceed through one, two, three, or all four of the steps.

One person indicates they want to speak (by bowing in or by your other chosen method).

If you are going around the circle you can ask for a volunteer to begin.

The person who has indicated they would like to speak picks up the flowers or plant and puts it in front of themselves as they sit back down, to remind themselves to use loving speech.

The speaker then begins with flower watering, saying one or two things they like, appreciate, or value about the other person or people. Everyone else just listens.

The speaker may then stop here after flower watering, or continue by expressing regrets, expressing a hurt, or asking for support, according to how they feel or their inspiration.

When the person has finished speaking, they **bow** to indicate they've finished, and/or return the flowers to the center of the room, and/or pass them to the person next to them.

Then **someone else takes a turn**. A long pause between sharings is fine and probably a sign that the group is processing carefully and deeply. Everyone can enjoy their breathing while contemplating the flowers.

3. Bell and Ending

You may like to share a brief heartfelt reflection from your point of view as the group facilitator.

Invite three sounds of the bell, with three mindful breaths between each sound, to close the sharing.

If appropriate, e.g., with younger children, you might sing a joyful song together. If your group will be comfortable, you can have everyone hold hands and breathe for a minute like this.

—

variations on beginning anew

- It is often helpful just to do "flower watering" as the only activity, or just flower watering and expressing a regret. "Water flowers" as often as you like, even outside of the formal practice of Beginning Anew.

- With younger children, you can do "flower watering" using pictures, which is helpful in a big group, so everyone receives positive affirmations quickly. You might do something like give every student a card with a picture of a stalk and the middle of a flower without petals. Give out the petals of a flower, four for each person, each petal with some other classmate's name on one side of it. Invite the students to write something on the other side that they like about the person named on the petal—and sign it if they wish. Quietly make sure the things written down are positive, perhaps by walking around or collecting them to distribute and looking at them as you give them out. At the end, the student receives "their" four petals and sticks them on their card to make a flower.

looking deeply: reflection questions for beginning anew

You may feel that the practice itself is sufficient. If you want to explore the process further, here are some suggested questions to discuss or just drop into the mind.

- How do I feel right now? Where is my mind, body, breath? (Can be asked at any point in the practice, with the help of the bell.)

- What was the effect of the practice on my mind, body, breath?

- How did it feel to have my flower watered? (Accept all answers—people often feel embarrassed and unworthy.)

- How did it feel to water someone else's flower? Did it feel authentic or forced?

- What part was the easiest for me?

- What part was the most difficult or challenging?

- Are there other times either inside or outside the classroom when we might want to apply the practice of Beginning Anew?

Add other questions as appropriate. Keep them simple, open, nonjudgmental, encouraging, and accepting of all kinds of responses including "negative" ones, e.g., "I feel angry/hurt/misunderstood." Take care not to immediately react and try to "put it right."

being together in our lives and in our teaching

Being Truly Present

Becoming more mindful often helps us become more present for others as Gloria Shepard, a mindfulness educator from the US, reflects.

> The most important thing I do is to actually be present with the people
> I'm working with. Teaching them how to "do it" is not the real thing; being
> deeply present with them is the real thing.

Many of our students may have no one in their life who is truly "there" for them, present, listening, and caring. Marcela Giordano a Uruguayan volunteer in the Children's Program at Plum Village, reminds us that experiencing the mindful presence of a teacher can help our students build a sense of connection, which is deeply nourishing for their personal well-being and essential in helping them find the motivation to learn.

> The most wonderful gift you can give a child is presence and connection,
> make them feel seen, trusted, and accepted.

To be present we need to be focused, which can be hard for the teacher in the classroom with thirty students—with so many things happening at once—in the middle of a busy timetable with lessons occurring all day. French teacher Murielle Dionnet reflects on the value of learning through mindfulness practice to actually be fully with the students right in front of her, not "fragmented" and with her mind on other students.

> I was a kindergarten and elementary school teacher, and I had to manage
> four levels. When I was with one group, I often got distracted thinking about
> what the other groups were doing: I felt like I had a broken spirit with a
> sense of fragmentation. The practice helped me to focus on the students
> with whom I was working, to really be with them and agree to "leave" the
> other classes while I worked with this one group. Later, as a specialized
> teacher, I was asked to work with twelve pupils with mental disabilities:
> twelve students, in twelve levels. I saw the benefit of the practice in allowing
> me to really be present with each student, to focus entirely on one at a
> time. I felt more united within.

The beginning of each year is a key opportunity for teachers to get off on the right foot with their classes. This can include helping every student feel seen and known by the teacher, which is the start of an authentic relationship. Goyo Hidalgo Ruiz, a secondary school teacher, takes time to stop and "contemplate" his students as he meets them at the start of each year, ensuring that he connects with them more fully.

> I teach Spanish Language and Literature in a public, secondary school in Seville, Spain. At the beginning of the year, I introduce myself, call roll, and give the course syllabus to my students. Then I dedicate some time to approaching each student at his or her desk, to shake hands with them with a smile, and ask their name and other questions about him or her. I like to keep his or her hand in mine throughout these introductions.
>
> Every time I go into a class I stay in the doorway—silent, smiling, and breathing mindfully—I look directly at the students, I contemplate them until they take their seats without passing judgment or giving directions. I gaze at them with a smile in silence and in full awareness. Once they were just a name and a student at a desk. Now I see them as human beings, as people with their own fears and desires. You could say that the practice has brought me closer to them and therefore they have come closer to me.

Pilar Aguilera, who has been training teachers for the past three years in the Escuelas Despiertas (Wake Up Schools) program at the University of Barcelona, when preparing for the teachers in her class, takes time to ensure she is fully present herself so she can be there for others.

> The music from the CD of Plum Village songs, *A Basket of Plums*, sounds on the stereo while I am preparing the centerpiece for our session. It makes me feel at home and connected with the beautiful seeds radiating in my heart. The centerpiece is a metaphor of our togetherness and deep aspiration, the heart of our collective presence. At the start of the course, everybody brings an object they love and puts it in there for the whole course around a vase of fresh flowers. The objects represent our own diligence and determination to bring mindfulness and joy into our daily lives. They bring light and love all together as a community. The fresh flowers inspire the quality of our true beauty. We start building a feeling of belonging and connectedness

from the first day of the course. Then this feeling of interbeing is expanding in a spiral and in a holistic way from session to session through a methodology based on presence.

Having a sense of relationship, engagement, and connection are the foundation of helping our students feel motivated to learn, and they are based on deep listening, as Julie Berentsen, an elementary school teacher in the UK, observes.

Taking time to listen and build trusting relationships is the key to engaging students. Deep listening and speaking from the heart have shown me how to hold a safe, authentic space for the young people I work with. I trust that everything I need is with me right now, that each moment is a wonderful opportunity to share mindfulness, and that whatever arises in the group can be held and looked after in a way that will water the seeds of happiness for us all.

deep listening and loving speech

Listening deeply and using compassionate speech help move our students toward greater happiness, as Tony Silvestre, Professor of Infectious Diseases and Microbiology and Director of the Center for Mindfulness and Consciousness Studies at the University of Pittsburgh, says:

By touching my students' suffering, I am able to offer them the opportunity to "change their channel," as Thay tells us, and to move from being caught in thinking and emotions that cause suffering to the joy and happiness available in the present moment. Listening deeply to my students allows me to generate the compassionate speech that may lead them to happiness.

Deep listening and loving speech help people build feelings of love, compassion, and empathy, and make these feelings apparent to others. They don't have to be practiced only in the context of a formal sharing; they can permeate our day. Alison Mayo, our preschool teacher from the UK, reflects,

In my work as a nursery class teacher, Plum Village teachings have given me greater confidence to be myself in the way I work: making kindness, patience, and the well-being and happiness of everyone my top priorities. One teaching that really helps with this is deep listening, allowing me to really tune-in to what is happening for individual children and give them my full attention. I also now give more priority to allowing plenty of time, during lunch breaks and after school, to listen to colleagues and understand their needs.

The tendency of teachers to want to "fix the problem" can get in the way of being of help; sometimes just to be heard is all we need. One special education teacher notes,

With adults and children, making space to be heard with compassion, without trying to fix the problem, is very helpful. I'm so grateful when someone does this for me and I diligently try to do this for others.

Deep listening and loving speech can transform relations right across the school, with adults as well as young people—as retired high school teacher and mindfulness trainer, Christiane Terrier from France, notes.

The practices of deep listening and loving speech helped me a lot in my relationships with students, colleagues, and the administration. My relations with them were already good before, but it allowed me to improve them, offering me a way of doing things where I had once improvised rather intuitively. Like Thay, I love my job as a teacher and my students. For me, the practice that bears the best fruit is: "Look deeply to understand. Listen deeply to love better."

Christiane goes on to describe how her school created an imaginatively named "drop your bag" listening space for students. Its profound impact deeply impressed students and staff.

We wanted to offer students the benefits of deep listening. In doing so, we could become more aware of their suffering. So we came up with the idea

of a listening space for students—"Drop Your Bag"—for which we created
a charter and a poster. Teachers made themselves available to listen to
students. They practiced listening without judgment or advice, knowing
full well that young people have the ability to find for themselves their own
solutions. The student "puts down her bag," while the teacher "takes off the
teacher's cap."

The students who attended the listening space repeatedly expressed
the belief that it offered them a lot. Young people who came discouraged,
anxious, stressed, subject to academic and/or family pressures, went
away relieved, smiling, and relaxed. This creates a real quality relationship
between youth and adults. Colleagues could also see the impact of their
investment on the students in their classes. Listening without discriminating
even helped prevent several dropouts.

In addition to listening, we can convey our concern to others in how we speak as
well as what we say. As Mary Lee Prescott-Griffin, a professor of education in the
US, says,

> In teaching, I am able to pause and plan my words so that I communicate
> more precisely and from a place of caring and compassion.

Our colleagues can also benefit from honing their listening skills. Lyndsay Lunan, a
psychology lecturer we met earlier, teaches the skills of deep listening to the senior
management team at her college. She describes an exercise in which she asks pairs
of staff to repeat a short period of listening to one another, having practiced mindfulness in between. Her colleague found that pausing to be more mindful can help
them to feel "more honest and authentic."

> I've taught mindful listening practices to staff and our college Senior
> Management Team. The group moves into pairs, and one person is asked to
> speak on a topic (such as what is most challenging about your job) while
> the other person listens. They then swap roles. After this, I guide a mindful-
> ness practice that directs the whole group to awareness of their body and
> their current feeling state, and that also focuses on appreciation for one

another (for all trying their best, for turning up every day in this difficult job). After this, we repeat the paired listening exercise. Then I invite folks to share as to whether there was any difference in what they shared or how they listened in the second listening pairing. Often several people in the group will find that they were more honest or authentic in their sharing in the second activity and that they paid more attention when listening. It's nice then to explore mindfulness itself as a synonym for listening: how listening inward gives us the space to be able to listen outward.

circle sharing

Circle sharing is a more formal way of practicing our deep listening and loving speech with others to open up about our thoughts and feelings. Plum Village's Brother Phap Lai summarizes the essence of circle sharing and comments on its profound value for teachers who come on educator's retreats, helping them feel safe enough to open up and start to heal the suffering which so many carry.

In our "discussion families," maybe twenty-five people who have never met each other before just sit in a circle and share. People get so much from this experience because we set it up in such a way that everybody has a chance to share and be listened to, and the energy of concentration and listening is quite profound. We don't go into dialogue, and we're not interrupted. You don't get or give advice. You get people sharing their experience, and it may relate to somebody else's experience. You get authentic sharings from people. People open up, sharing from their heart what is going on for them: their experience, their difficulty, their success, what they've found to be helpful for them. So, we exchange experiences that are beneficial, and we get to put down our load if we're having a difficulty. A lot of healing takes place, and people experience a feeling of brotherhood and sisterhood in the circle in a way which seems miraculous.

The circle is an endlessly rich teaching method, and we explore some examples below. US environmental educators Bobbie and Boz use the circle to help young people express gratitude.

[We have] a practice with kids called the "alphabet of gratitude" in which
we go through the alphabet with something to be grateful for at each letter.
This can be done nicely in a circle or at a dinner table with a family.

Yvonne Mazurek, an educator at the high school and university level in Italy, gives
a vivid and very human account of a circle sharing that cheered students at a dismal
time of year by helping them experience gratitude for the good that can come out of
difficult experiences.

I've often seen students feel blue in the winter, but the whole faculty
noticed something heavier than usual that January. The students seemed
to complain a lot, feeling tired and lacking motivation. I asked permission to
offer an afternoon of mindfulness. My otherwise skeptical colleagues agreed
that it couldn't hurt, and one colleague offered to help. So, one wintery
Friday, a colleague and I held a quiet afternoon for the eleventh and twelfth
graders during which we did a range of creative things.

When they "came to" after the deep relaxation session, I invited the
students to preserve the rich silence and briefly described circle sharing
along with the topic of gratitude.

Each student shared spontaneously and expressed thanks for things
that go unnoticed: their families, living without war, and being able to go
to school. This prompted one girl to think back to how much she hated
her long commute to and from school at the beginning of the school year.
One fellow student in particular rubbed her the wrong way. Over time, she
realized that missing buses, dark evenings, and dropping temperatures had
helped her get to know the girl she so disliked initially. During all the travel
difficulties, they'd started joking around and even studying together. As she
spoke, she realized that the girl, who was actually sitting next to her, had
changed from being an enemy to a friend. Some students laughed during
this story, since they'd witnessed the ups and downs of the girls' relationship through the year. The students who followed talked of how their own
emotional challenges have also helped them become stronger and wiser.

At the end of our time together it came naturally for everyone to pitch in and clean up together. The next day there was a group of twenty people roaming the school who smiled warmly to each other.

Lyndsay uses the circle as the architecture for an experiential listening exercise to help her psychology students be more aware that the origins of prejudice and discrimination are inside us all. She uses a "listening stick" to encourage taking turns.

With students in my psychology class, I've used the "listening stick" in group discussions, so that only the person holding the stick is allowed to speak. We study group prejudice in social psychology and I use this as pretext to do a "class experiment" on how prejudice and discrimination begins in the mind. The group is given a provocative topic to discuss using the listening stick. Then, periodically during discussion, I ring a small bell and ask the students to check in with what's happening internally (to their breathing, tensions in the body, their emotion state, and the kinds of thoughts they're having). They begin to see how their minds generate "like me" and "not like me" thoughts that can turn into strong emotions such as anger and blame.

beginning anew/flower watering

As described earlier in this chapter, Beginning Anew is a structured method for sharing, and potentially resolving, difficulties.

The opening stage, flower watering, is a way of articulating our appreciation of others, and it's often used on its own as a deeply nourishing practice. Students and teachers are judged a good deal, and we rarely experience hearing simple appreciation: when we do, it can be profoundly uplifting.

Sarah Woolman found her class of younger children in the UK so "massively" responded to flower watering, that they wanted to do it every lesson. Judging this to be too much, she still found ways to incorporate the spirit of appreciation of others on a regular basis.

The class massively responded to watering the flowers; it is a precious and healing activity. The class insisted that I was included in the activity so that they could water my flower. We talked about how to make the comments meaningful and particular to each person. The class wanted to do watering the flowers every lesson that I taught them—which says something about our need to appreciate one another. I felt it might lose its meaning if we had done that, however an adaption of going around the class in a circle and appreciating the person next to you is another way to create that feeling.

Pascale Dumont from France found she could get through to some difficult children with flower watering, and help them appreciate positively what they had in common—provided she got on with the practice and not the boring theory!

[Working with three very disruptive nine- to ten-year-olds] I decided to introduce the practice of Beginning Anew: a practice that allows us to renew, refresh, and improve our relationships with others. I brought a little plant with a pretty yellow flower that day and I had placed it in the center of our circle. Very quickly, I realized that my talking about this practice was boring them deeply and so I dove in straight away. I took up the plant and I talked about the fine qualities of each of them. From this very moment, they immediately understood the principle and they continued. It was really touching and above all unprecedented for them to find positive similarities between themselves! I have also been fortunate to benefit from their flower watering and hear them wishing me a nice career in the public educa-tion system.

Flower watering is just as useful for teachers as it is for students. Bea Harley reflects on the experience of a teaching team at an elementary school in the UK when they realized this simple truth.

The practice of flower watering was, I felt, one of the most wonderful prac-tices our friends shared with us. For years we have done what we call "Sun in the Center" with the children. Each child will sit in the center of a circle and their classmates and teacher will take it in turns to say what they really appreciate and love about them. As a staff body we had never considered doing this for ourselves, but we were shown the power of taking the time to stop and really consider our colleagues and to voice, and thank them for, the qualities we appreciated in them. I found it a beautiful and healing experience.

Teachers experience a good deal of exhaustion and are likely to be overwhelmed by this work. Kaira Jewel Lingo notes how the experience of flower watering regularly has a "refreshing" impact on herself as the teacher facilitating the practice in many different contexts.

I am surprised over and over again by the power of flower watering to restore my freshness and energy. I have experienced many times being quite tired and low energy from teaching a lot, and maybe not getting enough rest. When it's time to sit down for a flower watering practice, whether in the monastery or in the context of teaching mindfulness at a school, sometimes I am so tired, I don't know if I will have the energy for it. Inevitably as people begin to open up and share their appreciation for each other, their laughter, their tears, my fatigue drops away. My heart is touched and I am inspired, which always brings energy. I find myself smiling, and the refreshing water offered to another is also water offered to me, even if the person is not appreciating me directly. I always think of any expression of appreciation as a water sprinkler that waters the whole garden without discrimination. Even if someone isn't speaking about us, we benefit from kind words spoken. These uplift everyone. The whole community becomes happier and healthier when we do this practice. And we are energized and renewed.

PART TWO

BRINGING IT ALL TOGETHER

The way out is in.
THICH NHAT HANH

nine
cultivating
mindfulness
in ourselves

in this chapter

- Find further guidance on practical ways in which we can begin, build, deepen, and sustain our own mindfulness practice and integrate it into our lives.

- Read examples and reflections from teachers on how the Plum Village approach has positively shaped their lives, and discover what helped them to cultivate their own mindfulness.

mindfulness begins with ourselves

If there is one central message of this book, it is that mindfulness begins with ourselves. Thich Nhat Hanh is very clear that "coming home to ourselves" is always "the first step."

> There is a habit energy in every one of us. Usually, people don't like to go home to themselves and get in touch with the suffering inside. They try to run away and cover up the suffering inside—their loneliness, their fear, their anger, and their despair. For a teacher the first thing to do is to go home to himself or herself. The way out is in. Go back to oneself and take care of oneself: learning how to generate a feeling of joy, learning how to generate a feeling of happiness, learning how to handle a painful feeling or emotion, listening to the suffering to allow understanding and compassion to be born, and suffer less. This is the first step.[1]

Teachers often focus on others' needs rather than their own. We can get so committed to our job and immersed in our role as teachers that we forget that we are first and foremost human beings. Michael Schwammberger, an experienced Plum Village educator, was struck by the wisdom of a participant in a group he was leading in a Plum Village retreat, who remembered the important truth that we are "more than a teacher":

> One person in my group said: "It's not just the teacher we are trying to heal; it is the 'human being, the person.'" This teacher may have a wife, children, and many different other relationships. So how can we really support this person as more than a teacher—as a human being?

We all have the need and the human right to take time for ourselves, to heal our own suffering and cultivate our own happiness and well-being.

Br. Phap Luu, a lead figure in Wake Up Schools, has been one of those at the helm of many educators' retreats. He has found that teachers are often surprised by the idea of starting with themselves. They come to the retreat expecting, and probably hoping, to be given a curriculum to teach mindfulness to their students. However, once they relax into it, they usually find the personal care the retreat offers them to be a powerful and transformative experience.

> We get teachers in our retreats who want to come and learn curricula and techniques, but, in the end, we teach them how to transform themselves, and to bring about happiness in their own lives. That is more powerful than any curriculum or technique. After four or five days of just being in this collective energy of peace, quiet, mindfulness, ease, not having any projects to work on, any meetings to attend, just letting go of their thinking, coming back to their breathing, being aware of their body and their emotions—I think they feel very touched that we care so much about their wellbeing. That will always be a core part of Wake Up Schools—taking care of the teacher.[2]

what do teachers gain from practicing mindfulness?

We have heard a good deal about the changes the practice of mindfulness brings to teachers' lives, their teaching, and their relationship with their students. In this section we will reflect a little further on some of the changes and transformations that teachers report mindfulness brings to them personally.

Losing the Stress of Having to "Get Somewhere"

Targets, goals, and end points may tend to drive us as teachers. Stressful environments, pressure, and scrutiny from without may impose these on us. We can also drive ourselves with the well-intentioned impulse to help others and "fix it" for them. Mindfulness can bring about profound relief from all this driven-ness. It helps us relate to our experience in a different way, giving us the time and space to just be in the present—the only moment in which anything can actually change—rather than always planning for the future.

Thich Nhat Hanh warns of the danger of making mindfulness into an instrument or tool, reminding us not to *use* mindfulness to attain something in the future, but rather to simply arrive right now wherever we are.

We speak of "right mindfulness." If there's such a thing as right mindfulness, there must also be wrong mindfulness, and we all need to be able to distinguish between the two.

Right mindfulness is, first of all, not a tool or an instrument, but a path. Right mindfulness is not a means that can be used to arrive at an end. A tool is something that can be used in different ways, like a knife. If you give someone a knife, he might use it to chop wood or cut vegetables, but he could also use it to kill or to steal. Mindfulness is not like a knife. It's not a tool that can either do good or bad. And yet many of us speak of mindfulness as a tool. We say that with mindfulness we can heal; with mindfulness we can reconcile; with mindfulness we can make more money; even the military now says that with mindfulness we can kill the enemy more effectively.

True mindfulness is not only a path leading to happiness; it is a path of happiness. When you practice breathing in mindfully, your in-breath is not a means to an end. If you know how to breathe, then you get pleasure, peace, and healing right away while breathing. If you suffer while breathing in—if you have a tendency to think, "I'm suffering now so I can experience something better later on"—that's not right mindfulness. In right mindfulness every step is the path itself. We need to keep reminding ourselves to practice in such a way that we have a sense of peace, calm, and joy right away. Whether you're sitting, walking, breathing, cooking, or sweeping the floor, mindfulness makes it pleasant and offers you joy, peace, and insight—insight into your body, your mind, and your situation.

21-DAY RETREAT 2014

The relaxing sense that it is okay to be in the now, not planning for the future all the time, resonates with many teachers. This insight can enable us to slow down and let go—to continue to do our work of teaching, but also to enjoy life and trust things will "unfold."

One thing I have learned, or rather a view I try to adopt in doing this work, is not to get too goal-oriented to any particular outcome. Indeed, just do the work, and things will unfold as they need to.

—MICHAEL BREADY, MINDFULNESS TRAINER, UNITED KINGDOM

Responding with Skill to Our Challenges, Difficulties, and Suffering

In chapter seven, we explored the role of mindfulness in helping us embrace our difficult emotions and transform our experience of suffering. Mindfulness can help us meet the inevitable challenges of our lives with greater calm and equanimity, as the following stories illustrate.

Focusing on what seems like the "small stuff" can build peace, calm, and inner resilience, as Alison Mayo observes.

> The impact on my personal life has been considerable, and the teachings have helped me stay afloat and ride the waves through many busy, stressful times. The two aspects I find most helpful are the emphasis on practice being about enjoyment, ease, and happiness, and the guidance on bringing conscious breathing and mindfulness into your everyday activities. I now do walking meditation up a hill near my house most evenings, which I find clears my mind and also gives me some good exercise, fresh air, and connection with nature.

The rejuvenating sense of being present can be experienced throughout the day, in the details of everyday life. Gloria Shepherd, a mindfulness educator from the United States, confirms that, for her, simply practicing being more present with the little things—such as the daily dog walk—gives her something in reserve to deal with more difficult moments.

> The most helpful for me, I think, is Thay's saying, "This is it"—reminding us to be present with life as it is, kids and parents as they are, my own family, circumstances, and so on. It creates so much more space in me. I sit with this one often. It has helped me through really difficult moments when my kids have been angry and yelling at me—with mindful awareness, I feel

my resistance and then can often remember "This is it," and soften to the moment as it is, listening deeply, softening also to my own pain or response. I practice it in little moments. When my dog was still alive and I walked her at night, sometimes I would be in a hurry for her to go to the bathroom so I could just go back in and go to bed. But after an educators' retreat with Thay, and making "This is it" a constant formal and informal practice, I started to remind myself, This really is it. Here I am! Then I would look at the stars or clouds, feel the air—cold or hot or rainy or whatever—breathe, enjoy the moment, even the moment of cleaning up after my dog. For me, this constant practice during small moments of my life has helped me to be present with the more challenging moments.

Mindfulness can also be there to help us when we are faced by life's more serious challenges, such as, in Mariann Taigman's case, the illness and death of a beloved parent.

Thay's teachings really helped me "be present in every moment" with my father in the last few days before he transitioned, and made it a much richer experience than I thought it would be, even though it was difficult to watch him suffer. I caressed his brow, fed him, helped with his catheter, helped transfer him and deal with his wheelchair (I am an occupational therapist by trade), helped him to laugh, and sang retreat songs to him. It was the most profound, wonderful (and sad) experience of my life, as hard as it was.

Mindfulness can be our friend through all the most extreme moments of life. Jenna Joya Blondel, a college instructor from the United States, has been faced by serious difficulties, including deep early trauma, physical pain, and a broken relationship with those she cared for most. For her the teachings have helped "make my life my practice" and to be able, against all the odds, to lead a peaceful life with both happiness and compassion.

With the practice of mindfulness I have learned to embody peace, to meet the world and its suffering with an open heart, to make my life—walking, eating, talking, listening, breathing—my practice. I suffer from PTSD (from verbal and emotional abuse in my family of origin and my first marriage,

and from estrangement from my three children following my divorce).
Thay's teachings helped me deal with PTSD through the practice of mindfulness, of being present in the here and now, not in painful memories or
fear of the future. I have chronic pain (from fibromyalgia), and mindfulness
of my breath helps handle the pain. I am remarried, and Thay's teachings on
communication and true love have helped both me and my husband create
a peaceful, happy, heart-to-heart relationship. Thay's teachings have helped
me heal and grow. I am so grateful, and I try to pass on the teachings that
helped me so much to others.

Gain Freedom from Our Mental Habits

We can find ourselves mindlessly trapped by our taken-for-granted views and
outworn opinions, habits, and behaviors. Thich Nhat Hanh reflects on the freedom
that mindfulness, concentration, and insight bring, changing the way we relate to
our thinking and thus giving us greater choice about our actions.

> Everything evolves according to the principle of interdependence, but there
> is free will and the possibility to transform. Free will is mindfulness. When
> mindfulness intervenes, we are aware of what is going on. If we like our
> action, we allow it to continue; if we don't like our action, there are meth-
> ods to change it with concentration and insight. We don't want to take a
> path leading to ill-being; we want to take the path leading to the cessation
> of ill-being, to well-being. Free will is possible, because we know that we
> can handle our thinking, we can handle our speech, and we can handle our
> action. We are responsible for our action, and it is possible to assure a good
> continuation. Freedom begins with mindfulness, concentration, and insight.
> With insight and right view, we can practice right thinking. We can change
> ourselves; we can change the world. Everything is the fruit of action.[3]

Teachers who practice mindfulness find it can help them to reflect on their routine
habits and taken-for-granted judgments, identify those judgments that are getting
in the way, and become more flexible and open to change. This is exemplified by the
experience of Ranjani Shankar, a high school teacher from India.

I have been a very critical person all my life, perhaps judgmental too, but now forgiveness comes to me quite easily. This has made my life less miserable. Others can also see the change in me.

Valerie Brown, an experienced senior educator who leads a mindful leadership program in the United States, reflects on how mindfulness helps her recognize her own closed-mindedness, increasing her ability to pause long enough to be aware of habitual responses, to get behind the well-traveled pathways of the mind, and see a situation more clearly for what it is. This brings her and her students the freedom to make healthier choices.

Clarity is generated by the capacity to notice what is arising in the present moment, to be aware of how you are feeling, emotionally and physically, and the flexibility to pause long enough to choose how to respond, and not to react out of habitual or unconscious patterns. Seeing the situation clearly, not what you want to see, hope to see, or expect to see, you know how best to respond, to choose wisely. Skillful action based on insight supports wisdom. One of my course participants, a teacher-leader in a private Quaker school in the Midwest of the United States, uses mindful pausing to slow down her autopilot reactions. She says that these mindful moments to pause are really "moments to choose."

becoming more mindful ourselves: first steps

How do we make mindfulness a reality in our everyday lives? What is the path and what steps along it might we follow, where others have already found a way? How do teachers start to cultivate their own mindfulness? And how do they continue?

We find, of course, that there are many inspirations and many routes. There is no one right way—but there are some useful signposts.

Hearing about Mindfulness—through a Book or a Talk

For many people, simply hearing the principles of mindfulness outlined resonates with an inner sense of truth, striking a "bell of mindfulness" within. This can be enough to get us started on this path. Indeed, if hearing about mindfulness does not resonate with us, we are not likely to begin.

A familiar story from teachers who enjoy the Plum Village tradition is of a first contact through one of the many books by Thich Nhat Hanh, an experience shared by Mack Paul, a teacher from Oklahoma.

> When I started teaching, I didn't have faith in my ability to do the very big job. I became anxious and angry to the point that I suffered frequent bouts of stress-related illness. I tried meditating and could do it for a few minutes, but then, when I got off the seat, I'd be as stressed as ever. A friend gave me the book *The Miracle of Mindfulness* and I began learning to remain mindful. It made it possible for me to actually enjoy my years teaching. I retired from being full-time in the classroom after thirty-two years and now work as an assistant for a special ed teacher. It made me a better husband and father too.

For Valerie, whom we met above, the starting point was an inspirational talk she attended, which brought home to her the gap between Thich Nhat Hanh's vision and her own life in the present:

> Nearly everything he said during the talk was the opposite of the way I was living my life. He talked about cultivating happiness from within and sharing this with others. He talked about stopping and calming the mind and body. I was intrigued and puzzled because my life was largely about running. I decided to start practicing mindfulness at work, in my daily life.

We have provided a list of resources, including books and Web links, some of which link to talks, in the "What Next?" section at the end to help you explore mindfulness further.

Starting Mindfulness in Response to a Personal Experience of Suffering

There is no need to seek out suffering: suffering of some kind comes knocking on our door anyway. Sometimes those who take to mindfulness started practicing following a difficult personal experience—serious health issues, life-threatening events, and family crises—that challenged their existing ability to cope.

University academic Michele Chaban's account below is an astonishing and humbling story of how mindfulness helped her, not only in facing the impacts of a catastrophic event but even in managing to be appreciative of the experience.

> One day, a drunk driver ran into me and took my legs and my arms away from me. And in the years that ensued, I lost my ability to talk and walk. You have a choice in that kind of suffering about whether you are going to stay alive, go mad, or do something different with it. I decided that what I would do is to study about suffering. So I have to say that the practice of mindful meditation came to me through a drunk driver. And I am deeply appreciative for him and all he has done.

An extraordinary and inspirational example of the principle "No mud, no lotus," Michele's story demonstrates how mindfulness can sometimes help us integrate and draw strength from the most painful experiences in life.

Finding a Mindfulness Teacher

To deepen and sustain mindfulness, it can be useful to find a local teacher to continue to guide and inspire our path. One special education teacher in the United States shares how practicing in community helps her at all times, when practicing with a sangha (or group) or even when alone.

> For me, practice with a dharma teacher, Eileen Kiera, over the past twenty-three years and practicing with sangha has brought me happiness, understanding, and great relief. My husband, sister, and friends have commented on the positive changes that have happened in me over the years. When I practice walking in nature silently, practice in the car by myself on the way to work, wait prior to reacting in order to understand, know when I need a quiet moment, hold difficulties in sitting practice and letting what arises come forth, all of these practices continue to support me.

We can find mindfulness teachers right across the world, many of whom work particularly with the teachings of Thich Nhat Hanh and Plum Village. You may find them online or through contact with Plum Village or the other retreat centers. We provide a short list of Plum Village teachers in the "What Next?" section at the end of the book.

Linking with Other Mindfulness Approaches

As we have seen, work on mindfulness, compassion, contemplative approaches, positive psychology, and social and emotional learning has proliferated across the world in many contexts. We are currently experiencing an exponentially increasing wealth of work—research, scholarship, theory, centers, teachers, courses, teacher training, self-help, and teaching resources.

The teachings of Thich Nhat Hanh and the Plum Village approach are a foundational part of this fertile field, and inspirational for many. In this book we are attempting to make clear what the distinct voice of Plum Village and Thich Nhat Hanh bring to this burgeoning field, but the teachings are not a dogma and make no claims to exclusivity. In turn, Plum Village teachers are well integrated into this wider world and draw on it to support their theory and practice, while appreciating the solidity their grounding in these particular teachings gives them.

Many educators successfully combine the Plum Village approach with other sound and readily available programs, such as Mindfulness-Based Stress Reduction (MBSR) or one of the many school and university mindfulness curriculum-based programs and courses. For example, Michael Bready has developed his own program in the United Kingdom, "Youth Mindfulness," which combines the Plum Village approach with several other strands; he calls it a "hybrid of Plum Village practice, MBSR, and positive psychology."

Others have skillfully integrated the Plum Village approach with approaches rooted in their local culture. Norma Ines Barreiro is a social worker teaching in Mexico, where sympathetic aspects of the Mayan culture are easily intertwined with the teachings of mindfulness.

Something that really helps is that the ancient Mayan cultures have much in common with our tradition and this makes it easier to absorb for young people. For example, in two of the Mayan languages in which we work

(Tzeltal and Tzotzil), the founding principle of language is the *tik*, which means "us." There is no individual removed from a sense of community. Another affinity is the concept that we are one with Mother Earth. The weight of the ancestors in everyday life and the co-presence of individuals and communities is another aspect that facilitates the appropriation of mindfulness practices in the Plum Village tradition.

We hope we are helping you to choose your own path and, without overwhelming or confusing you, to integrate Plum Village ideas into whatever related approaches you feel are compatible in ethics and values, are easily available, suit your culture and context, work practically for you, and speak to your heart and mind.

Practice, Practice, Practice

Many people accept mindfulness in theory and dabble with a little practice now and then, but find it a challenge to sustain the ongoing practice that really makes positive change possible. If we want to become mindful, rather than just *knowing* about mindfulness or recommending it to others, we need to establish our own regular practice. This takes commitment, time, and effort. So after the initial inspiration, the real work—often joyful but also diligent and disciplined—begins.

Michael Schwammberger, whose wise and experienced voice we have heard throughout this book, gives those he teaches the simple message to "just practice."

> Teachers have ideas about what they would like to do in the class with the students, or maybe like to fix or improve. Often we have to go through a process with them to let go of those ideas, because the ideas can become an obstacle keeping them from actually experiencing the practice. So we always have to come back, again and again: first, just practice. Experience the practice. Come back to yourself. Come back to your breath. Slow down. Let go. Enjoy. Come back to the basic mindfulness practice first—actually experience that yourself.

Humans are creatures of habit. As with keeping up a long exercise regime, rather than just going for the odd run for a few days every new year, we need to establish a daily routine to develop the "mindfulness muscle." It helps, particularly at first, to identify a small simple practice we can do and stick to the same time and place every day. We then try as best we can to stay with it, recognizing that mindfulness is about being with what is, not a tap to turn on instant bliss. We continue to practice however it goes on any particular day.

Our practice does not have to be sitting meditation, and the first part of this book provides many options and starting points with basic practices, including eating, movement, and walking. We have heard earlier from Valerie about her initial inspiration to begin following a talk from Thich Nhat Hanh. We pick up her story again where she starts to practice, in small ways at first.

> I started very small, with tiny moments of awareness: eating one bite of a sandwich with as much awareness as I could, noticing my feet on the floor, becoming aware of my heart racing and calming and soothing myself. Gradually, my workday was filled with these mindful moments, which changed my thinking, speaking, and acting.

Where we choose to practice can be as important as when, and it helps to choose a space and practice there regularly while we establish a routine. We might create a breathing space or "breathing room," as Thich Nhat Hanh calls it, where we can take refuge. We can start very simply with a chair, or a cushion on the floor, maybe near a plant or a window. Our space can be as simple or complex as we wish, or can afford, in terms of space. We may be lucky enough to be able to transform a corner of a room, or even a whole room, into such a space, with soft colors, cushions, a bell, maybe inspiring calligraphy. If we live in a family or group, we may eventually create a communal space where anyone can go to practice or retreat to as a quiet refuge when things are difficult.

deepening our practice: going on a retreat

Attending a retreat involves spending some time away from our daily lives, removed from the usual distractions, taking part in a structured program of practice and instruction. Retreats are, for many people, an integral part of their mindfulness practice. They help us cultivate mindfulness and a sense of reflection and contemplation, supported by the context of simple communal living in a peaceful and refreshing environment. We might be there a few days, sometimes for extended periods of time.

Some retreats are silent, which some find a refreshing and transformative change from the noise and constant interaction of our everyday life. A retreat run within the Plum Village tradition is not silent, although it will offer some short stretches of silence, together with time for listening, sharing, and reflection. It will involve engaging in the core practices described in this book, as well as spending time sharing and reflecting with others in small "family" groups each day. We provide a list of retreat centers in the "What Next?" section at the end of the book.

Retreats are valuable at any point on our mindfulness path. They can inspire us when we are beginners and help get us started with basic instruction and periods of solid practice. For those farther along they can reinvigorate, consolidate, and deepen our skills and experience. We can reenter our everyday world feeling refreshed, understood, better connected with others, with our intentions strengthened and our mindfulness skills more honed. Many students of the Plum Village approach report that both their initial inspiration and also their deeper involvement have come from attending retreats.

Some teachers like to attend retreats for educators, emphasizing the importance of feeling safe, heard, and understood by other teachers in the same situation, and experiencing how healing that can be.

> The retreat helped teachers address certain issues that they felt they could voice clearly when there was a space of understanding for that issue. That is so important because the teacher holds so much. Where can he or she share or drop that? Where there's an understanding—like in the dharma discussions, panels, or the silent spaces that are so crucial on retreat. The question is not just how can we bring mindfulness into schools, it is more precisely: how do we heal the teachers? It is quite touching to see this happening . . . and it is recognized by everyone. **—MICHAEL SCHWAMMBERGER, MINDFULNESS TRAINER AND RETREAT LEADER, SPAIN AND UNITED KINGDOM**

Retreats are often personally and professionally transformative. They can provide unexpected solutions by helping us see a problem differently, realize that the block lies within us and not outside, and even sometimes go to places we did not know we needed to go. Sara J. Kein, now a professor of psychology teaching at a Navajo college in the US Southwest, reflects in an article she wrote for *The Mindfulness Bell.*

> Arriving at the retreat last November, I kept having one recurring thought: I want to learn how to connect to students. It didn't take long before the collective consciousness at Deer Park cut through my reality. The issue wasn't about connecting with students. If there was a missing connection, it was with myself.[4]

Julie Berentsen, an elementary school teacher from the United Kingdom, outlines an experience of a retreat that reflects the path that many teachers find they take. At the start of the retreat she first finds herself contemplating how far she has come from the intentions she had when she began teaching, then realizing the need to take care of her own well-being, and moving on to feel reinspired to approach her teaching with a new and different perspective, focusing more on joy, kindness, and compassion.

> I was drawn to teaching as a profession with the hope that I could make a difference to the lives of young people. I wanted to create a nurturing classroom that would support young people to realize and fulfill their potential in life. However, the pressures and strains of the profession and my own desire to be "the best" and give everything I had meant that I had forgotten to take care of myself.
>
> I saw and experienced for the first time how to live mindfully—to make mindfulness my life instead of solely a formal practice for a given amount of time each day. This has filtered its way into my everyday life—as I remind myself to stop and breathe, come home to myself . . . resulting in a deeper relationship with myself and those around me. The self-care and community aspects of mindfulness that are a part of Plum Village have helped me to deepen my communication with my friends and family. The PV educators' retreats taught me about deep listening and speaking from the heart, to heal myself and water the seeds of compassion. By slowing down I was able to see clearly what the children I taught needed and joyfully meet their needs with kindness and a full open heart. I now have an understanding of how to look after myself and others—with joy.

building a local community

To sustain our practice, we need to connect with other people. Thich Nhat Hanh is clear about the vital importance of finding or creating a mindfulness group or community (sometimes called a sangha). Drawing pragmatically on a long lifetime's experience teaching mindfulness across the world, he repeatedly asserts that without such a supportive group we are most unlikely to keep it up.

> Building a sangha is a very basic practice. If you have a deep aspiration, or a dream to realize, you cannot do it without a community. That is why building a community is very important.
>
> In your hometown, you can create a group of practitioners who practice together. Every weekend you come together to enjoy walking together, sitting together, or having tea together, sharing the practice together. That would be wonderful, because that community will help you to continue the practice for a long time. Otherwise you will be carried away and you'll abandon the practice after few weeks.[5]

Thich Nhat Hanh's view on the central importance of the group or sangha is echoed by the lived experience of many teachers.

> My sangha helps me a lot in my practice. I noticed that Thay attaches great importance to the sangha, and I fully understand that without it, everything would be much more difficult. —GOYO HIDALGO RUIZ, MIDDLE AND HIGH SCHOOL TEACHER, SPAIN

> People often ask for advice about their difficulties at one of the monthly meetings of the Barcelona Educators Sangha. I always answer the same way: the community of practice gives you refuge, as we are all here to nourish and refresh ourselves. —OLGA JULIÁN SEGURA, PROFESSIONAL DEVELOPMENT TRAINER, SPAIN

If there is no mindfulness group where you live, maybe, like Giorgia Rossato, an educator in France and Italy, you could start one in your neighborhood.

> I don't have opportunities to share the practices with other teachers or
> parents, so I decided to start a Wake Up group in Bordeaux. It took a little
> while to get going, but I dedicated myself to it. To start, I took cues from
> [the book] *Planting Seeds*, and we did sitting meditation, then walking
> meditation, followed by short sharings.

To start with, you need simply to find one other person nearby—in your school, university, family, or neighborhood—who shares your interest in mindfulness and with whom you can give and receive mutual support. You might go to a talk together, or a course or retreat, or share a reading, as well as, of course, doing the vital practice and reflection together.

Many countries have Plum Village sanghas (community groups)—the "What Next?" section at the end of the book helps you find them. Mariann Taigman, an occupational therapist from the United States whom we met earlier, finds her local group supportive professionally as well as personally; other participants are keen to help her with the practical task of spreading mindfulness in schools.

> Being part of a local sangha group based on Thay's teachings rounds out
> my days. Some of my sangha sisters are interested in assisting me in bring-
> ing more mindfulness trainings to the schools and the community, and it's
> nice to share my vision with others.

The final chapter explores in more detail how we might work with our colleagues to support mindfulness practice across the school.

cultivating mindfulness in our everyday lives

Our mindfulness practice comes alive as we live it in the present through concrete action. The chapters in part one explored the myriad ways teachers are integrating the core practices into their daily lives and work. There is no need to seek or build a rigid program or regime around these practices. Provided you practice daily, find some supports in your local community, and find time for yourself to go on retreat, you will gradually find your own unique way to cultivate mindfulness in more and more aspects of your life.

Pilar Aguilera, who teaches Escuelas Despiertas, an advanced course on mindfulness in the Plum Village tradition for teachers at the University of Barcelona, is aware of the impact of her small daily choices about what she allows into her mind and body:

> I am aware that keeping a genuine practice every day, by having a healthy and compassionate diet and looking deeply at how sense impressions influence my daily life, is a key element.

All kinds of small domestic events can be included in our practice. Thich Nhat Hanh's famous reflections on the practice of "washing the dishes to wash the dishes" are pasted over many a kitchen sink—to inspire the laborer just to focus on the suds and the water,

> If while washing the dishes, we think only of the cup of tea that awaits us, thus hurrying to get the dishes out of the way as if they were a nuisance, then we are not "washing the dishes to wash the dishes." What's more, we are not alive during the time we are washing the dishes. In fact we are completely incapable of realizing the miracle of life while standing at the sink. If we can't wash the dishes, the chances are we won't be able to drink our tea either. While drinking the cup of tea, we will only be thinking of other things, barely aware of the cup in our hands. Thus we are sucked away into the future—and we are incapable of actually living one minute of life.[6]

When we begin mindfulness we often worry that there is not enough time for it. Many, like Christine Petaccia, an occupational therapist from the United States, find that, as we cultivate mindfulness during everyday activities, we enhance our energy and add effectiveness to what we do, adding rather than depleting precious time.

> When I walk through the school, I use walking meditation and I have infinite energy and patience. I have very little time, but I can take a few breaths at least every hour, and when I walk, I try to do walking meditation. I feel so very peaceful and have so much more energy. Problem solving is so much easier with students and teachers because no one gets worked up. It is hard to express the profound effect this has had on my teaching.

let the path unfold

We have said that mindfulness is a path, not a destination. By steadily and joyfully walking this path, in no hurry to get somewhere, we can just let the path unfold before us. Chelsea True's story illustrates what can happen over the course of ten years by simply putting one foot quietly in front of the other. She moved from a personal challenge, which mindfulness helped heal, to founding an organization to spread mindfulness in schools.

Just over a decade ago, I suffered a stress-related illness that caused me to have to leave work. During that time, I found Thay's book *Touching the Earth*. His teachings were a soothing medicine. I began sitting in meditation every day. I changed my diet and began eating at least one meal in mindfulness each day. I spent more time in nature. I looked at each of my daily activities as a chance to practice mindfulness. As I began feeling the fruits of practice, the sunlight began to feel more vibrant. The sky became more spacious. I realized that those sunbeams, and that spaciousness, were within me too.

I began sharing mindfulness with my daughter, then age three. As the years went on, friends and families encouraged me to share mindfulness with them too. Last year, my organization, Joyful Mind Project, received nonprofit status in California. We're now bringing mindfulness to schools and families throughout the northern San Francisco Bay Area.

My daughter and I shared a trip to Plum Village in 2014. It felt like a pilgrimage home. Living at a time when these teachings are available, practicing as a community, beholding the wonder within the eyes of our children, these are true treasures. Just to be alive is a miracle.

In time, for some of us, mindfulness practice can shape how we are in the world: our view, our core values, and our deep sense of purpose and meaning. For some of us, our practice can become part of every portion of our lives.

We have heard from Valerie Brown several times in this chapter—how she was inspired to take up mindfulness after hearing a talk by Thich Nhat Hanh, and how she gradually integrated mindfulness into her daily routines. Concluding her story, she observes the shift in values she slowly experienced, and how for her mindfulness became the core of her life.

> It changed how I felt about myself, and again, slowly, my values and priori-
> ties shifted from a powerful work career to a deep desire to help others.
>
> With this shift in values, I began to study and practice mindfulness in
> earnest. I sought out ways to heal myself and attended retreats across the
> United States and in Plum Village. I attended every retreat I could with Thich
> Nhat Hanh from 1995 to 2014. . . . I have helped to organize many retreats
> for people of color, lawyers, and educators at Blue Cliff Monastery and
> elsewhere. Before I really understood how the practice of mindfulness was
> working within me, in 1998, I cofounded Old Path Sangha in my small village
> of New Hope, Pennsylvania, which continues to meet today, and which has
> spawned several other area sanghas. In 2003 I was ordained by Thay in the
> Order of Interbeing.

Valerie is now an educational consultant, leadership coach, writer, and retreat leader.[7] This was her particular journey, and we are in no way suggesting this is a path, goal, or blueprint. Many educators start to practice mindfulness as a tool for dealing with stress, for improving their classroom environment, and to relate better to their students and colleagues. For some of us this is all we need or want. Others of us find that as we progress through our days with mindfulness, it enhances other aspects of our lives, and becomes an enjoyable end in itself. Those of us who feel a long way from Val's dedication and achievements (most of us, in fact) may be reas-sured to note that "She firmly believes that ice cream and carousel rides are critical to a better world."

Teachers are so desperate. We have tried everything with our kids. And mindfulness works. It simply works. So teachers love it, and so do the kids.

DEREK HEFFERNAN,
HIGH SCHOOL TEACHER, CANADA

ten
cultivating mindfulness in our students and classrooms

in this chapter

- Explore further how we can cultivate mindfulness in our students.

- Reflect on how the nondualistic approach of mindfulness might help us respond to student behavior more skillfully.

- Bring together some overall principles that support teaching mindfulness in the classroom.

- Consider how mindfulness relates to effective learning.

- Reflect on when, where, and how to teach mindfulness, and the methods and approaches we might use.

- Explore how mindfulness and applied ethics can be taught within broader frameworks such as social and emotional learning, well-being, happiness, and violence prevention.

- Share approaches to handling difficulties and resistance when teaching mindfulness.

cultivating mindfulness in our students

We have already considered how we might cultivate mindfulness in our students through teaching them the core practices and integrating them into our classrooms and our students' lives. We have explored how all this is predicated on our own embodied mindfulness as teachers and in particular our ability to be present authentically for our students. This is all the essential foundation for what follows in this chapter, in which we will explore some further areas that build on this foundation.

relating skillfully to student behavior

Behavior that teachers and other students experience as troublesome is a major cause of stress and disruption to teachers and to the students themselves, and all teachers are interested in how to relate effectively to student behavior. Many find mindfulness essential in helping them discover skillful and effective ways to do this.

The concept of "store consciousness" in chapter seven provides a thought-provoking alternative to dualistic thinking, where we can get caught in simple opposites such as right-wrong, reward-punishment, or perpetrator-victim. When we look deeply into ourselves we may see more continuity than differences and polarities, and realize that we all are all made of the same stuff. We can discover that we all have within us the same potential, using the Plum Village metaphor, with wholesome as well as unwholesome "seeds" that we can choose to "water" or not. We can experience the feeling that we all have the ability to transform and begin anew in the right circumstances, especially when we feel understood, loved, supported, and forgiven. Looking at student behavior in this light of nondualism can radically change how we approach it.

Brother Phap Dung, a monastic who is helping to lead the Wake Up Schools movement, outlines his experience of working in a nondualistic approach when relating to children's behavior. He explores the shift of focus to developing skills rather than punishing "right and wrong," and reports that his nonconfrontational and investigative response to incidents is a surprise at first to the children he works with during retreats.

We teach children about people being skillful rather than being right or wrong. I think our approach in terms of ethics is not right or wrong, but that it is about the seeds you water. There are conditions around that child that made him more difficult, angrier, and more violent.

We need to teach children a more considerate and well-rounded approach to resolving conflicts. A kid hits another kid, and they expect me to come and yell. And I come and say, "Hey, what did you think about that?" And they look shocked, because I'm not angry and I'm not going to punish them. I really don't punish. Many times I ask what went wrong. I always get them to sit down and have them discuss. That has always been my approach. To work with children and not have them be told by me what should be done, not give them a punishment. I actually try to get them all together and ask what happened.

Bea Harley, whose wisdom we have heard many times throughout the book, is a retired senior manager at a small elementary school in the United Kingdom that is explicitly based on the principles of mindfulness. She outlines what a nondualistic approach means in practice for the approach to behavior across the school.

The school's approach to behavior and discipline lies in an expectation that all members of the community contribute to and support the learning environment. Difficult behavior is seen as "unskillful," and our intent is to facilitate children in understanding the consequences of their actions both on themselves and others. Through the practice of mindfulness and self-reflection, our aim is to nurture the qualities of respect, kindness, and consideration for oneself and others and the positive and lasting transformation of unskillful behaviors.

This nondualistic approach to behavior is, in theory at least, what many more far-sighted schools aim to achieve. Modern evidence-based responses to student behavior have moved on a great deal from simplistic, behaviorist, and punitive approaches.[1] Modern approaches to behavior see the whole child behind the difficult behavior, keep clear sight of the child's positive characteristics, and encourage teachers to understand the underlying meanings, attitudes, and feelings the behavior represents rather than taking the challenge personally. This approach recognizes that behavior may stem from previously undisclosed causes, such as unmet mental health, bullying, or relationship problems, issues in the home, or medical or learning difficulties—all of which can be addressed. Challenging behavior and difficult incidents are seen as golden opportunities to teach skills and help students choose better alternatives, with adults modeling the skills and attitudes they wish to impart. This is not a laissez-faire approach, and does not mean there should never be consequences for difficult behavior, but it ensures that when responses are needed, they are proportionate and tailored to the student, with students experiencing the logical consequences of their actions and being supported with warmth and kindness to learn and practice the positive skills that repair and reconcile, rather than shame and punish.

Applying this sound theory is easier said than done, but mindfulness practice can give us the support we need. When we are faced by difficult and troubled young people, we can be aware of the natural human emotions—such as the frustration, anger, fear, confusion, and despair that often accompany these challenges. Without this awareness we may be tempted to become angry, to raise our voice, to judge someone negatively, or to punish or blame.

The practice of mindfulness can provide a way for us to walk the talk—the missing key to make the noble aspirations of positive behavior management a reality. Mindfulness can help us learn the embodied skills that can support us to stay solid, relaxed, open-minded, calm, and reflective so that we do not take challenges personally and can better manage our own emotional stress. Our steadiness can help a pupil calm down, stand back, and reflect on the meaning of his or her behavior, allowing him or her to make more positive choices in moving forward. If our students learn mindfulness too, and everyone shares the same practices and manages their own behavior mindfully, our task is easier; but even without such conditions, mindfulness helps the teacher stay solid.

Christiane Terrier stresses the importance of not taking student behavior that we find difficult personally, but instead to focus, much more productively, on the underlying needs of the student. She finds mindfulness very useful to help us keep this solid ground.

> When a student is aggressive with the teacher, instead of reacting and responding immediately or giving a punishment, stop and breathe, trying

not to take personally what we have just heard. In dialogue with him, as a human being to human being, we can practice deep listening to understand what is happening. We realize that his remark was not unpleasant, nor directed against us, but is caused by great suffering.

The sense of our calm presence may be all a child needs. Michael Schwammberger notes the particular value of simply being with the child when he is being apparently difficult, tuning in with mind, body, and breath, and soothing the emotions that are driving the behavior.

You notice the child has suffering. He or she may not do or say something or may be voiceful and reactive. If the child is being a real nuisance, often what you need to do is just to embrace that child, or touch that child on the shoulder. Just be, sit with him, and look into his eyes and say, "Okay, what's going on? What are you feeling?" Or just be present without any kind of plan; just be there. I notice that somehow unconsciously there is a process for that child. It's like he or she can begin to feel that it is okay to feel what you are feeling—no need to be afraid.

preparing to teach students mindfulness

Is the Time Right?

Many teachers who become enthused by mindfulness in their own lives are naturally keen to integrate mindfulness-based routines into their classrooms and explicitly teach mindfulness practices and skills to students. As always, the message is that there is no need to hurry. We can take our time to reflect realistically about ourselves, our motives, our skills, and the level of challenge we can comfortably take. We can assess carefully whether the context is right, and ensure we do not turn off our students by mistiming our offering.

Chris Willard teaches mindfulness to children in a health care setting, but his honest and humorous comments apply equally to school and university classrooms. He has used his own mindfulness practice to slow down and catch his unconscious ingrained habits of mind, finding he needs to let go of the urge to teach mindfulness right now, inspired by heroic fantasies on how well it might go. He advises us to reflect carefully about whether our students are really yet ready to learn about mindfulness, or to learn about it in ways in which we envisage they should.

I've often found dealing with myself and my own expectations a more difficult challenge than dealing with some of the toughest children. I've worked for a long time with troubled children, and when I started out I had high expectations for the power of mindfulness, imagining the chaotic classroom I taught in at a mental hospital suddenly transformed into an oasis of peace to rival any monastery. In the fantasy, not only did the kids come to practice mindfulness on their own—their emotional and behavioral issues cured—but the other teachers and staff sought out my wisdom in classroom management and clinical theories. This hardly happened, but once I let go of the struggle, I came to appreciate the somewhat more frequent moments of peace that came with patience and practice.

It is vital to keep checking in with ourselves and our intentions, as well as our expectations for the children. Ask yourself: What are my goals? Are they reasonable given the child I am working with? Have I become too attached to the idea of this child changing or learning to meditate? Have I become too attached to my role as a teacher? And no matter how important meditation or mindfulness practice may be to you personally, it may not be the right time for the child you are trying to teach.[2]

Morrakot "Chompoo" Raweewan shares, with refreshing honesty, an experience of teaching university students where "the more I tried, the more uncomfortable I felt." Her experience suggests that we can face any experience of apparent failure to connect with our students with realism, equanimity, and self-compassion, simply returning to our own practice for a while to rebuild the vital sense of joyful presence for our students.

I work with undergrad and grad students. At these ages, students have their own way of thinking, so it was difficult for me to introduce mindfulness to them without forcing. The more I tried, the more uncomfortable I felt. In a twenty-one-day retreat in 2012, Thay said that if we want to teach, we should teach from ourselves—the way we speak, the way we listen, the way we carry our life. If we are mindful, it shows. His advice is an answer. So I continue my practice, and some days there are students asking me how I feel when I teach a class, why I am not angry, how I handle my anger, and how I practice. Students who need help, either in study or in personal life, have the courage to reach out to me. The class atmosphere is better. Now it is easy to advise them, and they actually listen. I am a happy teacher now. As Thay said, "Happy teachers will change the world."

We come back to the realization that we, the teacher, are always our main teaching aid, and our own embodied practice of mindfulness is the chief gift we give to our students, our colleagues, and ourselves. We may at times decide that on reflection it is wise to wait for a while before teaching mindfulness: the pause can give us all the more time to focus on our own practice to make sure it is a solid base for all we do, and hope to do, in the future.

Are Our Own Classroom Skills Well Developed?

Much of this book has focused on the need to develop our own mindfulness practice before teaching others. But teaching mindfulness in schools and universities also involves the skills of classroom teaching. An experienced classroom teacher will intuitively understand the difference in approach needed when moving from learning mindfulness for ourselves, as highly motivated adult volunteers, to teaching mindfulness to students in classroom situations. Our students have not chosen to learn mindfulness, they have as yet expressed no interest, they cannot leave the classroom when they wish and are in the middle of a routine day with its taken-for-granted expectations and habits.

We cannot rely simply on how we learned mindfulness as adults, and assume that the fascination of practices that inspire us will inspire our students too. We have to invite, engage, and motivate. Every skill an experienced teacher has in their repertoire—their lively and varied methods and resources, their ability to start where students are and make their teaching relevant to the needs and preoccupations of their students, the clarity of their aims and the strong structures they provide, their warm and humorous but professional relationships with their students, and their robust skills in calmly managing the hurly-burly of a class of maybe thirty students—needs to be brought to bear on the teaching of mindfulness in the classroom.

If you are a young teacher, new to teaching, without a wide range of methods and techniques yet at your disposal, and with only rudimentary classroom management skills, then of course practice mindfulness yourself when you are with your students—it will help you greatly—but do not rush to teach mindfulness directly. Go slowly and build up your classroom craft. If you are not a classroom teacher but are bringing mindfulness into a school or university from the outside, then it is wise to respect the art and science of managing the classroom—it is not nearly as easy as a professional can make it look. Consider buddying up with an experienced classroom teacher. If you are invited in to teach mindfulness, make sure you have an experienced teacher who stays in the class with you and who knows the class, to help keep things on track.

Assuming the time is right, that we and the students are ready, that our intention to teach mindfulness is based on the students' needs and not our own fantasies, and that we have a solid bedrock of mindfulness practice and classroom skills on which to draw, we can move now on to consider how we might teach mindfulness in our classrooms.

methods and approaches for teaching mindfulness

Varied, Lively, Fun

The full wealth of teaching methods, approaches, and resources that experienced teachers have at their disposal all have a place in teaching mindfulness. We can use these imaginatively and flexibly to maintain interest and meet the different and changing learning needs of our students. Youngsters have lively minds and lower concentration spans than adults, so we keep our teaching lively and fun. Michael Bready, a mindfulness program developer from the United Kingdom, advises,

> I use lots of different methods and approaches. I like to use kinesthetic activities where possible. I also like to use videos to illustrate different concepts and ideas, such as gratitude and kindness. I also make use of written activities, such as writing down three things you're grateful for, or writing a gratitude letter, and games, like noticing where your attention goes if it

wanders from the breath. Movement is really useful in helping the children balance their energy—if they're too hyper, it lets some of their energy dissipate; if they're too tired, it can wake them up.

We keep lessons simple, immediate, and repetitive for younger children, as Niki Smith, a teaching assistant from the United Kingdom, suggests.

In our class we have continued to use many of the practices introduced to us by our Plum Village friends, but of these, the ones that I feel are the most deeply understood and embraced by the children, ages five to seven, are the simplest and most immediate: inviting the bell and singing.

Knowing when less is more is a vital skill. Chris encourages teachers to hold realistic hopes and intentions for themselves and for the children.

Be patient, challenge yourself and those you work with, but do not push too hard. Experience (and research) suggests that children do best with shorter meditative activities practiced more often. Thich Nhat Hanh suggests letting children mindfully walk five or ten steps, and then rest and run around a bit before trying again.[3]

Unpacking the Practices with Discussion and Sharing

In addition to the basic practices of mindful breathing, walking, eating, and being aware of the body, we need also to help our students unpack their experience of practices and meditations with periods of guided discussion. These open-ended periods of sharing and looking deeply help students become more aware of and sensitive to the detail and nuances of their experience, and to be able to voice it within the group, viewing "what happened for me" in the context of other people's experience. This helps students to realize they are not alone in their difficulties, and gives them support to work through them. They come to see there is no one right way to be; mindfulness is about simply being with whatever is there, in the now. Teens can be suspicious of adult enthusiasm and are particularly keen to have a reason for doing what they are doing, which discussion can help tease out in an experiential and peer-led way.

In part one of this book, in which we outlined core practices, we suggested some looking deeply and reflection questions teachers might like to draw on to guide discussion. We emphasized the particular quality of the questions we might gently pose, the tone of which reflects mindfulness itself. They are simple, open, nonjudgmental, encouraging, and accepting of all kinds of responses, including negative ones and "I don't knows." Gently, we bring the sharing back to real life experience to help our students move away from their stories and judgments and into the present moment.

Dzung X. Vo, the adolescent medicine specialist we have met throughout this book, reinforces the need to use this open style of questioning in his outline of his own skillful use of what he terms "inquiry" with teens.

> I've also found that teens learn from each other, and that their peers can be their own best teachers. This process emerges in the inquiry phase of our training. At the beginning of each session, we start with a ten- to twenty-minute formal guided meditation (typically sitting or body scan). Then we'll go around the circle with an inquiry on the practice we just experienced. The facilitator will guide a discussion, exploring, "What did you notice during that experience? How was that different from your normal way of being? What does this have to do with health, stress, depression, anxiety, pain, coping, and so on?"
>
> Then we'll have a check-in and inquiry on the previous week's practice. For example, I might open the discussion by saying, "Last week we focused on informal mindfulness. For the home practice, we invited you to bring mindful awareness to some activity that you do every day, like tying your shoes or walking to the bus. Did anyone try this? If so, what did you notice?"

Young People Learn from One Another

We can use wider discussion to help our students apply their mindfulness in the real world. Teens in particular appreciate being able to connect mindfulness with their everyday experience and challenges. They learn a great deal from their peers, deriving, as David Viafora says below, confidence, faith, and inspiration.

> It has been my experience that youth, and especially teens, are most often better teachers to each other as peers than if I or my cofacilitator or other

adults teach them. During our teen or children's mindfulness groups, we often encourage those who have been coming longer to explain certain practices or comment about their own experiences of practice with the newer students, right from the beginning. This elicits a different kind of authenticity and confidence in the group when the experience comes from a peer that they naturally relate to developmentally and don't consider as someone in a position of authority. It allows the new child or teen to enter the group with respect for what their peers have already learned, and builds faith and inspiration that he or she too can learn and grow in practice like that.

We can teach mindfulness wherever we find students, not only in classrooms. There are many contexts in which to offer mindfulness teaching outside the compulsory timetabled day. Lunchtime and after-school clubs have the advantage of being voluntary, so our practice there can be both deeper and more relaxed than with compulsory classes. The group atmosphere is more likely to feel safe enough to allow vulnerable students to open up about their emotional needs.

mindfulness and learning

Mindfulness Helps Students Focus and Be Ready to Learn

All teachers want their students to be able to focus, concentrate, and pay attention: this is the basis for any kind of learning. Helping lively and impulsive young people to focus has always been a challenge, but teachers are only too aware that it is increasingly difficult in the modern digital world, with its proliferating distractions and deliberate encouragement to switch tasks. As noted in the preface there is clear research evidence that mindfulness helps with the learning process, helping students to settle, focus, and concentrate and start to watch the inner workings of their own mind and body. The regular practice of mindfulness can gradually bring a state of calm, peace, and relaxation, which is both enjoyable in itself and which also allows the mind to work with greater clarity.

Imagine a child in school—how many feelings and states of mind a child goes through in the course of a day: maybe feeling confused, or excited, or rejected, or cared for, or lost, or proud, and on and on, sometimes in rapid succession. If children were taught meditation, if they could have a way of noticing these different mind states and know that these are "not mine, not me, not myself," then they could be saved from a lot of suffering, and have more attention free to learn. —JOHN BELL, CONSULTANT AND MINDFULNESS TRAINER, UNITED STATES

When children arrive at my class, they are very scattered, agitating over another class. Instead of asking them to calm down, which often leads to the opposite effect, I try to listen deeply: "Can you tell me what is happening to you?" I can then show understanding and compassion, and offer them a few minutes to relax. We would waste much more time if I imposed the work on them right away. When they feel understood and recognized in their feelings, they are much more open to learning. —CHRISTIANE TERRIER, RETIRED HIGH SCHOOL TEACHER AND MINDFULNESS TRAINER, FRANCE

Mindfulness Helps Students to Look Deeply

Mindfulness can water the seeds of concentration and insight, or deep understanding, that we all have within us, and which grow as we quietly focus on whatever we are contemplating—our breath, our next step, our thoughts, our sense impressions, or the spoken or written words of another person. Mindfulness can help us get beyond the habits and thought patterns we take for granted and experience the world differently. It can help us develop the ability to reflect, contemplate, exercise wise discernment, and look behind outer appearances to see interconnections and deeper truths. Through mindfulness practice of all kinds we can build the ability to look ever more deeply, and to experience more directly the complex and subtle nature of our physical and social world. We can bring a more open and focused mind, and a more finely tuned set of bodily reactions, to our interactions with ourselves, our encounters, and our discussions with others. We can learn to appreciate needs, feelings, and ideas more directly. We may well approach our studies with a sharper mind and greater wisdom. Richard Brady, who has decades of experience in mindful teaching, reflects on this process.

> My foremost goal in teaching—whether meditation or mathematics—is the same: to offer my students opportunities to be mindful of their minds, of their breath, of mathematics and math problems, of other students, and of their own ways of learning. As I create opportunities for mindfulness, students discover the meaning and value of their own experiences for themselves.

Mindfulness can help us stand back and reflect on our very thought processes. This ability, termed metacognition,[4] is increasingly being recognized in mainstream education as a foundational skill that assists every kind of learning.

Active Listening and the Value of Silence

Schools and universities are generally busy places, full of noise and talk, not all of it useful or beneficial. Learning to listen deeply and actively is not only helpful in getting on with other people, it is also central to all learning. Sara Messire, a teacher in an elementary school in France, practiced this core skill of mindfulness in mainstream lessons.

> This year, my students particularly needed to learn to listen. They were only interested in what the teacher would say, not in what their peers would share. I wanted them to be able to analyze their work or that of others in order to reflect more effectively. I set up a ritual to promote active listening: when a child hears speech and chatter continue, he said, "Listen to me, please," and everyone replied "I'm listening," putting his or her hands wide open behind their ears. In this way they became more involved with their whole body to receive the word of the other. They cooperated more effectively.

Young people often associate being asked to be quiet with discipline and coercion. Mindfulness practice can bring teachers and students a new appreciation of the positive value of quietness, stillness, and silence by providing a space for contemplation and looking deeply. It can help them to see the invitation to silence as a gift that they are happy to accept voluntarily.

Didde and Nikolaj Flor Rotne, the Danish authors of the mindful education book *Everybody Present,* teach that "the power of silence is one of the greatest gifts we can offer to others and ourselves in our hectic world." They have identified four steps of deepening silence into our lives, which they teach to their students and which help them create "an inner sanctuary of peace" inside themselves.[5]

Teachers can find silence unnerving, and Julie Berentsen from the United Kingdom concludes that being happy with silence in the classroom is the greatest thing that mindfulness has given her. She shares an instance of needing to become more comfortable herself with a student whose silence preoccupied her but who nevertheless turned out to be learning some profound truths.

Just before Christmas I asked the group what they thought of the sessions. They replied with things like "fun," "interesting," and "a good time." I was of course happy with their remarks but I also wanted to know what they had learned, if anything, from the practice. There was one girl who had been very quiet, and I had often wondered what she was taking with her from our time together. She shared with us that she felt that mindfulness had helped her to get to know herself better, to understand that she had many emotions, and that that was okay. She ended by saying that she had learned to be kinder to herself.

From my observations and reflections on the sessions, the children value having space to connect with themselves physically and emotionally and appreciate having an adult deeply listen to them. Perhaps the greatest thing that has been shown to me is the importance of space and silence: the joy of sitting together without feeling the need to fill the time with the busyness of school life.

integrating mindfulness within an ethical and social and emotional curriculum

Teachers often wonder where in the curriculum and on the timetable they might teach mindfulness. It can be taught on its own, of course, as a special class, and this is often an effective starting point for a school. Over time it has more long-term impact and credibility when it becomes normalized and integrated within broader frameworks that are routinely used to organize teaching and learning in schools and universities.

Given the generic and foundational nature of mindfulness and the varied way in which schools and universities across the world organize their curricula, there is no one way to do this: there are countless potential homes for mindfulness. We will explore here just a few of the most obvious ones, focusing particularly on those that have actually been used in practice by teachers inspired by the Plum Village approach to mindfulness.

As we have already discussed, schools and universities are increasingly interested in explicitly developing a cluster of social, emotional, and ethical qualities in their students, using a range of terms including *character, values, morals, ethics,* and *social and emotional learning.* Below we will explore ways in which mindfulness is being taught in this context under a range of headings; later in the chapter we focus on mindfulness within school subjects. There is no one right way. We can just use whatever words and opportunities work in our context, while holding true to the principles that inform our practice.

We begin with the framework and terminology that Plum Village itself uses, which are around ethics and the mindfulness trainings.

Applied Ethics

The various core practices we have explored already could be said to make up a basic curriculum of mindfulness, but to experience them as a coherent whole and with a sense of deeper purpose, it helps to integrate them into a set of broader principles, sometimes called "applied ethics" in the context of education. As we said in the preface, mindfulness is just one part of a 2,500-year tradition concerned with how to live a wholesome life. Mindfulness is not something we just practice as a tool or for our own quiet benefit; it comes to life when it is applied through our relationships and our actions in our daily lives out in the world.

The Plum Village approach provides an ethical framework to help us deal with our daily challenges. The simplest set of trainings, the Two Promises, is for younger children.

- I vow to develop understanding in order to live peacefully with people, animals, plants, and minerals.

- I vow to develop my compassion in order to protect the lives of people, animals, plants, and minerals.

Many teens and adults also find these two simple formulations helpful.

The Five Mindfulness Trainings

The framework used most often with young people is the Five Mindfulness Trainings, the full text of which can be found in appendix B. The trainings focus on five areas: *reverence for life, true happiness, true love, loving speech and deep listening,* and *nourishment and healing.* At a May 10, 2014, Educators Retreat in Barcelona, Spain, Thich Nhat Hanh said:

> The Five Mindfulness Trainings are the very concrete expression of the practice of mindfulness. If we ourselves and the young people live according to the five practices of mindfulness, then happiness, compassion, and healing are possible. A schoolteacher should embody that kind of mindful living, that kind of compassion and understanding. They will help the young generation tremendously in their transformation and healing.

Teachers can be concerned that mindfulness, especially when it moves into the sphere of ethics, is too close to religion. Brother Phap Kham, a monastic at the Asian Institute of Applied Buddhism in Hong Kong, is clear that applied ethics is not about religion or dogma; it is about universal human sentiments and principles.

> The trainings are secular, not religious, based on simple universal principles of compassion and understanding, and can be seen as a set of invitations, voluntary commitments, statements of intentions, and aspirations. Teachers who use them appreciate being offered an explicit and shared solid ethical foundation for their own actions and for the guidance they offer their students. They report that they find the Five Trainings to be workable in finding direction in their own lives and in guiding young people.

Young people also have their fears about the notion of "ethics," feeling fear that it is going to lead to moralizing and judgment. In contrast, Brother Minh Tam, who works with teens and young adults at Deer Park Monastery, a Plum Village Practice Center in Southern California, sees the Five Mindfulness Trainings as ever-tolerant friends who offer unconditional love, not judgment.

> I treat the Five MTs like five dear friends. They are always there, helping to remind us, to clarify our confusions, and to bring us back to our true selves, to our hearts. They will never walk away from or abandon us, no matter how circuitous or frustrating our path may be. They are in themselves exactly the kind of unconditional love we aspire to give to ourselves and the world. When we commit to practice them, we are only making a commitment to ourselves, not to any outside authority or judge. Our teacher doesn't even mind if we only practice one or a few of them. He had seen clearly that when you have even one true spiritual friend by your side, you are practicing all of the trainings.

Ethics in the Classroom

Some teachers use the terminology of ethics and the mindfulness trainings directly to shape their own teaching. This language and approach fit especially easily into contexts where ethics is routinely taught explicitly, such as in the training of medical students.

Neha Kaul, who teaches medical ethics to medical students in the United States, looked deeply inside herself when she found herself feeling uncomfortable with the argumentative ways the teaching sessions were going. She realized she had to be aware of her rigidity of mind and make a shift toward greater openness and letting go of the idea of right and wrong views, and allow her students to think for themselves. She had the further insight that this opening and allowing was in fact vital to empower her students to manage the many ethical dilemmas they would meet in their medical practice.

> Initially, I found myself feeling tense at the beginning of each session and during the discussions I struggled many times in wanting the students to think in certain ways, and would often lead, or even try to dominate, the

discussions. I had to bring the eyes of practice to look more deeply at what was going on inside me that left me tired and feeling worn out. I found a strong habit energy within myself of rigidity over what I thought were right and wrong views. I was experiencing a certain rigidity and fear of my students making an unethical decision.

Medical ethics involves thinking about an ethical dilemma or a difficult medical situation, using different approaches and finding ways to resolve the ethical tension that exists between more than one applicable ethical principle. I realized that if I wanted my students to succeed in doing this in real life, when they were busy with their medical practice, I had to inculcate their comfort with this process right here and right now in class. I had to accept that there was no way for me to control their thinking. What I could do was facilitate their understanding of the concepts, and encourage them in holding challenging ideas through the ethical reasoning process.

Social and Emotional Learning

As we explored in the preface, a widely used and well understood term to describe this whole area of education is *social and emotional learning* (SEL). SEL aims to help us understand ourselves better and relate effectively to others, developing skills such as self-awareness and managing our emotions, motivation, resilience, social skills, and empathy. SEL is increasingly accepted, taught, and sometimes integrated into schools and universities as part of their programs. SEL and mindfulness have powerful synergy, and schools already engaging with SEL are finding it a congenial home for the teaching of mindfulness.

In the preface we explored what mindfulness brings to SEL and why mindfulness is often described by those who work in this field as the "missing piece." For Constance Chua Mey-Ing, an elementary school teacher in Singapore, mindfulness, "working from within," is the "missing link" in teaching what she calls social and emotional competences, which "works from without."

Since 2004, MOE, the Singapore Ministry of Education, had mandated the teaching of social emotional competencies in schools. Mindfulness is the missing link in the teaching of SE competencies, therefore a perfect solution [is] mindfulness-based social emotional learning. Mindfulness works from the inside out, raising one's self-awareness by placing one's attention on the body, the moment, the present, while social emotional learning is the learning of skills to manage one's emotions, working from the outside. For young children, mindfulness is necessary yet not sufficient, as they are not equipped with skills to handle their emotions when they arise.

Mindfulness fits well with many other developments within education that aim to help students develop values, ethical standards, and a sound set of emotional and social skills, using different terminology. For example, Dzung sees a clear overlap between the Plum Village concept of interbeing and the concept of "sense of connectedness" found in the resilience and positive youth movement.

The resilience and positive youth development literature shows us that a positive sense of connectedness with peers, schools, and caring adults is a tremendously powerful protective factor for youth. To me, this is very consistent with the spirit of interbeing and can be taught in a nonreligious way.

Let us use whatever terminology and language fits and works to make links with the very many areas with which mindfulness interfaces.

The Prevention of Aggression, Bullying, and Violence

The First Mindfulness Training is concerned with reverence for life and the prevention of violence, aggression, hostility, and intolerance.

The Wake Up Schools initiative was inspired initially by a concern to tackle violence and aggression in French society, and the first mindfulness training of reverence for life directly addresses this issue. Many schools and organizations that work with young people carry out explicit work on these themes—attempting, for example, to prevent bullying and violence, to help their students manage anger, to explore the origins of aggression and violence in human societies, to tackle prejudice and intolerance, and to teach the skills that resolve conflict and reconcile and heal difficulties. This whole area of concern presents a valuable opportunity to teach mindfulness and ethics.

Young people are often deeply concerned by the strong emotions they experience, including hatred and violence. Many, even those who seem to have had fairly easy lives, have experienced a degree of abuse and suffering. Tony Silvestre, a professor in the United States, found this out to his surprise when he explored the theme of "difference" with university students, who even he thought of as a fairly advantaged social group.

> It began when I first added an exercise in "Difference" to my Human Diversity and Public Health Course. I began the course by asking my students to pair up and talk about the first time they experienced feeling different. After twenty minutes, I bring them together and invite them to discuss their reactions. During every class in the last fifteen years, the discussions have brought tears to my eyes as the students described the pain of feeling different growing up as a transgendered child, living with an abusive and alcoholic mother, being a Jew in a conservative Christian town, being biracial and rejected by the black and white kids, being bipolar, being "too skinny," and on and on. Their stories shattered my views of my students as sweet, angelic-faced vessels waiting to be filled up with my ideas of what is important. My experience taught me to listen closely and to see and touch the real person sitting at the desk facing me. I realized that pain is no stranger to young adults despite my storybook notions about them.

If the young people in Tony's class, who have had the resilience and support to make it to university, are nevertheless suffering, we might consider the impact of the kind of toxic levels of aggression, abuse, and violence that threaten to destabilize completely some of our less advantaged young people. We may reflect on how mindfulness might help them.

John Bell runs the YouthBuild project using a Plum Village approach to working with disconnected youth who have been subject to extreme adverse conditions that have led them to marginalization, and often to crime, drug abuse, and prison. Rather than mete out punishment, or even the kind of well-meaning advice to which the young people are well accustomed, the project starts by creating the conditions in which they are more likely to heal and flourish, providing a "sanctuary of safety and caring."

YouthBuild is a program that engages disconnected low-income sixteen-to twenty-four-year-olds in full-time comprehensive year-long education and employment training, through which they build affordable housing for homeless and low-income people in their neighborhoods, and simultaneously work toward their own high school diploma or GED, and gain experience and training as community leaders.

In some ways, YouthBuild is like a mini monastery. Young people come in pretty beat up by poverty, racism, or abuse of all kinds. They may have been dodging bullets and the police. They may have been victims of sexual or domestic abuse. They may have been incarcerated. What do they find? A sanctuary of safety and caring. They don't believe it at first. "No one ever cared about me before." For some young people, it is the first time they genuinely feel loved. As a YouthBuild counselor said, "They don't care what you know until they know that you care." Then they can take advantage of the learning opportunities, skill development, and leadership roles. As the process of transformation unfolds, a young person gradually makes a shift in identity.

Thich Nhat Hanh, my teacher, uses an image of the flowers that close up at night. In the morning, the sun comes up again and shines its photons indiscriminately on all things. The flower responds to these gentle photons and gradually opens up to reveal its full beauty. It is the nature of the flower to open up to the sun. The young people that find their way to YouthBuild are like that closed flower. If the staff keep beaming love, care, and respect at them, gradually, over time, in fits and starts, they open up. It is their nature to move toward their health and well-being. It's not easy to change long-standing, culturally ingrained habit energies. But it is possible.

J., a student on the program, said, "I used to think I was a bad person. Staff helped me find my real self. Now I just want to belong to a great movement to bring respect to my peers."

Acknowledging that all of us have a darker side, and encouraging forgiveness and compassion for all, is courageous work that may sometimes be difficult for others to understand. Cara Harzheim, a German teacher of older teens, clearly lives out the principles of respect for life, nonattachment to views, and the belief in forgiveness and healing in her philosophy classes. She felt it important that her students hear from a mother who, with extraordinary openness, was able to forgive the person who killed her son. She invited the mother to the classroom, despite the other teachers in her school not feeling open to doing this.

> Another subject we treated in philosophy was the death penalty in some countries. That is in the first mindfulness training: not to kill. By chance I was asked by the headmaster if I would accept an American woman in my classes to bear witness of what she was doing—her son had been killed in the streets. She had forgiven the murderer and she didn't want him to be killed. She explained this to the students. We were very moved by her bearing witness; she was making a tour of Europe to explain this to people. I had fifty students because the other teachers did not want her to come to their classes, but I said, "We want her because it is very important."

Teaching Well-Being and Happiness

The Second Mindfulness Training is to cultivate the value of true happiness (see appendix B for the full text). As we explored in the preface, happiness and well-being are increasingly seen as legitimate to introduce into the classroom as topics for investigation in their own right, thanks partly to the rising evidence base for their importance and their links with learning. In this section we present several powerful and inspiring examples of the ways in which teachers have used the Plum Village approach and the spirit of the second mindfulness training to invite students of all ages to reflect about how their habits and choices influence their happiness.

Adults often worry that young people pursue happiness in misguided ways, are over-materialistic, and use media and technology, and often recreational drugs, as their main emotional escape. When we talk with young people, however, we tend to find that they are often clear, at least in theory, that such things do not actually make them happy. Mike Bell discovered, when exploring the theme of happiness with his class of teens, that they had no difficulty in coming up with some detailed rules for a happy society.

> The students came up with a list of what they called "Rules for a Happy Society," which included: 1. Consideration for others—no discrimination on

the basis of age, sex, religion, or disability. 2. No stealing. 3. No hurting, violation, or murder. 4. Protection for religions and cultures. 5. Accept a reasonable level of risk—do not look for blame. 6. Welcome asylum seekers, but deport illegal immigrants. 7. Make facilities available for people of all ages. 8. Limit the use of addictive drugs.

I have tried the same exercise with twelve-year-olds. I introduce the practice as "the science of happiness," and tell them not to believe what I tell them, just to examine the facts. On one occasion, without any prompting, they did indeed group their concerns into the same five areas as the precepts: violence, stealing, speech, sexual misconduct, and consumption. I found from experience that I needed to include a second question, such as: "What things that you eat, buy, or consume can make you or other people unhappy?" Once prompted, they easily came up with overeating, getting drunk, and using drugs.

In another practical teaching example, Mike used the simple aids of a stone and a plant to trigger some profound thinking about the complex needs of living things, helping his students see the conditions of happiness are all around, and that these conditions necessarily include our relationships.

This year I was planning to teach eleven-year-olds about the characteristics of living things. I asked the technician to bring me a green plant and a large stone. Showing these items to the pupils, I asked them what would happen if I put the stone in a cupboard and left it for a year and took it out again. They had no trouble telling me that the stone would be roughly as it was before—perhaps a little dusty or even moldy, but basically the same. When I asked them what would happen to the plant if it were kept in a cupboard for a year, they readily agreed that the plant would be dead, all rotten or all brown.

I then asked what would happen if the pupils were shut in a cupboard for a year (pointing out that I had no intention of doing this). They easily agreed that they would be dead and rotten and smelly. I asked them what they needed to stay alive, and they first thought of food, water, and air; they soon added friends, family, and a house. They were ready to acknowledge that they could not live by themselves alone. I then asked them what they needed to be happy, and again they had no trouble listing the things that would help them.[6]

Lyndsay Lunan from the United Kingdom uses a particularly student-centered approach to the topic of happiness, asking her college students to map and reflect on their emotional reaction to different parts of their day. This approach helped increase their awareness of what nourishes or depletes our happiness, in a natural and indirect way.

> I had them draw a map of their typical day and we explored how much time in their day produced negative, positive, or flat emotion. They found that a lot of their negative and bored feelings came from things that they did out of habit, like Facebook and TV, and this led to very interesting discussions about what really nourishes us. The happy experiences were almost always something to do with being with people they loved or being outside. So that gave us a basis for doing the practices on generating positive emotion. Instead of me suggesting things as "conditions of happiness" that they might not really connect with, they chose something that had emerged from the exercise and sat deliberately bringing these experiences to mind, using the breathing techniques we'd practiced and focusing on how these experiences felt at their heart. This was a very accessible way in for them—and is probably consistently the most powerful practice for these kids.

Angelika Hoberg, a retired elementary school teacher in Germany, engaged her third-grade students in a powerful term's work using mindfulness notebooks to help them record their success in watering seeds of goodness inside themselves. Through their reflections, and through her expert coaching in the classroom, they were able to develop their own skills to move toward greater happiness and compassion, and come naturally to an appreciation that the conditions for happiness are here and now. This highly practical exercise not only motivated the students (and her) to reflect and act, but also drew in the students' parents.

> I invited my third-grade class to create a mindfulness notebook. I made a large drawing of the mind and store consciousness diagram, and then we brainstormed together which kinds of seeds we wanted to water. I wrote

down all their suggestions and hung them up together with the drawing. The children copied the drawing into their mindfulness notebooks and wrote down which seed they had selected from the list we made. The point of the exercise was to water the chosen seed for one week, and to write next to the drawing the situations where they succeeded.

Once, a child was spontaneously complimenting another on her success, and I asked him how he felt at that moment. He paused. "Good?" "Isn't it wonderful that you feel happy just by helping someone else and giving a compliment?" I asked. Afterward, the child ran around busily helping others for the rest of the lesson. I must say, this was never his strong point in the past. Acting this way was a startling discovery for him.

Even for me, there is so much to discover. I have my own mindfulness notebook. It makes a real difference if I give a loud and angry child a warning to be quiet or if I ask him or her, "Which seed are you watering at the moment?" All the other children help to think about it, and the angry child stops reacting and listens to her feelings. "The anger-seed?" "And which one have you chosen for this week?" "Happiness." A smile. There is nothing more to say. In situations like these, the children learn that they are able to choose their way of looking at things, to have an influence on their own attitude. They are not just the victim of external conditions.

At one parents' night, I shared about our mindfulness notebooks. Only after they promised not to criticize their children back home for misspellings or mistakes were they allowed to take a look at their notebooks. Of course I had asked the children's permission beforehand. The parents did not comment directly on the work, but there was a respectful and contemplative atmosphere in the room.

mindfulness and the mainstream subject-based curriculum

We have explored teaching mindfulness in classrooms, both in its own right and as part of a course on ethics or some variant on a social and emotional curriculum. There is a further level of potential integration. Mindfulness is most likely to be seen as truly significant and credible by students, colleagues, and parents, and lead to longer-term changes in students' attitudes and ways of being, once it moves across the whole school and university day and starts to permeate the mainstream-taught subject-based curriculum.

As we explored earlier in this chapter, the skills that mindfulness practice brings support academic learning and have the potential to weave right through the curriculum, and the timetable, while mindfulness and the associated skill of metacognition (reflecting on thinking) can help our students navigate across ways of knowing represented by different subjects. With mindfulness, students can stand back from surface facts and detail and see the underlying assumptions and processes, perceiving the various subjects as different paradigms or discourses with different truths and procedures.

Mindfulness trainer and retreat leader Michael Schwammberger reflects on the ways in which effective teachers teach mindfulness in their own ways, in line with their subject-based strengths and skills.

> Each teacher has different skills. Some teachers can be very skillful, very playful, or use the subject matter as a tool to communicate the practice. Like the philosophy teacher—he's wonderful. He has been practicing for a long time and he uses philosophy. That is what he teaches in order to open spaces of awareness, to awaken reality in the kids, open their curiosity, their interest, their attention, the presence.

Richard Brady comments on how mindfulness gradually shapes what he terms the "pedagogies" at the very heart of how we teach in ways that are "obedient to the truths of particular subjects."

> With the support of our practice, we can teach in a mindful way, a way that is much appreciated by our students. Additionally, employing pedagogies that promote mindful learning enables us to more effectively create spaces obedient to the truths of particular subjects and particular students. Familiarizing ourselves with some of these pedagogies is a second support for us as teachers of mindfulness. These pedagogies are as simple as mindfully erasing whiteboards and as complex as helping classes to mindfully make decisions by consensus. Some are spatial, such as arranging desks in

circles or groups of four. Others are temporal, such as periodically providing time for reflection or free writing. With our mindfulness we can successfully employ mindful pedagogies in teaching many subjects to many different kinds of students.

He comments on how some well-known educators are developing ways to help students use mindfulness to engage with different subject areas.

Drawing on their own practice, educators are increasingly developing ways to invite their students to mindfully engage with course content. Three times during the fall, Denise Aldridge's third and fourth grade students sit for forty minutes in their school's garden and observe and draw what they see. They discover how to look at one thing and observe both details and change.

English teacher Hope Blosser's twelve- and thirteen-year-old students read Sandra Cisneros's *The House on Mango Street* and learn to engage in contemplation and self-reflection in the process of writing their own micro-fiction. Professor of Information Science David Levy asks the students in his Information and Contemplation course to record their thoughts and experiences in journals when they use a particular form of information technology. Students in Economics Professor Daniel Barbezat's Consumption and the Pursuit of Happiness course discover the effect of doing a well-wishing meditation on their generosity.

We look next at how mindfulness can be taught within, and contribute to, subjects within the mainstream curriculum. We will take as our examples some of the subject areas with which Plum Village teachers have made concrete links to date. In this relatively short section we can only illustrate, not present an exhaustive account of where mindfulness might fit into every part of the curriculum. We hope it may inspire you to apply mindfulness to your own teaching, including within the subjects you teach.

Creativity

Creativity is a natural ally of mindfulness and core to the Plum Village approach.

Young peoples' retreats buzz with song, drama, art and crafts, food preparation, little ceremonies, and opportunities to create and share. Brother Phap Dung, who works enthusiastically with young people in Plum Village and beyond, conveys the feelings of warmth, community, and family that the sense of going beyond this engenders.

> Making a classroom feel like a community, like a family, is a skill. It's creating opportunities that are beyond the objective, using your creativity to create other ways to relate. Community involves music, play, dance, and heart-to-heart sharing. If you keep meeting and all you do is have the same discussions, it gets stale: you need to also have a potluck, a barbecue, go to the beach together—these other elements create this novelty, this sense of going beyond. So making a community involves a lot of creativity.

The previous chapters have included many examples, across all the core practices, of finding creative ways to teach mindfulness. Pilar Aguilera, who teaches Escuelas Despiertas, an advanced course for teachers on the Plum Village approach to mindfulness at the University of Barcelona, describes the warmth and creativity of the final session of her course.

> For the last session of the course we celebrate a "be-in" all together as a way to share our beautiful garden grown during the whole course. Educators bring, to the be-in, their abilities to do things from the heart: creative objects inspired by Wake Up Schools, songs, cakes, mindful activities, anything they love to offer to the group as a gift. We all finish the course with many gifts in our hands and with our heart full of kindness and gratitude.

Chelsea True's account suggests many ways in which teachers in schools, especially at the elementary level, find it easy to integrate work on creativity and mindfulness into the daily routine, to help children, as she says, "really come alive."

> When we enter mindfulness practice through the door of the imagination, the children really come alive. Storytelling, art, and poetry honor their inner lives and create images that they can feel and embody. I've written and told

stories that accompany many of the practices, using playful images to help children enter practice through the door of the imagination. I also share art and contemplative handwork projects with the children to help us deepen our understanding and embody the teachings. We share a period of mindful eating in each class and recite a special poem together each time that speaks to our interbeing and the sunbeams in our food.

Creativity, like mindfulness, helps us apprehend the world in innovative and fresh ways and break out of habitual patterns. Bea Harley reflects on the way in which, for her, creativity is more or less synonymous with mindfulness—a way of experiencing the world in an embodied and immediate way. She has found her personal experience of learning art profoundly contemplative and transformative, bringing her to a deeper sense of connection and an ability to see to the heart of things, an ability she has been keen to share with the young children she teaches.

While a student at Art College, after a particularly long thirty-six-hour session of drawing the same plant over and over again, there came a point where I experienced the realization that I was the plant and the plant was me, no boundaries. With this insight of interconnectedness came a world of potential and wonder, which changed the course of my life forever.

Since that time I have always believed there to be a strong relationship between the practice of mindfulness and the process of creativity. When teaching art I would try to encourage students to put judgment and expectations aside, but to hold a singular focus and concentration, to endeavor to see beyond what is in front of us, to truly understand the nature of what we are seeing in order to capture that essence. At times, I have wondered whether these moments of inspiration captured within a work of art, music, or literature are what move us, as if perceiving the symbols we experience an unconscious recognition of our own universality. It is these moments of insight gained through the practice of mindfulness that can launch us into a world of infinite possibilities. Through an understanding of our minds and once able to master our own projections (a lifetime's practice, I fear) to free ourselves of our incumbent anxieties, we might, with a somersault of thought and a quantum leap in our perception, become the very stuff of our dreams and go on to create a more loving and peaceful world.

Creativity can help young people express themselves directly, expressing what is in the heart in ways that engage with their experience of the world. Sister Hai Nghiem, teaching teens at a retreat in Plum Village, reflects on how young people use creative methods such as song and drama to process the teachings in direct ways that are different from the cerebral ways adults tend to prefer. She found inviting teens to write a rap song about "messes in this world" far better than asking them to study a text. It revealed in the process how it brought out the best in the young people.

> That year was really fun because we had the Five Mindfulness Trainings (ethics) workshop without presenting the text. We wrote a rap song. They were sitting together, and we wrote on the board about the messes in this world that we would like to fix. What do you see are the solutions? They came to deep insights about this suffering both personally and on a global level. This brainstorming turned into a song, and they turned it into a performance for the be-in at the end of the week.
>
> At the performance we realized how much they get out of the dharma talks and the experience. They take a song that they love and they change the lyrics and reveal what they've understood from the teaching. Or they make a skit where they exaggerate the dark path and what happens if you don't listen to the trainings. It's so striking that they really get the point. They express it in a way that's different from the adult sharings, where people sit around and share their thoughts and feelings. The teens are so smart and witty. The way they reveal what they've learned speaks greatly to the grownups too.

Art

Bea reminds us that art has the ability to shift us to experience a different way of seeing, one that links easily and directly to our emotional experience. Expressing a difficult feeling through art can help us embrace it in a safe way that is soothing and healing, as Barbara Calgaro, an educator in Italy, experienced powerfully in her classroom.

We built a 3-D rainbow together. Each child finger-painted one of the bow's stripes and glued the colorful stripes onto cardboard. Then we talked about how each color was linked to a feeling and the importance of each feeling. We discussed how all these colors have to come together to shine like a rainbow in the same way all our feelings need to come together inside each one of us.

We placed our rainbow in the corner of our room. That became the place where we could recognize and welcome our emotions or simply have some space for ourselves. If the children were fighting, they knew they could go there to embrace the feelings that came up or meet with the person they were having trouble with—whether a child or an adult—to talk about their strong emotions.

Elli Weisbaum, a mindfulness trainer in Canada, uses an art activity to help students routinely share their inner emotional state, or "weather."

Weather Check-In Art Activity

At the beginning of Circle Sharing in the Plum Village tradition we sometimes go around and share how we are feeling by describing our feelings as weather. We may be sunny with a chance of rain, or filled with thunderstorms. When sharing this activity to classrooms I often introduce it as an art activity. I have found this to work really well for elementary and high-school students, and also for college students and adults. First we gather and I explain the basic activity, which is to describe your internal feelings as weather. For the younger students it is nice to review what different weather options there are and what feelings they might represent. I then invite participants to go back to their tables or desks. We listen to the sound of the bell and take a moment to check in with ourselves to see how we are feeling. Then everyone draws what their weather is that day. Once the drawing is done, and if time allows, everyone who would like is invited to share his or her weather. The impact of this sharing creates a greater sense of community, understanding, and compassion within the classroom, as each student and teacher present becomes more aware of the different emotions that exist within the space. Some teachers have then continued to do a weather check-in journal each day with their students. This activity allows students to gain insight into their ongoing weather patterns and also, if the teacher is given permission, for the teacher to get insight into what is going on emotionally for the students.

Elli found that the activity proved invaluable in disclosing some difficult emotions that a student was holding, of which his teacher had been unaware.

In a grade three classroom I worked in, the teacher had a student who was always smiling, but had been acting out with harsh words toward some of the other students and creating distractions during class. The teacher was starting to feel irritated by this behavior, which was out of character for this student. This same week the teacher started doing the weather check-in journal. She asked permission to look at the journal, and the student said yes. When the teacher looked in the journal she was surprised to see thunder and lightning every day for the past week. The teacher asked the student what was causing the thunder and lightning, and the student shared that their father was away on a business trip, which was very upsetting. This gave the teacher understanding and compassion for what the student was going through, and without the journal she would not have known what was happening internally, when externally the student was projecting sunshine.

Stories and Poetry

A well-crafted story or poem, read or skillfully told, can convey essential truths in a vivid and direct way. Gail Silver's Plum Village–inspired story and picture book for young children on embracing anger with mindfulness, titled *Anh's Anger,* is a favorite in elementary classrooms, and was one that Adriana, a mindfulness mentor from Italy, read to her grandson. He then demanded that it be read to his whole class.

In the "What Next?" section, we provide a list books for children and young people in the Plum Village tradition, with their content briefly described.

A few years ago I read *Anh's Anger*, about how to transform anger, to my grandson Ariele when he was five and a half years old. He was so impressed that a few days later, while we were at home enjoying a party around the fireplace, and two little boys were having a tough fight, he whispered in my ear: "Shall we read the book to them?" I did it, and the miracle of reconciliation happened almost instantly. In fact, they all wanted me to read it once more. The following day, Ariele asked me to go to his school of four- to six-year-olds and read it to the whole class. We had to wait quite a few weeks to receive permission from the principal. Finally, one afternoon, there I was, in a circle of twenty-five kids with their teacher, sharing the story of how to transform anger. I introduced the little bell to them, and we breathed and sang practice songs. How impressive their presence! How joyful their participation!

Richard describes a creative method he devised in a teachers' course to explore a poem by Thich Nhat Hanh. He used mindful communication in pairs, boldly putting together those who felt they understood the poem and those who did not.

Inspired by Parker Palmer, I like to use poetry to teach looking deeply. I was planning to use the poem "Please Call Me by My True Names." I realized that this could be very problematic given the number of teachers relatively new to the practice and unfamiliar with interbeing. On that day I made a modification of my usual procedure. After the participants had read the poem and sat with it for a full three minutes, I asked them to stand and silently form a line across the room. At one end would be those who had little or no idea of the poem's meaning, at the other end people who felt they really understood it. This was accomplished in short order. I then asked the participants to pair up in the following way. Those at either end became a pair, then the next ones at the ends and so on. After all had found their partners and sat facing them, I asked the person who was less sure of the poem's meaning to share first. My impression was that it went very well. Afterward, someone already very familiar with the poem shared with me how much he'd learned listening to a partner with a very different understanding.

Music and Song

If you spend time on a Plum Village retreat, you will encounter music and song of many kinds—of happiness, love, celebration, contemplation, and peace. The extensive repertoire of Plum Village songs is extremely popular with teachers, who use the songs to inspire their own lives, and share them with their students. In chapter seven, on "The Emotions," we explored how powerfully these songs can transform feelings.

In a 2012 question-and-answer session at a retreat in the United Kingdom, Thich Nhat Hanh reflected on the direct appeal of music and song and their ability to shortcut the need for much explicit teaching about mindfulness, offering instead a whole-person experience of embodied peacefulness, which harmonizes the many elements our complex being.

> We don't have to teach the students everything in the book. We just use a number of things that they can understand to begin with. In order to understand ourselves, we have to go back to observe our body, our feelings, our perceptions, our mental state, our consciousness in order to really understand how they operate, so we can help them to function, to work together in peace. For instance, when you practice mindful breathing, you can practice with a song. You use music. And when you sing inside that song and breathe in and out, you bring all these five elements together, and you create harmony within the five elements. They do not oppose each other; there is no fighting between the five elements anymore. The music that you produce brings them together, and you have peace and harmony in you during the time you breathe in or you practice mindful walking.[7]

Retreat facilitator Nhu-Mai Nguyen reflects on the many potential values of a song: to remind us of the essential elements of a practice, to raise the spirits, to create or shift a mood, to provoke reflection, and to bring people together.

> Songs are very effective educational tools, mainly because songs aid in memory, influence mood, and bring collective focus to the group. For example, "Breathing In, Breathing Out" is basically the Pebble Meditation put to song. Many people have expressed that after a five-day retreat, they do not remember anything they've heard from the Dharma Talks, but they always remember one or two songs they learned.
>
> Songs can be used to uplift mood or calm emotions. "I Like the Roses" is a popular song for uplifting emotions. "Breathing In, Breathing Out" is

also very effective at calming strong emotions. Some young people even reported singing this song any time they felt anxiety or despair, and it has been a life preserver to help them navigate difficult situations.

Everyone can be invited to sing a song together at the beginning of the session in order to collect the group's focus, and songs may also be used to close a session. The facilitator can rest in knowing that the purpose of practice songs isn't to sing well. The point of singing practice songs is to be in touch with the meaning of the words.

Elementary school teacher Elia Ferrer Garcia teaches in a disadvantaged neighborhood outside Barcelona where students and families often struggle with unemployment and resulting difficulties. Like many teachers, she routinely integrates song into her classroom, finding that it brings group harmony and a "smoother and calmer" day.

I find it beautiful and nourishing when the children arrive at school and we start with the song "Dear Friends." We sing in a circle, remembering that each and all of us are important, that we are a group, a team. In that moment we are all the same—no social differences. We feel our togetherness through our feelings and sense of being. The day seems to run smoother and calmer, and the relationship with our fellow colleagues does as well.

Young people love to write songs themselves. Songwriter and environmental educator Joe Reilly talks about his experience of writing songs with children in a detailed *Mindfulness Bell* article well worth reading in its entirety.

As I share my songwriting process with the children, I understand that it is a way for me to also share the practice of mindfulness with them. In my life these art forms inter-are. I have found that I can help water seeds of mindfulness, hope, and creativity in children while watering the same seeds in myself.[8]

Song, intimately associated with breath, can reach parts of the mind and body that more cerebral approaches cannot, shifting mood directly and often swiftly. Special education teacher Tineke Spruytenburg worked with a child whose anxiety about swimming was calmed by singing a familiar Plum Village song, "Breathing In, Breathing Out."

> There was a boy in grade three a few years ago. He was extremely active and easily distracted. His life wasn't simple due to family circumstances and he had little motivation to learn. He lacked self-confidence, hence he lacked motivation. Yet he did want to show off his capacities during swimming lessons. There, at least, he could be one of the top-level students.
>
> One day I taught the class the "Breathing In, Breathing Out" song. They loved it, and this boy especially found some calm inside from singing it. We sang it with the gestures and explained how breathing calmly and consciously could help you calm down in "stormy weather." A few weeks later, our class had swimming lessons. I was watching the children swim while talking to the swimming teacher when he ran towards me. He was upset: his heart was beating so fast I could see it move in his breast. "Teacher, please sing me the song about breathing," he stuttered. "Otherwise I cannot practice swimming any longer." I kneeled down and softly sang him the song. His face lightened up, and with a big smile he went back to his "work."

Several websites featuring Plum Village and related songs on video are listed in the "What Next?" resources section.

physical education

Mindfulness is now almost routinely used in the world of sport, often to help athletes deliver the performance of which they are capable when they have let go of their worries and thoughts, and are fully present and focused in the moment, a state sometimes called "flow."

Julian Goetz, a US educator, describes the importance of "still moments" to teach students potentially lifesaving sensory-motor skills when riding their bicycles, building on the embodied nature of mindfulness.

As a New York City cycling instructor for three years, I embedded mindfulness into all of my lessons. There is a great advantage to introducing the practice of mindfulness during a physical education class—the students are already required to be aware of their bodies. With cycling, the risks are clear. We were riding in the streets of Manhattan or Brooklyn or wherever, and if they should lose focus or pay attention to the wrong details, we'd be up a creek. They understood this so long as I made it apparent to them, but I think the same could apply for any sport or physical endeavor. I would usually introduce the practice during the explanation of the brake system. Most people generally believe that squeezing the left brake is always dangerous, or squeezing only the right brake is ideal. Both of these are false, which is easy enough to explain. But to get someone to squeeze both brakes gently and evenly in a crisis moment, let alone children and adolescents, is another picture. For this, mindfulness was extremely helpful.

With both hands on their brakes, squeezing gently while rocking forward and backward, I would encourage them to close their eyes for a minute, to feel what it's like to be sitting on a bike, safe, collected, calm. I would have them take a few breaths, feel the sensation of the breath entering and exiting their bodies, sometimes including a bit on how our breathing connects with the work our muscles do, and then have them store that memory, of stillness, breath, and of squeezing the brakes gently, for when a crisis eventually occurs. Something always happens when you're riding bicycles. To be ready for it, you can use the still moments to inform the crisis moments.

That's how I would teach them. Before heading out on rides, or before getting into hairy intersections, I would have them pause, and do the exercise again, peppering the lessons, as it were, with mindful pauses. I believe those are the keys to teaching mindfulness to youth, particularly in a sports setting.

science

Mindfulness can help us look deeply, get behind outer appearances, and perceive interconnections and deeper truths, rather than being distracted by sensory-based impressions and our mental habits and prejudices. This process is of direct support to the objectivity, clarity, and dispassion we hope students will gain when they learn about science and its processes and methods.

At family retreats, Thich Nhat Hanh helps children contemplate the nature of reality by using examples from the natural world of apparent defined objects that change form and may therefore seem to disappear—such as flowers, flames, water, the seas, rain, and clouds—but which actually simply transform. His best-known and iconic teaching example is to give each child a seed of corn and invite them, for homework, to go home and plant it. As he talks to them in preparation, he invites them to contemplate a plant of corn and reflect on what has happened to the seed.

> The seed of corn has not died; it has become a plant. It does not retain the form of a seed but the seed is always there. If you look deeply into the plant of corn, you can still see the seed everywhere in the plant. Originally, the seed was small and yellow in color, but now it is big and green. But if you are intelligent, when you look at the corn plant, you can see the seed of corn still there. You can say, "Hello, my little seed of corn. I know you have not died. I can see you in the plant of corn."[9]

University instructor and mindfulness teacher Marianne Claveau uses the opportunity of a biology lesson to help her teenage students explore such fascinating territory, helping them contemplate and experience directly the complex and ever-changing nature of phenomena, and our own interdependence, with the help of a simple glass of water.

> I used to teach biology and sustainable development. The practice helped me to make the student understand more deeply complexity and interdependence and to develop a systemic view of each situation. I start by drinking a glass of water. I do it this way. "I invite you to look carefully into this glass of water. So who made this glass? Who had the idea one day to use sand and fire to manufacture it? Who first took a container to put water in? Can you look into this glass and see the skill, the ingenuity, the knowledge, and the intelligence of all humanity? Could you look into this glass and be in contact with all the human beings that reflected and worked in the past to

make this glass available for you now? We may think we are independent, but simply by holding a glass, are we not linked with so many people?

"And now, look carefully to the water inside the glass. Where was it yesterday, last month, last year? Where was this water one hundred million years ago? Has it been a cloud, an ocean, a bird, a dinosaur? And where will it be in a few hours? Could you imagine the trip that each drop of water has made before being gathered into this glass and before becoming a part of your body soon? Our body is made up of 75 percent water. Getting in contact with this water in each of our cells, could you reflect on what is the body, on what this form is that you usually call you, on what you are made of?"

After that, I invite the students to drink the glass of water mindfully, and to get in touch with their sensations, with the freshness of the water, to taste it just like if it was the first time they drank. I invite them to drink the water being aware that it has been a cloud.

I'm always surprised how the students are touched by this practice. Most of them suddenly understand that they are part of the whole, I mean not as a concept but as a physical sensation.

Earth sciences provide opportunities to explore interdependence. Bobbie Cleave and Gordon "Boz" Bosworth, the environmental educators we met earlier, build on mindful eating practice and on the Five Mindfulness Trainings to help their students generalize the concept of mindful consumption into the wider areas of sustainable energy consumption and a reduction in pollution.

We mention global climate change in our daily prayer at the practice centers. To have teens and all kids learn to eat mindfully in silence and focus on their food is the first step. We also started doing this practice with kids in public and private schools, starting with a raisin. The steps are to look at the raisin or the plate of food and trace it back to all the causes and conditions that brought it to the consumer—the trucks, people, factory, farms, soil, sun, rain, worms, and so on. This can easily lead to a discussion of what kinds of food are the softest on the earth to grow, which the least violent, or that cause the least harm. Without getting into the large amount of data here, meat production is not only huge in its impact on global warming (more than car pollution), but also the violence involved and suffering can be heartbreaking. It is all about raising awareness.

We also take children here at Deer Park and show them the solar panels. This leads to discussions of solar power; pollution sources, including noise pollution; and their own practices at home in daily life. There has to be a connection to their personal lives for kids. How does what you do impact the planet and everything and everyone on it? The five mindfulness trainings are our guide to do that: how we eat, grow food, have fun, travel. All of it deeply impacts our planet earth and ourselves.

sexuality and relationships education

In many societies, schools are charged with teaching young people about sexuality and relationships, which many find challenging. In industrialized countries, at least, young people often see sexuality as their private domain and are generally very suspicious of being lectured or moralized to by adults, preferring to come to their own insights. Mindfulness can help us connect more effectively with the needs and concerns of young people around sexuality, helping us to listen in an open and nonjudgmental way with kindness, compassion, and empathy, while also encouraging the young people to consider their values around sexuality and to listen deeply to themselves and to one another.

We may be concerned that if we are too laissez-faire, we will fail to give sound guidance to our students on how to take care of themselves and others. But if we take an open-minded and exploratory approach, we may well find that young people themselves are often aware of the need for responsible behavior to others, and the value of love and commitment in satisfying relationships. Professor of creative writing in the United States, Fiona Cheong, listening deeply to her university students, finds them both much preoccupied with romantic relationships, and also feeling strongly that a satisfying relationship has to be loving rather than just sexual.

Our responsibilities to the people we love and our desire to protect them from worry and suffering have an energy that is always present, even in the classroom. Add to the mix the various anxieties and fears common especially to young people. For instance: Will they have a date on the coming weekend? And if they do, will they have a good time? Will their date think they look fat? Will they say something stupid? Will there be expectations of sex? More importantly, will they ever find someone (aside from family members) whom they can love deeply? Will that person love them deeply back?

Norma Ines from Mexico works with teens to empower them about their own sexuality and health, using an imaginative and creative range of methods to help them build respect for themselves and their bodies.

I am working with adolescents aged ten to nineteen in elementary, middle, and high school. The themes are strengthening life skills, decision-making, teen pregnancy prevention, and taking care of sexual and reproductive health. We use the mindfulness practice and art to allow young people to express their voices and deeper desires.

We invite teens to consider their bodies as sacred, learning to care for their bodies and hearts. We made an educational campaign to reflect on the unintended and unplanned pregnancies. We supported artistic projects made by adolescents of both sexes. Through theater, radio, and video, teens explored how to take care of our body and sexual energy. The whole process explored how we can all learn to make better decisions, to live our lives responsibly and be happier.

media literacy

Chau Li Huay, working in the context of media literacy in Singapore, uses the Fifth Mindfulness Training to help high school students make more conscious choices about the media they consume. Chau helps them sensitize to how the thrilling sensationalism and taken-for-granted violence of movies can affect our moods and perspectives.

The topic I taught was on Media Literacy, in effect being aware of media messages. A common theme found in videos and movies is violence, a big thrill factor. Students actually laugh a lot and are very excited when the characters are flung over the hill, meet a tragic death, or meet a comical death, like banging their head against the wall. Most students are gratified to see the characters getting killed. As part of the lesson, apart from identifying what is the message and the meaning (for example, a thriller movie, and everyone is dead except the hero), the reflection is whether killing is really necessary. Or is it greed, jealousy, or a quest for power, loyalty, national pride, or ideals such as saving the world that is justifying this act of killing, and can the same outcome be achieved without killing? Can killing put an end to a thing or event?

The connection with the Fifth Mindfulness Training is to show them that even the act of getting in contact with media is already consumption. If they really understand the awareness of the media messages, and recognize it is giving unwholesome messages, then they will know whether to consume it or not.

Chau also used media literacy as a vehicle to explore the conditions of happiness in ways that engage the sophisticated and skeptical minds of teenage students, helping them see for themselves how advertisers use the idea of happiness to sell their products.

The Second Mindfulness Training taught us that happiness doesn't depend on externals, but it is very hard to say it like that literally to young people. What I tried to do [to connect with the Second Mindfulness Training] was to teach them to discern the media messages, and get them to reflect: is it true that happiness is only when you have to buy this particular product or service, as what the media is telling you, or is that really only an artificial message? Can the advertisers be using happiness as bait, because happiness in the media equals youth, fancy clothes, flashy cars, and popularity? What exactly is this thing we call happiness? If they really understand the awareness of the media messages, and recognize that it is giving unwholesome messages, then they will know whether to consume it or not.

We do not have to use only examples from the present. Yvonne Mazurek, teaching young adults in Italy, uses images from art history to help her students become more critical and thoughtful about the body imagery that currently surrounds and oppresses them.

> I began to brainstorm about ways to help students recognize unhealthy images in pop culture. I decided to focus on body image, since many teenage girls had spoken to me over the years about their mounting insecurities. Over one month, I dedicate a class a week to look at ways in which bodies have been portrayed over time. We compare idealized bodies from the past—like a statue of a heroic Greek athlete or a Renaissance portrait—and a contemporary advertisement, mostly based off images they've brought in. When looking at images from contemporary media, students begin to recognize how so much points to individual wealth, power, control, and immediate gratification. By contrasting today's advertisements with images from different places and eras, students realize that there are many kinds of beauties and many different value systems. With this awareness, they talk about some of the choices they have and how they can become agents of social change. They begin to see the limits of material consumerism and see the deep impact media can have on our psyche as individuals and a society. Once students recognize that a picture is worth a thousand words, they discover their ability to hear and discern messages that once engulfed them.

when mindfulness is difficult to teach

Our teaching of mindfulness will not always go according to plan. Rather than becoming discouraged, we can reflect that we often learn most when this happens. We hear next from teachers who are open and confident enough to share their difficulties and challenges with us.

Creating Difficulties for Ourselves—the Tyranny of "Ought"

When we look closely at our own reactions and perceptions, we can often conclude that the difficulties we are having have their origins in our own mental habits. A recurrent block we teachers can put in our own way is our judgment around what we think "ought" to be happening, and the belief that we know what is best for others.

Teachers can suffer particularly from the rescuer's urge to fix things for students, and from wanting to hear them supply us with our preconceived answer. It is tough to change this habit and just be with how things are right now, giving students space to work things out for themselves in their own way to fit their own needs.

Richard reflects on his experience of teaching mathematics in a secondary school. He describes his attempts to model for his students how to shift their perceptions of difficulties. His aim was to help them to learn to welcome obstacles, "seeing what gifts of understanding they have to offer" rather than trying to overcome or avoid them.

> When my students encounter obstacles, their first impulse is usually towards one of two extremes: they try to overcome them or they give up. The approach of welcoming obstacles, sitting with them, and seeing what gifts of understanding they have to offer is foreign to my students, yet it is one that could serve them well in life. I ask myself how I can do a better job of modeling this way of relating to difficulties in the classroom. I realize I can begin by curbing my impulses to diagnose and suggest remedies for students' problems, and learn how to just be with the students and their problems.[10]

Gloria Shephard, teaching mindfulness to parents in the United States, came to similar conclusions about the need to identify her own unhelpful tendencies of rushing to answer for her students when they met a challenge.

> I think the Plum Village teachings often come with a smile and a lot of quiet space. This experience has helped me to infuse my own teaching with a tendency to look past the things that present as challenges (someone not listening or doing something distracting) and smile at the being in front of me. Also to respond more slowly, letting a question sit for a bit before rushing to answer, letting people take time to describe their experiences.

When to Stick and When to Change

Things do not always go as we hope when our classes are learning mindfulness. When this happens we need to use our wise discernment and calm mind to see whether to stick to the process and allow more time or adapt what we are offering.

As Julie Berentsen reminds us, we sometimes just need to stick to it and allow students to adapt to the new demands of mindfulness, and trust our own teaching skills, which in this case were for Julie to provide a clear structure, listen deeply to her students and engage in authentic, two-way conversation.

> I have been sharing mindfulness practice with small groups of children in an inner city London school for a few years now. We meet once a week for around thirty minutes. That is not to say it was an easy ride to reach this point. It has taken time to build trust and understanding. The children needed to understand that this is not a lesson with a right answer or the expectation of achievement. They found it hard to sit and observe the breath. By having a clear structure to the sessions and deeply listening to the needs of the children, I have used different aspects of the practice to support and nourish them. For example, if they share in the beginning that they were up late the night before, I will guide them with a total relaxation which often ends with them telling me that they have realized how tired they were when they came to school.
>
> At times the groups' behavior can be challenging. The following week I take time to share with them honestly about what happened. I let them know they have been in my thoughts, that I respect them, and that I want to understand them, so it would be helpful if they could share their thoughts and feelings about a situation that has come up. They have valued these conversations and so have I.

Similarly, Sarah Woolman, when her class was "giggly and distracted," found it worked to just stick with the practice "without fear."

> The class found it hard to take the pebble meditation seriously, and I found I had to sit with my discomfort while some of them giggled and got distracted. I worked hard to keep my voice neutral and to breathe with each pebble even if the whole class was not with me. At the end of the meditation one of the girls approached me and said, "The mountain and space meditation let us experience some quiet, which we don't usually have when we are all crammed in a classroom together." This was a teaching for me to continue without fear even if it looks like it isn't working, because you never know what the children will get from it.

Sometimes, however, we need to be flexible and change to suit the group, as Michael Bready did when he found that speaking too directly about cultivating happiness and kindness with young offenders did not go down well.

> In my work with young offenders, the emphasis is more toward the foundations of mindfulness and less toward cultivating happiness and kindness. When trying to bring in these practices it has been met with some resistance, so instead I try to impart these elements of the practice in an unspoken way rather than in a direct way.

Tineke similarly dropped mindful walking in favor of mindful working when families were simply not enjoying it.

> On our days of mindfulness, we do not practice walking meditation any more. Usually we host about twenty adults and twenty children between four and twelve years old, and no matter what fun forms we came up with, the families did not enjoy walking meditation much. Often parents were annoyed by noisy children, and a lot of irritation was generated. Because we aim to have the families practice mindful skills for everyday life situations, we replaced the walking meditation with working mindfully. Each family does simple gardening together, plucking weeds between the sidewalk tiles. Even the youngest family member gets a suitable job, like helping bring the wheelbarrow to the shed while riding it.

Once again we honor the pragmatism and adaptability of the experienced classroom teacher.

All of this can sound very complex. We might reflect that it is sometimes the simplest and most spontaneous creative impulses that give rise to the most engaging and delightful moments in the classroom, as Elia Ferrer Garcia of Spain experienced.

> The children love it when I pick up the watering can and I pretend to give them a shower. I tell them they are flowers and that in order to keep our garden growing beautifully, we need to water every flower. One day, as a surprise, I poured some glitter into the watering can, and I told them they were shining even brighter. They loved it.

I have arrived; I am home.
THICH NHAT HANH

eleven
cultivating mindfulness across school and university communities

in this chapter

- Reflect on how to introduce mindfulness to our colleagues, administrators, and senior managers, to students' parents and families, and into the structure, values, and ethos of the whole school or university.

- Hear some inspiring examples and reflections from those who have begun to reach out to colleagues and parents, and in some cases right across the organization, to help their school or university become more mindful.

cultivating a sense of family

Thich Nhat Hanh encapsulates a vision of the kind of schools, universities, homes, communities—and indeed the world—we might hope to cultivate with his frequent use of the word *family*. Family to him means a place of warmth, acceptance, and nurturing, where members are deeply connected with one another. In a 2012 Plum Village Educators Retreat, he said:

> It's very nourishing and healing to be with your classroom, your community, your students, and your friends. I get a lot of joy, nourishment, and healing from that kind of life. It is a second opportunity for the child, because the child may not have had love and happiness in the family. Maybe their parents fought each other, and suffered a lot; they did not have a chance to learn how to love, how to experience happiness in family life. So as teachers we have an opportunity to give them a second chance, by transforming our community into a family, where a good relationship can be established between teacher and students.[1]

This warm and welcoming vision naturally includes actual families, as Shantum Seth, a senior Plum Village teacher working in India stresses.

> What we are really trying to do is create the school as a family, the classroom as a family, and all these elements in it, the teacher, child, parent, make that into a whole.

Brother Phap Dung further explores this vision of the school (and by implication, university) as a family, reflecting on the need to focus on joy and happiness in the present moment, shifting the focus away from being solely on the future, to make the school or university a place where young people, and their teachers, can enjoy living and learning—right now.

> What we are really trying to do is to make a school become a second family where the teacher, the students, and the whole school—the parents as

well—see it as a joint effort—a joint effort to create a place where it's not about the future, about your career, job, position, or your money, but a place where you actually enjoy living and enjoy learning, and enjoy exploring.[2]

This chapter explores how we can gradually extend the practice of mindfulness, the idea of a warm and nurturing family, and the idea of happiness in the here and now. We can move, outward from mindfulness in our own lives and our classrooms, and into the lives of our colleagues, into our students' homes and families, and across the school and university as a whole.

sharing mindfulness with our colleagues

No Need to Hurry

Happiness is here and now / I have dropped my worries / Nowhere to go, nothing to do / No longer in a hurry.

Happiness is here and now / I have dropped my worries / Somewhere to go, something to do / But I don't need to hurry.

"HAPPINESS IS HERE AND NOW," PLUM VILLAGE SONGBOOK

As we learn to enjoy our own mindfulness practice, it is tempting to think how desirable it would be to share it with our colleagues, to help them with their own stress, and to work together with them to develop mindfulness for our students. This may well be true, but there is no need to hurry. Enthusiastically sharing mindfulness with colleagues who currently have no interest is likely to demotivate them. Mindfulness, in the sense of the core meditative practices, is not for everyone, and if it is, people need to come to it in a way and at a time that is right for them.

We may well find that when we start out, most of our colleagues are not in the right place to want to hear about mindfulness. Indeed, they may even, like Goyo's teaching colleagues in Spain, be quite resistant to the idea.

> I wish there were more teachers practicing this. I feel like a *rara avis*
> (rare bird) among my peers. My colleagues are touchy about things
> like mindfulness.

Our colleagues may be too stressed to want to consider the possibility that mindfulness can provide any relief, as Matt Spence, teaching high school in the United States, found.

> Many of my colleagues seem skeptical of practicing mindfulness and resist
> the idea of being still and quiet for more than a few minutes. I don't think
> they understand that they are contributing to their own stress and that of
> their students.

Some of our colleagues may even find any apparent success we may have with our students threatening rather than motivating, as happened in the experience of Pascal Dumont in France.

> This year, one of the first-year teachers was particularly emotional, fragile,
> and nervous. She had three very disruptive students in her class. I offered
> to support these three nine- to ten-year-old children every afternoon after
> recess. We went on to practice different mindfulness exercises together:
> guided and silent sitting meditations; we did deep relaxation exercises; we
> trained to listen openly and attentively; and we learned to express ourselves
> with gentleness and understanding.
>   The teacher came to me and looked visibly annoyed: "What are you
> doing with these kids? Fabien blew up in class today. He took a chair. He
> was ready to swing it across the class and suddenly stopped. He said, 'Uh-
> oh! I better meditate,' and he bolted to the back of the classroom and sat
> with his legs crossed. It was something like yoga. The whole class burst out
> laughing. He said he was doing it with you. This is unbearable."

While such responses can be challenging for us, we can try to not be defensive, downhearted, or even worried about these attitudes. If we face these challenges calmly and with open-mindedness, we can come back to our own mindfulness practice as a refuge, continuing to practice quietly in our own lives; teach mindfulness, if we are able, in our classrooms; and extend our loving kindness to our stressed colleagues. Our own mindfulness is the solid groundwork for anything we do or may hope to do in the future.

We have the satisfaction of knowing, like Maggie Chau, who teaches at a university in Hong Kong, that through our own practice we can immediately create a better school and university environment, with warmer and more empathic relationships.

> I have been able to understand the feelings and limitations of my colleagues better. I can then work with them accordingly.

Starting to Teach Our Colleagues Mindfulness

It is a familiar story that, as we continue to practice, the impact of mindfulness on ourselves becomes apparent, and some colleagues can become intrigued and interested.

> I can only say that my own enthusiasm for the practice and describing the joy that I derive from the practice has cultivated interest in the people around me. —PAUL BREADY, EDUCATION STUDENT AND TEACHER IN TRAINING, UNITED KINGDOM

> Once when I was associate dean, I was meeting with my home department about an issue that had gotten a few people fired up. Rather than immediately responding, I consciously breathed a few times and replied calmly. One of my colleagues was very impressed. —GAIL WILLIAMS O'BRIEN, UNIVERSITY AND YOGA TEACHER, UNITED STATES

> I also have found that I am more receptive and nonjudgmental in professional relationships with fellow teachers and administrators, and no longer waste energy on worrying about things that would have made me stressed in the past, like deadlines, curriculum directives, meetings, and so on. I am now able to breathe and allow whatever is to be, and as a result I feel like I go through my day much more peacefully. Several colleagues and others have observed this peacefulness in me as well, so I believe it is having a

positive impact on those around me. **—ELIZABETH KRIYNOVICH, HIGH SCHOOL TEACHER, UNITED STATES**

When colleagues start to express an interest, this is often a good time to start to talk tentatively about our practice. Goyo, who spoke earlier about his colleagues' "touchiness" on the topic of mindfulness, found a skillful but sensitive way to do so.

> Sometimes if the time is right, I make comments about my practice to my colleagues and friends, but I do not like to talk much about it because I feel like I'm proselytizing. I talk about it if it is applicable or if they ask me. Otherwise, I kept silent. It is true that some colleagues say they notice I have changed. Then I tell them it is because of my practice of mindfulness.

With interest in mindfulness and its applications to education growing in society and in education, we may be asked to teach mindfulness to our colleagues. With any luck it will go as well as it did for Jasna K. Schwind, an associate nursing professor in Canada:

> I was invited to provide a series of mindfulness workshops to the staff in the School of Business with a positive response from participants. Some responses were: "I had less anxiety and I realized I could not control every situation." "I am less quick to make a rash decision or to answer quickly." "The mindful eating session. I felt so satisfied eating this way, I could barely finish my meal." Participants were interested in continuing with their own mindfulness group.

We may even find, like occupational therapist Mariann Taigman, that once the spark has struck, the fire takes hold quite fast and we become involved in a good deal of activity.

> I am working on putting together in-services for school staff and for my occupational and physical therapy department coworkers to teach them about mindfulness and also how to teach children, using Thay's teachings and books as my foundation. Thay's teachings have increased my awareness

of my relationships with many different school staff members and the students I work with. I try to help others see the miracles of daily tasks (taking a shower, eating, washing dishes, and so on) and to enjoy every moment, frequently using humor like Thay does when he teaches. It seems almost daily that I'm recommending books on mindfulness to others.

Usually it takes time. It took two years for Grace Bruneel, who was training teachers in Hong Kong, to move from a situation of great resistance to one where colleagues became receptive to new ideas.

Our idea was not totally supported by the school management, not to mention the resistance from the much-stressed teachers who thought it was a good thing for the students to learn, but that they were too busy to do mindfulness. With strong volition, we just kept trying, with no expectations. In the teachers' training last month, we finally saw the first sprouting of seeds sown in the last two years. From resistance, doubt, and feeling forced to do it, our teachers are finally truly experiencing the benefits of mindfulness practices. One after another they shared their insights, revelations, and their happiness in their growth. Our session ended with reconciliation, understanding, and reaching out to each other. It was just so beautiful.

Keeping Mindfulness Invitational

However enthusiastic we are, and however much we are encouraged by others to share our practice, it is vital to continue to offer mindfulness to colleagues as a gift and an invitation, and not make it compulsory. Otherwise, like Tineke Spruytenburg, who shares her experience below of being asked to teach it to colleagues who it turned out had to be there, we may get walkouts and even risk totally putting people off who are not yet ready—and may indeed never be.

When bringing mindfulness to schools, my colleague and I only work with people that show an interest in mindfulness practices. Once we were asked to give an introductory workshop for a whole team. Most of the twenty-five workers had chosen this possibility, yet some of them showed resistance. They had to cooperate because participation was obligatory.

We offered them basic practices such as walking meditation, sitting meditation, and eating meditation and refrained from using any spiritual-sounding explanations or ritual. We asked the participants to reflect on what was happening inside when practicing, and there were enough people responding.

The resistance of the minority of teachers that did not have an interest in the workshop was felt during the coffee break. Some six or seven people left the room, taking their cellphones along. They did not return when time was over, and the whole group had to wait more than fifteen minutes to restart the workshop. We learned from this experience and try to prevent school managers from imposing mindfulness practices on their colleagues. Mindfulness can only be practiced when the mind and the heart are open to the experiences.

Where teachers are really suffering, being with them on a one-to-one basis can often be more helpful than a group, as retreat leader Valerie Brown found in her work with stressed school leaders.

Outstanding school leadership rests on focus, clarity, creativity, compassion, and connectedness—bringing yourself to your work and to life, being fully present. However, stress, fractured attention, and crazy-busy overwhelm steadily erode your capacity to lead. Sonia's crazy busy schedule left her with chronic panic attacks, which she managed with medication. At school, she found herself unable to focus and to concentrate. Her attention was constantly being rerouted by "one emergency after another." I began work-ing with Sonia to develop mindfulness practices. We began very slowly and simply with mini pause moments of fifteen to thirty seconds several times each day, to breathe and to feel her feet on the floor. Sonia also began taking mini mindfulness moments of two to three minutes daily by walking outside the school building every day to look up at the sky and to breathe. Slowly, these and other practices helped Sonia to put herself first, to take good care of herself. She began feeling greater acceptance of herself and greater ease with school colleagues. Her ability to focus improved as she became clearer in setting boundaries.

Seize the Day

We may want to take advantage of any inspirational events that happen in our locality. It can sometimes have the effect of validating our own efforts if, like Alison Mayo, we invite an external teacher or expert to visit our school to offer an introduction or practice session.

> We are very fortunate to have had visits from the Plum Village community, which have involved Days of Mindfulness for staff, parents, and the wider community, and there is now a sangha group that meets regularly at the school.

We may find that a local mindfulness retreat catalyzes enthusiasm on which we can build.

> After a local retreat, two members of our teachers' sangha arrived with loads of ideas about what they wanted to do in their shared classroom. They introduced the practices to their students bit by bit. The fifth graders were so happy to practice that they turned their end-of-the-year recital into a morning of mindfulness for themselves and their families. The students led everyone through a guided meditation, walking meditation, relaxation, reading, and a mindful snack. Students, parents, and teachers were all so happy to dedicate this special time of year to their mutual well-being.
> **—ROSA MARINA DE VECCHI, SOCIAL WORKER, ITALY**

> We offered two retreats for teachers, one in Delhi for three days at Sanskriti School, New Delhi, and another in Dehradun for four days at The Doon School. A number of teachers and school principals asked us to come and lead retreats in their school for all their teachers to attend. Many expressed a strong desire for more regular training in mindfulness and on a larger scale. They asked for repeat workshops in each of the sixteen blocks around Dehradun. There was a lot of interest and feedback across the board, and the press was also very supportive with their reports. **—SHANTUM SETH, TEACHER, PILGRIMAGE LEADER, AND CULTURAL INTERPRETER, INDIA**

Building a Teachers' Mindfulness Group

Thich Nhat Hanh is a strong advocate for surrounding ourselves with a supportive group, or sangha. Over time we may find, like Christiane Terrier, that we can build a mindfulness group in our school or university, and that such benevolent places bring a great deal of joy.

> The team consists of adults who decided to meet regularly as a sangha, once a month, to share, and to practice together. Group practice is essential to keep relationships alive. These meetings were privileged moments, during which teachers can share about the quality moments they experienced in class, as well as their professional difficulties. This allowed us to break out of our loneliness, to support each other, and to work together to find creative solutions. Such a benevolent place of exchange and deep listening is precious and rare. My colleagues soon discovered that this profound listening already relieved much suffering. Many times at the quarter's end, for example, they got really exhausted and discouraged, but they'd leave our meetings full of energy. "It's helped me an awful lot," "It left me wanting more," "I leave feeling relaxed," they say. These benevolent spaces, where there is trust, loving speech, and solidarity, hardly ever exist in schools. Yet they offer a reassuring framework that is truly indispensable. My colleagues testify, like me, to becoming happy teachers and having better relationships with their students, who in turn are happier, which promotes learning.

Kenley Neufeld, working at a community college in the United States, started his efforts to build community with a weekly staff meditation group. Ten years later his group has grown, and he has been invited to speak on "mindfulness in the workplace" across the college.

> During the last decade of work as an educator at a public community college in the United States, I have had many opportunities to bring mindfulness practice to students, staff, administration, and faculty. The interest and opportunity arose from the establishment of a weekly meditation

group that met in the campus library. This meditation group provided the space for thirty minutes of silent sitting once a week—no readings, no form, nothing to believe. Once a semester I would send a campus-wide email that introduced the meditation group and invited any and all who are interested to join. That, and a few posters around campus, was all we did to create this meditation group, very simple and concrete. Over a decade later, the group still meets.

From this meditation group, awareness of my meditation practice grew, and I was subsequently invited to speak to classes, departments, and managers. The department and manager presentations focused on how to practice meditation in the work environment and why it might be important and beneficial to our campus culture. The presentation is simple, with a focus on breath awareness and examples to create conditions of mindfulness in the work setting, whether in your classroom or in your office.

A group of teachers—Dunia Aparicio, Karina Grau, Carme Morist, Toni Pujades, Montserrat Ramírez Sáez, Rosa Rodrigo—from a middle-high school in Spain share a practical experience of a weekly mindfulness breakfast meeting, with coffee, a short practice, and sharing. First we hear from the teacher who organizes it and prepares both the space and her own mind and body to be ready to take part.

For me, Wednesday is very special; it is the day when teachers meet for mindful breakfast and meditate for a short time; a moment to feel the bonds that link us. In the morning, before classes start, I go to our little practice room; I put a thermos of coffee on a little table. Then with all my full attention, enthusiasm, and appreciation, I prepare the place: I place the rugs, cushions, and some chairs in a circle around a focal point. I extend a pretty fabric placing a reproduction of one of Thay's calligraphies and a picture of the participants of the Wake Up Schools course on each side of it. Slowly, I add some elements of nature: pebbles, shells, leaves, and a candle in the center. It is my mindful practice before the start of classes. Then, I dedicate another five minutes more to strengthen my presence, paying attention to my breathing and visualizing students who will attend that day. I wish them, my teammates and myself, a happy day.

Her colleagues also speak positively about the sense of grounding, calm, and comradeship they derive from this little oasis at the start of the day.

> On Wednesdays I wake up in a different mood, with a kind of special joy; the first thing I do is remind my teammates that we have an appointment for mindful breakfast. When it's time, I walk to the mindfulness room we have in our institute, and I feel thankful for dedicating this time for myself, nourishing myself, and giving my best to my students. When I enter this room I can feel the love with which my friend has prepared the place. I sit and I connect with my breathing, other colleagues walk in, and we silently nourish each other.
>
> I am now a frequent participant in our Wednesday gatherings. It's a moment to stop, coming back to ourselves, to reconstruct our inner being on a day that I have many classes. It is also a moment for feeling the silent links we share with those from different approaches. It's a moment I really love.
>
> After these meetings, our classes have a different quality. They are nourished by our conscious dedication and our refreshed energy.

reaching out to students' families

Parents and families are at the heart of the Plum Village tradition. Families routinely come together on retreat to experience joy, fun, healing, and renewed communication. Thich Nhat Hanh takes great care to frequently mention parents and family in his speech and writings. He reflects on the need to use our practice of mindfulness in the present to repair and heal the communication and relationship problems that crop up so often in families. At retreats he often advises participants to phone home that very evening to reconcile and begin anew with anyone with whom they have a difficulty or estrangement. Many successfully do, and here, from a 2013 Educators

We will also be using the term *parents* in this section as shorthand, but we are fully aware that families and parents come in all shapes and sizes, and that our students come from many backgrounds and are cared for by many people. So we are including in this term the many adoptive parents, stepparents, foster parents, surrogate parents, and blended families who care for our students. We also recognize the informal caring relationships—the relatives, siblings, and friends who often parent our students, temporarily or permanently. Our attitudes and practices include all of these arrangements, with compassion and without judgment or discrimination.

Retreat talk, is his sharing of a story, which may seem extraordinary but which is quite common at his retreats:

> The miracle of reconciliation always takes place in our retreats, whether in Asia, North America, Europe, or anywhere. When you come to a retreat, you practice releasing your tension, touching the wonders of life, handling strong emotions, and looking at the suffering inside in order to understand the suffering outside. Then, on the fifth or sixth day, practitioners are asked to apply the practice to reconcile with another person. On the fifth day, we say, "Ladies and gentlemen, you have until midnight tonight to practice. If the other person is not there, you can use your telephone."
>
> I remember that in a retreat in northern Germany, four German gentlemen came to me and reported that the night before they had used the telephone and had been able to reconcile with their fathers. One of them said, "Dear Thay, I couldn't believe that I could talk to my father like that. I was so angry with him. I would never think that I could speak to him gently like that. But last night, I did! I had a little doubt when I dialed the number. But when I heard his voice, I suddenly and naturally spoke very gently to him." His father didn't know that the good seeds in him had been watered during the first five days of the retreat, and that he had been able to see his father's suffering by getting in touch with his own suffering, which is why, when he heard the voice of his father, he was naturally able to use loving speech. All four of these gentlemen had been able to reconcile with their fathers in just one or two hours—something they'd been unable to do for many years. It's a miracle. And all of us can perform that miracle, if we master the techniques of deep listening and loving speech.[3]

Michael Schwammberger, whose wise experiences as a retreat leader we've shared many times here, reflects on how much the families he meets need help, how rarely they experience support and understanding, but how much they gain from it when they do.

> I supported for many years a family retreat in the United Kingdom because I felt that that was so essential. I notice that families need so much support, and it seems that not enough people understand that. But when you are in

a five-day retreat you see the reality of the parent's needs and the children's needs, and also their potential for healing. You just know you have to create that space. The most beautiful practice I experience with the family is the "Beginning Anew" practice. I am so amazed by the simple practice of just watering the flowers and sometimes expressing regrets. It is so powerful. It is something they never do without this kind of held space. They don't have the opportunity to do it.

Bea Harley outlines the connected relationship between school and home that mindfulness helped to cultivate at the small elementary school in which she worked. It is an inspirational model.

In my experience it is often through the changes parents see in their children that leads them to want to know more about the practice of mindfulness. Once a week the whole school community comes together, and this is an opportunity for us to not only celebrate the children and their work, but also to sing, chant, and breathe together and to share stories that underpin the qualities of compassion, wisdom, and kindness.

Involving parents from the onset and having their support and understanding is vital. Over the years we have offered parenting courses and after-school meditation classes, and since the monastic visit, a Conscious Parenting group was set up which meets at the school once a month. At other times parents support each other via social media.

Bea is fortunate to have worked in a small independent school shaped by the principles of mindfulness. We are a long way from this vision of a mindful partnership between home and the school in many of the communities in which we teach. What steady steps might we take to get there?

Relating to Family Members Mindfully in Everyday Interactions

The starting point for reaching out with mindfulness to families is to ensure, when a routine opportunity to connect occurs, that parents and other family members experience us as walking the talk—kindly, compassionate, empathic, and embodying deep listening and loving speech.

Staying mindful and compassionate may be relatively easy when a parent is calm and friendly, but often the most significant encounters are at the sharp end, when parents are complaining, upset, or angry. As every teacher knows, the parents we most want to connect with are usually those we see least, often because their own negative experience of education has left them frightened of educational establishments, so they tend to avoid contact. When they do come, they often arrive at the school or university in a tense and defensive state. Our mindfulness can help us remain solid and stable so we can seize such golden opportunities to listen, soothe, and heal the relationship, realizing, with compassion, that the parents themselves are actually suffering.

Bea reminds us how important listening is in our dealings with parents, helping us avoid defensiveness when faced with a parent who is expressing difficulty. She sees that mindfulness practice can allow us to be more open and compassionate and lead to healthier communication.

> For me the practice of deep listening has always been a humbling experience. At times it can be challenging to face a concerned or anxious parent and not to feel defensive, particularly if the concern is around some aspect of our own teaching practice or management. To put judgment aside and to deeply listen can bring with it the opportunity to truly connect with another human being. At times the realization that some of these concerns may come from the individual's own pain or past experience can enable us to be more compassionate and loving in our communication and actions.

Through her own conscious breathing, Murielle Dionnet manages to listen mindfully to a parent she was finding very difficult.

> I had to manage very difficult relationships in my professional life. There was a student's mom who was ill and had very paranoid tendencies. Sometimes it was very hard to listen to her. So from time to time I would focus on my breath, practice mindful breathing, and then listen to her again. While I listened, I practiced conscious breathing. I could accept things as they were, and that she was doing her best. So, my breathing allowed me to stay connected with her while taking care of myself. This strategy was important for

the good of her son. A colleague told me "oh, yeah, you're just pretending," but no, I really listened, I listened to who she was.

Judith Toy, a mindfulness mentor in the United States, has developed a program to strengthen skills for families who live in challenging circumstances marred by poverty, intergenerational violence, and injustice. She finds her own mindfulness practice is vital to keep her empathetic and steady for both a parent and a child with whom she is working.

Mindfulness helped me put myself in [the child] Dee's shoes. What would it feel like to have no father, to lose your mother, to be abused by your grandmother? Through mindfulness, I could model a calm and patient authority for her newly sober mother.[4]

We may even be called on to use our mindfulness to help expedite communication between our students and their parents.

When students have a problem in their studies and don't know how to talk to parents, they sometimes invite their parents to my office. I listen to both sides and assist them through Beginning Anew. —MORRAKOT "CHOMPOO" RAWEEWAN, UNIVERSITY PROFESSOR, THAILAND

Students Take Mindfulness Practice Home

In our efforts to reach out to families and homes, our students are the chief emissaries. One of the most satisfying steps along the path to becoming a more mindful school is when children and families report that mindfulness has made its way home and is supporting family communication, positively affecting life. The following are some accounts of the kind of impacts parents routinely witness and learn from; they are often stories of reparation and healing.

Parents often have stories of how their children have brought this technique home. For example, one student was arguing with his sisters about a toy and it was getting quite heated when he said "I think we all need to take a breath." Another parent confided that when she and her husband were arguing, her daughter came in and told her parents they needed to take a breath. —**CHRISTINE PETACCIA, OCCUPATIONAL THERAPIST, UNITED STATES**

I saw the fruits of the practice come alive one day when, during our weekly check-in, a teenager shared this story: "I came home one day from school, and I was really stressed and pissed off. Then, my dad told me to do something that pissed me off even more. But instead of yelling at him, I just breathed, and then I went to my room to do some meditation. My dad saw me do that, and followed me in, and sat down beside me and meditated with me. By the time we were done, we both felt better, and then we ended up having a great evening together." —**DZUNG X. VO, PEDIATRICIAN, CANADA**

A parent called me on the phone. She described to me how she supported her son, who was competing on a national youth fencing team by driving him three hours several times a week to practice. During the long commute, her son was usually fixated on his digital devices. During the drive that day her son had surprised her when he stopped and turned off his iPhone and iPad. She was delighted when he suggested to her that they simply spend time together in the moment, mindfully enjoying the scenery, clouds, and sky. —**BETSY BLAKE ARIZU, RETIRED HIGH SCHOOL TEACHER AND COUNSELOR, UNITED STATES**

Young people have a powerful role to play in teaching all of us adults, including parents, how to practice, if we are humble enough to realize it. Annie Mahon, a US mindfulness teacher, recounts an amusing and touching story of discovering that, although she imagined herself a committed mindfulness practitioner in the middle of a retreat, it took her nine-year-old son to teach her about truly savoring mindful eating—with loud pleasurable relish—instead of her usual approach, which was to look "very serious" while eating.

I learned what it meant to be in touch with my food from my nine-year-old son, Louie. Well, actually he only reminded me. . . . I was on a meditation retreat with my four young children, enjoying a silent lunch in a huge cafeteria. As I sat there struggling to eat mindfully, setting my fork down between bites, and looking very serious, the silence in the hall was suddenly broken. From across the room came the very loud moaning of my son, Louie, enjoying a piece of blueberry pie, "Mmm. Mmm. Mmm!" Louie was completely immersed in eating his pie, oblivious to six hundred pairs of eyes—some looking with annoyance, some rolling their eyes, some smiling, and many looking like they wished they could enjoy their food with as much intensity and pleasure as Louie was. . . . Watching Louie eat with such natural mindfulness and joy inspired me and gave me hope that I might one day rediscover that feeling for myself. Since then, I have a new mantra: I vow to consume my food with the joy of a nine-year-old boy eating a piece of blueberry pie.

Teaching Mindfulness to Parents and Families

Once a warm relationship between the school and the home is established, and when the bridge of mindfulness between home and school or university is being routinely crossed by our students, we may find we have an opportunity to share mindfulness with parents and families more directly.

An easy starting point is involving families in mindful activities, such as mindful picnics. As we learned in chapter six, US teacher Chelsea True shares a period of mindful eating in class as well as in an after-school program, which she encourages families to join. We can also offer mindfulness training to parents and children together. This is probably best done with younger children—teens are not usually great fans of learning directly alongside their parents. Tineke describes how parents and children regularly participate in days of mindfulness to experience total relaxation and be free of stress.

We invite parents and children to lie down in pairs (father and child, mother and child) or trios, so they can feel each other's presence. Younger children often like to lie on the belly of a parent.

Staff guide them through the children's version of total relaxation, using the big bell. There may be a little movement here or there during the practice, and we invite parents to move with the child, not going against it.

One of the mothers recorded her own voice reading through the text of a relaxation on her cell phone, and this helped her son go to sleep more smoothly. The boy explained how his body and mind get more and more relaxed while listening to his mom's voice and how he hardly ever gets to the end before falling asleep.

Richard Brady describes in some detail the process of developing mindful workshops for the parents at Sidwell Friends School in Washington, DC. After he taught mindfulness for stress reduction to the ninth graders for several years, he saw the potential for mutual support if school parents also had an opportunity to experience mindfulness practice. For several years he offered a stress reduction workshop for parents similar to the one he gave the students, but the turnout was disappointing. Were parents too busy, or did they feel uncomfortable revealing their need for help? Perhaps they would come if the focus was on how they could better support their children. This was the genesis of the much more successful workshop described below.

Workshops for Parents: The Joy of Mindful Parenting

Presence is the key ingredient of mindful parenting, being fully present both to oneself and one's children. In this workshop participants will engage in contemplative exercises that enhance awareness of one's thoughts and feelings, sharpen sensory awareness, and promote mindful speech and deep listening. These skills are important building blocks of rewarding relationships with children and adults as well.

My parents' workshops evolved, with opportunities to present them to other schools. We focused on communication and practicing with negative emotions. The starting point was to become present with nonjudgmental awareness to whatever was happening in the present moment. To do so, we took four minutes with closed eyes to simply notice whatever was passing through our awareness, whether it came in through our senses, was a body sensation, a thought, or an emotion. We then turned the focus of our mindfulness to another person. We all know that being fully present to our children, listening to them with all our attention, is a wonderful gift we can give them. I described deep listening, or "listening like a cow," as Mary Rose O'Reilley describes it, as giving 100 percent of our attention to the person speaking, not asking questions, not reacting, not comparing what we hear with our own views, not thinking. Parents paired up with someone they didn't know, read three inspirational quotes, contemplated one that particularly spoke to them, and then took three minutes each to share with and listen deeply to their partners.

I would conclude each workshop by talking about the difficult emotions that come up in response to our children's behavior. These emotions are entirely natural; it's not wrong to have them. It's what parents do in response to them that's important. In order to handle them in a healthy way, they must be aware of their presence and not act from them unconsciously. This goes back to the opening exercise of becoming aware of what is happening inside us as well as outside us in the present moment. We can see our emotions as a suffering part of us that needs our attention, much like a crying infant. At this point we might be able to redirect our attention from our child to our emotion, and embrace it with mindfulness. *Breathing in, I'm aware of my anger*—or whatever. *Breathing out, I cradle it with love.* I asked the parents to recall a recent experience of very minor suffering (such as an unkind word said to them or which they said to someone else) and practice in this manner with the emotion they felt.

I closed by inviting the parents to do these practices regularly so that they became more available for the parents to call on, especially in challenging times with their kids.

The need to start where people are, rather than where our own preconceptions say they "ought" to be, is foundational to sharing mindfulness with others.

a whole-school, comprehensive approach

In the preface, we looked at the increasing recognition of the importance of taking a school or university-wide comprehensive or "whole-school" approach to the kind of issues that work best when integrated at the level of the total organization. This is a concept that is becoming familiar within education, as research increasingly demonstrates how effective the synergy this creates can be when carried out with coherence and clarity.

The quotation from psychologist Chris Willard below captures some of what a comprehensive whole-school approach might look like when applied to mindfulness.

> We are planting seeds in a child to blossom in the community, and we must tend our entire garden. If you are a parent, practice as a family, and recommend a mindfulness curriculum at school or in your place of worship. If they don't have one, volunteer to come in and lead a meditation. Be a part of creating a mindful school community where teachers and students can all reinforce contemplative practice in each other. Advocate for the physical education teacher to incorporate yoga and tai chi into their lessons. If you are a therapist or doctor, teach the whole family you work with to practice together—the research shows that kids thrive in school when parents are involved, and the same holds true for medicine and psychotherapy. The more places that a child is reminded of mindful awareness, the more places the seeds you planted will be nurtured and can thrive.[5]

Moving Toward a Whole-School Approach: Four Examples

Mindfulness is now being taught in classrooms in schools and universities in some parts of the world. The vision of a more comprehensive approach to mindfulness, one that works at many levels, right across the school, and aims ultimately to create a mindful school, is also starting to have some reality, including in relation to the Plum Village approach. Here we share four inspirational examples.

Creating a Culture

Carmelo Blazquez Jimenezae, an educator from Spain, describes the profound impact on the atmosphere in a whole school team when everyone practiced deep listening and loving speech. The effect was even discernible to the visiting regional director of his program.

> Not long ago my boss, the regional director for Aldeas Infantiles SOS Cataluña, visited us and told me: "Every time I see the Barlovento program youngsters, I see them joyful and happy, and that is somehow the merit of your team and the good relationship you seem to have with one another." As a matter of fact, our educators' team in the program has been working

together for nine years; it's the most stable team, with the least turnover in the whole Aldeas Infantiles SOS Cataluña organization. The level of conflict in the daily coexistence among the youngsters, as well as with the educators, has diminished drastically. They understand each other much better, and take care of each other more lovingly.

From a Teachers' Group to a Taught Curriculum

Miles Dunmore, a teacher of English literature and experienced retreat facilitator in the United Kingdom, describes how he and his colleagues proceeded to set up a small teachers' group that grew slowly over many years and has now become a catalyst for curriculum-based programs with students at their international high school. He also reflects on the whole-school changes he hopes to make next.

In our experience, there are often like-minded or interested colleagues who are open to practice. Sometimes these are people we never suspected of such an interest.

At my school in London, following a retreat with Thay and the Plum Village community in 2012, several of us began sitting together for fifteen minutes once a week on Monday before school started. After a few months, we added a Friday afternoon meeting for thirty minutes. We would invite other colleagues to these sessions as a taster. People came, and often these meetings ran longer than the scheduled time.

As interest grew, we were able to begin sitting daily before school, at first in a quiet corner of the library, again for fifteen minutes. While we could not each make it every day, there were always some of us sitting. The benefits were that we felt calmer and more stable as we began the school day, and we could support one another in maintaining a more mindful approach to our teaching. A year on, we moved to a classroom with windows onto an open corridor. More colleagues and students began to see what we were doing. Something was happening. Initiatives began to develop. Students were invited to practice in the class and to make use of a quiet, mindful room at other periods.

As we deepen our practice together and raise awareness in school, we can begin to talk about good ways to introduce mindfulness into our own schools, about how to select and develop programs, where to find resources and training, and how to approach head teachers and curriculum leaders with proposals. Our support for one another means that we can proceed in a thoughtful and measured way, and we are not alone. That makes it easier to introduce mindfulness into school.

A Comprehensive Approach: Two Examples

Lyndsay Lunan reports impressive progress at her college in Glasgow, Scotland, in creating an authentically holistic approach. The work spread from her own teaching of mindfulness to students to training her colleagues, developing a whole-school student program, and involving parents and families. She supports the whole process with an online learning environment, providing mindfulness practices for all to download, including "stressed moms and grannies." She comments on the value of collecting and publishing data as she developed and evaluated these initiatives, which provided credibility with her colleagues.

I began by teaching mindfulness to staff ("staff" in the United Kingdom means all who work in a school) during lunchtimes and at the end of the day. The invaluable thing here was to measure the impact; I took a record of how many staff came and how many remained, and I produced feedback questionnaires that asked them to record any impact the sessions were having on stress and work performance. It was from this data that HR was then able to obtain funding to support a mindfulness for staff program, that I continued to measure, and which has now been running for five years.

In the second year, I asked if I could offer mindfulness to students, on the basis of success with staff, and we began a pilot study with students. Actually one of the main reasons that my program for students won an award was because I'd measured its impact; all the students completed anxiety and well-being scales at the beginning and end of a twelve-week course. The results were strikingly positive and led to enthusiasm to form the student mindfulness program.

For both staff and students, I created online learning environments that included MP3s of each of the guided practices we did together as a group. Staff and students can download these to their phones or iPods and continue their practice beyond the college environment. A number of students have shared these resources with their families and I've learned that stressed moms and grannies have been using the guided practices. And that has actually helped the students in their family lives. After two years of running the staff program, I was able to create a training program to invite staff with an established practice of mindfulness to learn how to share their practice with the young people they teach.

I've begun delivering mindfulness workshops to the Senior Management Team, with the real hope that an experience of this gentle listening presence might inform the way that the ethos of the college is shaped—that we might ultimately work together to become a community that lives and works in mindfulness.

The final example is a fascinating joint account by Gift Tavedikul, the assistant director at the American School of Bangkok (ASB) and Peggy and Larry Rowe Ward, the two mindfulness consultants who supported the school. They write about the considerable progress they have made over fifteen years toward a genuinely comprehensive school approach in which students, staff, and parents are now all involved. The account demonstrates the value of taking a slow and steady long-term perspective, getting some expert help, and involving senior management early on in the process. Here is Gift, speaking from a senior administrator's perspective:

Fifteen years ago, I shared my passion for meditation with my staff members, starting with a circle of four people. Joy and contentment were always present in our little sangha circle. Over ten years of voluntarily holding group practice, the group grew steadily from four to seventy people. Our school administrators started to join the sangha circle one by one until all members were in favor of applying mindfulness school-wide. One of the biggest blessings of my life was meeting Larry Ward and Peggy Rowe Ward in Saraburi, Thailand. Their expertise in dharma teachings, business, psychology, education, and spirituality laid a great foundation for various mindfulness teachings at ASB. Through their recommendation, I attended an Educators Retreat at Plum Village.

It took us fifteen years to lay a healthy foundation of understanding before our program established a strong foothold in our community. Educating our stakeholders about how mindfulness increases brain performance and develops compassion were key in helping us overcome these initial hurdles of resistance. Our school now has 850 students, 120 teachers, and 200 support staff, all of whom have been exposed to mindfulness theories and practices.

Peggy and Larry feel doubly blessed to have the support of the director and the owner of the school.

We offered our first faculty in-service on mindfulness. The focus of this first hour of training was on the neuroscience of mindfulness. We wanted to begin with the research that we have on the impact on the brain and the whole child. At the end of this in-service, more than half of the faculty requested more training. At our next in-service, we divided the faculty into three different groups, and Gift, Larry, and I offered three different mindfulness sessions: mindful movement, mindful breathing, and an additional piece on neuroscience. At the end of this training, almost 80 percent of the faculty requested more training.

We also offered sessions for the parents at both campuses. The session included our five-year plan for integrating mindfulness at ASB, and once again we practiced mindful breathing. We had some wonderful video clips of many different classrooms practicing mindfulness. This session was offered in English, Thai, Japanese, and Korean. We practiced Take Five (see page 14 in chapter one, "The Breath," for this game) with the parents and responded to questions. The parents were on board. We created a curriculum for K to 12 the first year; every grade had five sessions. We had a very happy time.

Peggy has valuable advice on what she feels they have learned about implementing mindfulness across the school.

While every setting is unique, we would like to share some of our insights:

- Start small, be patient, and have a plan. Teachers are famous for being critical and often resistant learners. To begin, we wanted to offer something that didn't take much time or training and that would be hard to fight, namely Take Five. While we heard a few whines, for the most part, we did not upset the culture. We had a five-year plan and we let our administrators know that cultural change takes time, patience, and practice.

- Engage the faculty early on. Teachers like to know what is going on, and they like to educate themselves. Give them a resource list and include them. And no forcing. The first in-services were mandatory. The mindfulness practice sessions, days of mindfulness, and retreats are optional.

- Every organization has the early adopters and the never adopters. Engage the early adopters, the lead birds, as quickly as you can and don't put your energy into the never adopters. The very first in-service we did, we had several teachers come up to us. One even said, "I want to do what you do." These teachers became our first mindfulness specialists.

- The trifecta is to have students, teachers, and parents engaged in cultivating a mindful school. Include all three in your five-year plan.

- Whoever teaches mindfulness has to have a personal practice. The research is very clear on this point, as is our experience. We all have to practice together. This cultivates the ground of the new culture. Our practice humbles us and strengthens us. Together, we are doing our best to wake up, to create a kind, wise, and compassionate culture where people treat each other with respect and dignity.

- Whatever you do, keep practicing and share with your students and faculty what you love. We are so fortunate to have found such a beautiful path.

happy teachers change the world

Richard Brady, a friend and mentor through many chapters in this book, shares a final story that gives us hope. He reminds us that we may be surprised over time by the deep impact of our work on the next generation.

Those of us who share mindfulness with young people often ask ourselves, "At the end of the day, has it made a difference?" We believe it has, but controlled research studies aside, do we really know? Four years ago, at my school's annual holiday alumni reception, I had a memorable conversation with Tom, a former student whom I had seen when he graduated in 1989. Tom shared something of his career path, ending with his current job as a compliance lawyer for the World Bank. When he asked me what I was up to, I handed him my Minding Your Life business card. "Mindfulness education," he read. "That's like the story you read to us about washing the dishes." (He was referring to Thay's story about being present to washing the dishes from *The Miracle of Mindfulness*.) I was surprised Tom remembered the story eighteen years later. It turned out that in the interim he had also read several books on mindfulness.[6]

With patience we see that we can change the world—one student at a time.

We end where we began, with a wise reminder from Thich Nhat Hanh to constantly return to ourselves and our own solid practice as the sure foundation for any change we wish to make.

As teachers, and as human beings, we are eager to help our partner, and other members of our family, to suffer less. We are also eager to help our colleagues in schools and our students, and even their families, to suffer less. We have the tendency to try to do something: "I want to do something to improve the situation." That's what we want.

But according to our practice, we should not be too eager to do something right away. The first thing is to go home to ourselves. When you have enough peace, joy, and compassion, and you suffer less, you can go to your partner—the person who is closest to you—and help him or her to do the same. When you have not changed yourself, it is very difficult to help change the other person. Of course, your partner, your loved one, then has to do the same as you. You help them to go back to themselves to take care of the situation inside. You show them how to release the tension in the body; how to generate a feeling of joy or happiness; how to listen to the suffering inside and understand the suffering inside. After having helped the people in our own family, we have a stronger foundation at home—we become co-practitioners. We share the same values; we share the same spiritual practice. Because we know that each day the situation improves; there's more peace, less suffering, more joy, and more happiness.

With that foundation, we can begin to help the people in our workplace, our colleagues and our students. The principle is very much the same: helping them to go home to themselves and take care. Within the school, first you have your class and you transform your class. Your class becomes a happier place. Your class can become like a family. Finally, with our families, our colleagues, our students, and the whole school behind us, we are stronger. Together we can take the next step and help still more people. The transformation begins to affect even the families of our students and our colleagues, and the ripples spread far and wide. But we always remember, the principle is this: the way out is in.

**THICH NHAT HANH, AUGUST 12, 2013, DHARMA TALK
AT TORONTO EDUCATORS RETREAT, CANADA**

appendix a
summaries of the core practices

These are *aide-mémoires* for the classroom only—not to be used alone and not be distributed. Full versions of the practices are set out in the chapters. Ensure you are fully familiar with them, all the details and teaching notes, before teaching them

1. Getting in Touch with Our Breath

2. Inviting and Listening to the Bell

3. Mindful Sitting

4. Mindful Walking

5. Awareness of the Body and the Breath

6. Ten Mindful Movements

7. Deep Relaxation

8. Mindful Eating (Tangerine Meditation)

9. Using Our Breath to Get in Touch with Our Emotions

10. Tree in a Storm

11. Pebble Meditation

12. Circle Sharing

13. Beginning Anew

getting in touch with our breath

Why?

See the breath as a friend, refuge, there for us right here, right now.

Cultivate concentration and attention.

Anchor body-mind to better manage difficult emotions.

Relax, relieve stress and tension.

Unite body-mind, get in touch with the wonders of life.

More present for feelings, self, and others.

Prep and materials

Teacher familiar with the breath, bell, and sitting practice

Bell and inviter (optional)

Steps

Prepare.

- Comfortable, relaxed, stable sitting position—like a mountain
- Chair, cushion, floor—comfortable
- Bell (optional)

Notice you are breathing.

- Close the eyes or soften the gaze.
- Become directly aware of the breath.
- Nothing to change.

Follow the breath.

- Focus on physical sensations.
- Follow whole length of the in-breath/out-breath.
- Feel air passing through nose, mouth, throat, lungs.
- When mind wanders, bring it back to the breath.

Breath in the belly (optional)

- Hands on belly, aware of rising and falling.
- Notice length of the breath, transition between in- and out-breath.

End

- Bell (optional)
- Three breaths
- Gently open the eyes (if closed).

Reflection questions

- How do I feel right now—mind, breath, body?
- What happened? How did it feel? Did anything change?
- How easy is it to focus on the breath? Did my mind wander?

Variations

- Practice lying down or standing. How does it feel?
- Finger breathing—run the index finger of one hand up and down thumb and fingers of the other hand in time with in- and out-breath.
- Place the finger under the nose, feel the current of air, changes in temperature, etc.
- Where in the body do you feel the breath right now?
- Aware of length of in- and out-breath—notice any lengthening.
- Combine breath with a smile.
- Gently count breaths, 1 to 10, then start again. Notice if the mind wanders.
- Fun practice: observe the impact of breath on different objects: e.g., feathers, paper, ice, balloons, etc.
- Recite the guiding words in the sidebar.

Teaching notes

No need to change, force, or control anything; simply be aware, observe.

Guiding words

Breathing in, I know
that I am breathing in.

Breathing out, I know
that I am breathing out.

Breathing in, I am calm.

Breathing out, I smile.

inviting and listening to the bell

Why?

Create and enjoy a mindful moment.

Stop and become aware of breath and feelings.

Calm and relax body and mind.

Improve the classroom atmosphere—more happiness, peace, relaxation, concentration.

Connect with oneself and others.

Prep and materials

Bell (chosen for context) and inviter (stick)

Teacher well-practiced in inviting and listening

Verse for listening to the bell

Listen, listen (on the in-breath)

This wonderful sound brings me back to my true home. (on the out-breath)

Invite the bell—clean, full, clear sound.

Steps

Prepare the group and explain.

- Become settled and focused, sit straight and relaxed.
- Explain practice below (briefly).

Wake-up bell half sound—indicates full sound is coming.

- Hold the bell in the palm at eye level, or on the joined tips of the fingers.
- Two breaths
- Bring the inviter gently in contact with the bell, leave it there for dampened sound.

Optional: silently recite the verses on the facing page before inviting the half sound.

Full sound.

- Mindfully breathe in and out once.
- Recite (silently or out loud) the verse on listening to the bell (optional).

Listen to the full sound.

- Focus fully on in- and out-breath; allow sound to penetrate deeply.
- Breathe mindfully three times to calm mind and body.
- Listen or recite silently with each breath the verse in the sidebar on listening (optional).

Reflection questions

· How do I feel right now—mind, body, and breath?

· What happened for me?

· Am I able to touch my center? Am I calm and grounded? Am I irritated, anxious, distracted?

· Am I able to return to the bell or breath when thinking arises?

· Is it easy or difficult to stay focused on the sound?

Variations

· Notice thoughts arising—gently let go.

· Smile.

· Allow the sound to penetrate every cell of the body.

· Use the sound to get in touch with the center, the island within.

· Count breaths with the bell.

· Students walk around—stop and breathe when they hear the bell.

Teaching notes

Invite the bell with care, aware of your attitude: relaxed smile, concentrated.

Treat the bell with care; encourage students to do so.

Do not use it as a disciplinary tool.

Keep the practice authentic and fresh, don't overdo it.

Verses for inviting the bell

Body, speech, and mind in perfect oneness

I send my heart along with the sound of this bell.

May the hearers awaken from forgetfulness

And transcend the path of anxiety and sorrow.

mindful sitting

Why?

Strengthen ability to settle, calm, and relax mind and body.

Bring the mind back to the body.

Practice to cultivate an awareness of being alive.

Build our awareness of thoughts, feelings, and body.

Increase a sense of connection to others.

Prep and materials

Teacher experienced in sitting meditation

Chairs, cushions, mats (something to sit on)

Bell and inviter (optional)

Steps

Finding a sitting position

- Find a comfortable sitting position, calm and at ease.
- Sit up straight, but relaxed—stable and solid like a mountain.
- Head sits comfortably on the spine, tuck the chin slightly.
- Feel free to sit on a chair, cushion, mat, floor, etc.
- Shut your eyes or rest them softly in front of you.
- Relax the face and jaw.

Contact

- If in a chair, get a sense of the contact your feet make with the floor.
- If on a cushion or mat, establish three points of contact with the floor (bottom and both knees). Support your knees with cushions if they don't touch the floor.
- Rest the body, sense the support beneath you.

Sitting

- One sound of the bell to start the practice
- Become aware of your in-breath and out-breath.
- Breathing in, breath becomes deep; breathing out, breath becomes slow.
- Breathing in, calm; breathing out, at ease.
- Breathing in, smile; breathing out, release.
- Breathing in, present moment; breathing out, wonderful moment.

End

- Three breaths; come back to awareness of contact with the floor, cushion, or chair.
- Invite one sound of the bell to end.
- Gently stretch, open your eyes, smile, and breathe.

Reflection questions

- How do I feel now in my body, mind, and breath?
- How did sitting practice feel? Were there changes throughout the practice?
- Where was my mind today? Stressed, calm, distracted?
- Where was my body? Did I sit still with ease? Did I move mindfully if I had to move position?
- When my mind wandered, was I able to bring it back to the present moment?

Variations

- Sit for a longer period of time.
- Further images for solid sitting position: (1) Tree in a storm (2) Rock in fast flowing river
- Further images for letting go of thoughts and feelings: (1) Traffic passing while on side of the road—"thought buses" coming and going (2) River flowing while watching from the bank (3) Characters coming and going across a stage or a film.
- Become aware of sounds. Observe pitches, volumes, rhythm, etc.
- End practice with a final reflection.

Teaching notes

In silence (except for guidance) to support concentration

Find an upright yet relaxed sitting position.

Feel stillness and the contact with the earth.

Be aware of your breath without attempting to change it.

Gently help students adjust their posture (optional).

....

mindful walking

Why?

Bring the mind back to the body in the present moment.

Enjoy slowing down, not rushing.

Cultivate awareness of the body through movement.

Awareness of the link between breath, feelings, and movement.

Cultivate attention and calm, relieve stress and anxiety, let go of thinking.

Come back to oneself and become aware of the wonders of life.

Teacher prep and materials

Teacher familiar with mindful walking

Choose place for intended path. First time: a small circle.

Rehearse instructions.

Bell and inviter (optional)

Steps

Prepare the group and explain (keep brief).

- Singing to gather the collective energy (optional).
- Demonstrate how to walk, aware of breath and steps.
- Bring the mind back to the breath and steps when lost in thinking. (Use verses on the facing page.)
- Let them know if they will follow you or walk slowly in a circle.
- Remind them to enjoy every moment.

Standing mindfully

- Bell: awareness of breath, body, and the present moment.
- Aware of contact of the feet with the floor or the earth. Aware of standing upright. Ground the body and mind.

Walking

- Begin, walking with ease and freedom.
- Aware of the feeling of touching ground with the soles of the feet.
- One step at a time, arriving fully with each step.
- When thoughts arise, notice, gently bring the mind back to step and breath.
- Coordinate breath and step (e.g., two for in-breath, three for out-breath).

Pause or End.

- Stand mindfully, aware of your breath and body.
- Bell (optional).
- Notice how stillness feels. Notice the intention to move.

Reflection questions

- Where is my mind, body, breath right now?
- What did I notice—in self, feelings, body, breath, surroundings?
- Was it different from normal walking? How?
- Easy, difficult, fun, boring, calming, challenging?
- How was the silence? How was walking with others?
- Mind wandering? Able to bring it back?

Variations

- Short straight line up and down, pausing before the turn.
- Recite mindful walking verses above, coordinating with the breath.
- Move awareness throughout the body; observe the feeling walking creates.
- Change speed—slower or faster. Notice impact on the mind and body.
- Walking as or with different moods, characters, animals, etc.; e.g., walking on a sandy beach, as an elephant. Observe how each impacts on walking, body, mind.
- Longer group walk, teacher leading, pauses for observation, poems.

Teaching notes

We walk in silence for concentration.

Aware of the breath and steps

Gently guide the wandering mind back to the present moment.

Notice the connection between breath and steps—no need to force one to match the other.

Keep a natural and relaxed rhythm.

Stay together as one collective, moving together.

Relax and enjoy the sounds, sights, smells.

Verses for mindful walking

I have arrived / I am home
In the here / In the now
I am solid / I am free
In the ultimate I dwell

awareness of the body and the breath

Why?

Mind-body connection

Focus and pay attention to here and now in breath, body, and mind.

Breath as a bridge between body and mind

Learn to handle difficult feelings and emotions.

Decrease stress; increase calm, relaxation, and happiness.

Prep and materials

Teacher experienced in the practice

Students and teacher experienced in bell, breath, and sitting

Chairs or mats

Bell and inviter (optional)

Teaching notes

Stopping allows us to release and relax our body.

Allow the whole body to become the object of our mindfulness.

Touch the quality of being alive, of everything inside and around us.

Steps

Start

• Lying down or sitting comfortably

• Settled, grounded, stable, aware of contact points

• Bell

Awareness of breathing and following the breath

Read the following aloud slowly, encouraging students to tune their in- and out-breaths to the rhythm of the words.:

Breathing in, I know that I am breathing in;
Breathing out, I know that I am breathing out.
Breathing in, I follow my in-breath from the beginning to end;
Breathing out, I follow my out-breath from beginning to end.

Aware of body

Breathing in, I am aware that I have a body;
Breathing out, I know my body is there.
Breathing in, I am aware of my whole body;
Breathing out, I smile to my whole body.

Calming and releasing tension

Breathing in, I am aware of my body;
Breathing out, I calm my body.
Breathing in, I relax my body;
Breathing out, I release any tension in my body.

End

• Bell

Reflection

• How do I feel right now?

• Was it easy or difficult?

• How much did my mind wander? Was I able to bring it back to my body?

• Any specific parts of my body that held a lot of tension?

summary of the practice
....

ten mindful movements

Steps

Start

- Explain—slow, easy, relaxed, no straining.
- Make sure everyone has enough distance between them and others.
- Stand with feet firmly on ground, shoulder width apart.
- Knees soft, shoulders loose, body upright and relaxed.
- Aware of in-breath and out-breath (optional: hands on belly).
- Aware of contact of feet with the earth.
- Coordinate the breathing with each movement.

Movements

1. Arm Raises

- Start with back straight, arms at sides, aware of the breath.
- Breathing in, slowly raise your arms straight out in front to shoulder level.
- Breathing out, lower your arms to your sides.
- Repeat two to three times.

2. Stretching the arms, touch the sky

- Start with back straight, arms at sides, aware of the breath.
- Breathing in, raise your arms to reach toward the sky.
- Breathing out, lower your arms to your sides.
- Repeat two to three times.

3. Opening the arms, arms unfolding (flower blooming)

- Start with fingers touching shoulders, elbows pointed out to the side.
- Breathing in, open your arms out to each side, palms up.
- Breathing out, fold your arms in to touch your shoulders again.
- Repeat two to three times.

Why?

Mind-body connection

Cultivate awareness, focus, and attention here and now through movement.

Decrease stress and anxiety.

Increase calm, relaxation, and happiness.

Prep and materials needed

Teacher practiced in mindful movements

Enough room to stretch arms and circle legs (if not possible, adapt)

Teaching notes

Aim is awareness, balance, flexibility—not strenuous exercise.

Adapt to age, mood, space and (dis) abilities of group.

ten mindful movements *continued*

4. Circling the arms

- Start with palms joined in front, arms straight and down.
- Breathing in, raise your arms in a circle up above your head.
- Breathing out, circle your arms behind you, down and back, forward together in front.
- Repeat two to three times, then reverse direction.

5. Circling at the waist

- Start, hands on hips, legs straight but not locked, bend forward at the waist.
- Breathing in, circle the upper body to the left and back.
- Breathing out, complete the circle to the front.
- Repeat two to three times, then reverse direction.

6. Stretching the body

- Start: bend at the waist to touch the ground; relax the neck.
- Breathing in, come up and reach your arms toward the sky.
- Breathing out, bend down at waist to touch the earth.
- Repeat two to three times.

7. Squats (like a frog!)

- Start with hands on hips, heels together, feet in a V.
- Breathing in, rise up, on the toes, heels still together.
- Breathing out, stay on the toes, and bend the knees to come down, back straight.
- Repeat two to three times.

8. Stretching the legs

To help with the next two balancing movements:

Focus your gaze on a spot on the floor about three feet away, or

Use one hand on the wall or chair back for support.

- Start with hands on hips and shift your weight to the left foot.
- Breathing in, lift your right thigh, bend the knee, toes pointed to the ground.
- Breathing out, stretch your right leg out in front, toes pointed forward.
- Breathing in, bend your knee back toward your body, toes pointed to the ground.
- Breathing out, lower your right foot back down to the ground.
- Repeat two to three times, then change legs and repeat.

9. Circling the Legs

- Start with hands on hips and shift your weight to the left foot.
- Breathing in, lift your right leg, point it straight out in front, and circle to the side.
- Breathing out, circle your foot around behind your body, back in, and forward.
- Breathing in and out, circle your foot back the other way, to return to the starting position.
- Make two or three more circles with the right leg, then change legs and repeat.

10. Side Lunge with Arm Stretch

- Start with right foot stepping to the side, turn out 90 degrees, left hand on hips.
- Breathing in, bend your right knee, bringing your weight over the right foot, while stretching your right hand out and up to your left. Look up at your raised hand.
- Breathing out, straighten the knee, lower your right hand back down to your side.
- Repeat two to three times, then change legs and repeat.

End

- Standing still, feet parallel, shoulder width apart.
- Bell and breathe three times.
- Allow your body to relax (optional: hands on belly).
- Thank everyone with a quiet smile or a bow.

Reflection questions

- How do I feel right now?
- How easy or difficult did I find it?
- How much did my mind wander? If I noticed it wander, was I able to bring it back to my body?
- Did I notice any specific parts of my body that held a lot of tension?

Variations

- Bring mindfulness to stretches you already do (yoga, exercise warm-ups), mindful with full awareness and breath.
- Students create their own alternate set.

....

deep relaxation

Why?

Reduce tension, relax body and mind.

Develop mind-body connection.

Be aware of, focus, and pay attention to what is happening here and now.

Decrease stress and anxiety.

Increase calm, gratitude, acceptance, and happiness.

Prep and materials

Teacher experienced in deep relaxation

Clean floor, mats, blankets

Comfortable clothes

Warm room

Bell and inviter

Songs to sing

Polite "Do not disturb" notice on the door

Steps

Getting settled

- Invite the group to lie down on their backs.
- Allow for time to settle, eyes closed if they wish.
- Sit where you can see every student clearly.
- Three sounds of the bell.

The practice

- Begin with awareness of the breath and inviting them to relax their body.
- Move steadily through the body, one part at a time.
- Suggested order: whole body, abdomen (rising and falling), eyes, mouth, shoulders, arms, heart, belly, hips, legs, feet, toes, whole body.
- Basic relaxation process: breathe in and out aware of that part of the body; relax and release tension in it; send it tenderness, care, and gratitude.
- When the mind wanders—note the wandering and bring it back to the body.
- Bring awareness back just to the in- and out-breath from time to time.
- Allow the space of at least one full in- and out-breath between sentences.

Music and singing (optional)

- Sing some gentle songs to bring the practice to a close.
- Allow time for rest and quiet between songs.

Getting ready to end

- Awareness back to your breathing, abdomen rising and falling.
- Aware of arms and legs.

- Let the class know that the sound of the bell is coming: half sound.
- Invite one sound of the bell.

Ending the practice (slowly)

- Invite students to move a little, wiggle toes and fingers, gently open their eyes.
- Invite them to roll onto their right side, stretch gently, then slowly sit up.

Reflection questions

- How do I feel right now?
- How easy or difficult did I find the practice?
- How much did my mind wander? If I noticed it wander, was I able to bring it back to my body?
- Did I notice any specific parts of my body that held a lot of tension?

Variations

- Add awareness to other parts of the body.
- Go into more detail when aware of each part of the body.
- Change the order that you move through parts of the body.
- Focus on bringing the mind to a part of the body that is sick or feeling pain, send it love, and allow the area to rest and relax.
- Practice outside in nature.
- Use imagery: a small rain cloud, a waterfall of light, or a laser beam gently moving across the body.

Teaching notes

Awareness of each part of the body begins with awareness of the breath.

Follow awareness of each part by relaxing and releasing tension.

Smile to each part of the body, sending love and gratitude.

Be aware of any physical problems students may have.

Students unwilling to lie down may practice seated.

mindful eating (tangerine meditation)

Why

Become mindful of what and how we eat.

Develop awareness of habit energies around food, eating, and consumption.

Develop a sense of gratitude through awareness of where the food comes from.

Prep and materials

One tangerine per person

Bell (recommended)

Paper towels, sanitizer, wet wipes to use before and after eating to clean hands

Steps

Prepare.

- Have tangerines (or selected food) ready.

Introduce the practice.

- Tell students that we will eat all together, and not to start eating until we are all ready.
- Invite them to enjoy the activity in silence.

Be with the breath.

- Invite the bell to give them a moment to sit quietly and get in touch with their breath.

Hand out tangerines.

- Distribute the tangerines—stay with the breath.
- Invite students to hold the tangerine in the palm of their hand.

Contemplate.

- Read the first two lines of the Food Contemplation: "This tangerine is a gift of the whole universe: the earth, the sky, the rain, and the sun. We thank the people who have brought this tangerine to us, especially the farmers and the people at the market."
- Reflect on the non-tangerine elements of the tangerine: the tangerine flowers, the tree, the sun, rain, earth, compost, and all the things and people that helped bring this fruit to your hand.

Look deeply.

- Look at the tangerine as if you have never seen one before.
- Notice color, texture, shape, reflection, etc.
- Notice the difference between one side and the other.
- Be aware of reactions in body: anticipation, salivation, aversion.

Smell.

- Smell—notice where you sense: nostrils, palate, throat?

Touch and peel.

- Peel—notice how it feels; examine the peel.
- Hold it to your ear while peeling to hear the sound of the peel tearing.
- Take off one segment.

Place it in your mouth and eat.

- Place a segment on the tongue; try not to chew it or swallow it.
- Notice how your mouth responds: salivation, urge to chew.
- Roll the segment around in your mouth—notice the texture, gently bite, notice the flavor, chew, and swallow; bring full awareness to each action.

After eating

- Sit and breathe; experience the aftermath of taste—notice the impulse to eat the next piece.

End

- Eat the rest of the tangerine.
- Sit quietly, in touch with the breath, with gratitude.

Reflection questions

- What was my experience at different points in the process, in mind and body?
- Was it different to how I usually eat? In what ways?
- How did it feel to contemplate where the food has come from? Gratitude, connection?
- How was it to eat in silence?
- How was eating with other people in this way?

Variations

- Mindfully eat any small item of food.
- Eat one piece of food normally and a second mindfully; notice any difference.

Teaching notes

Hand out and prepare food mindfully.

Intention to be present for the whole activity—mind, body, and senses.

Be aware and mindful of the whole group; use smiles and bows.

Contemplate food deeply: see the rain, sunshine, earth, air, and love in the food.

Consciously see, smell, chew, taste, and enjoy every morsel of food.

Habits and emotions can be connected to eating; be aware and ready to offer support and care to any strong emotions that arise.

Eat one or more mouthfuls of a snack or a normal meal mindfully.

See full outlines for these core practices in the "Mindful Eating" chapter.

using our breath to get in touch with our emotions

Why?

Calm and relax body and mind.

Get in touch with the breath in the belly, bring the mind to the body in the present moment.

Recognize feelings in mind and body.

Cultivate peace, joy, and happiness.

Aware of and embrace painful feelings.

Prep and materials

Teacher and students familiar with breath, bell, sitting, body practices

Bell and inviter

Steps

Prepare the group.

• Position: comfortable, relaxed, stable (sitting or lying down)

Bell

• Invite one sound of the bell to begin.

Notice you are breathing.

• Become aware of your breath.

• Nothing to change, just be aware.

Feel breath in the belly.

• Hands on belly, notice rising and falling.

• Notice lengths of breaths; notice pauses in between.

Use breath to calm mind and body.

• Become aware of mind, body, mood, feelings, tension.

• Nothing to change, be with what is.

• Breathing in and out, gently release tension and discomfort.

> Breathing in I calm my mind.
> Breathing out I calm my feelings, my emotions.

Optional: End here—bell.

Feeling joy and happiness

• Aware of the in- and out-breath.

• Aware of parts of body that feel okay. Enjoy, with breath.

• Aware of feeling of happiness. Enjoy, with breath.

> Breathing in I feel the joy of having two eyes.
> Breathing out, I smile to the joy in myself.
> Breathing in, I feel the happiness of sitting here peacefully.
> Breathing out, I smile to the feelings of happiness in myself.

Optional: End here—bell.

Being with painful feelings

• Aware of difficult feelings in the mind or body, e.g., anger, sadness, worry.

• Calm the painful feeling.

> Breathing in, I am aware of a painful feeling.
> Breathing out I calm my painful feeling.

• Breathe with it, say hello to it, and embrace it.

> Hello there, my feeling.
> Your name is (x).
> I know you.
> I will take good care of you.

Bell and ending

• End by breathing with one sound of the bell.

Reflection questions

• How do I feel right now—mind, body, breath?

• What is the effect of the practice on mind, body, breath?

• Was it easy or difficult?

• How to use it in daily life?

Teaching notes

Happiness and suffering inter-are—no mud, no lotus.

Mindfulness waters the wholesome seeds (happiness, joy, compassion) in our store consciousness.

Five steps to care for strong emotions: recognize, accept, embrace, look deeply, insight.

Go slowly; take several sessions if need be. Work from calm to joy and happiness to painful feelings.

....

tree in a storm

Why?

Experience the present moment through the breath.

Develop a sense of a stable core to remain calm whenever.

Calm and relax body and mind.

Increase the sense of emotional stability and safety.

Prep and materials

Teacher and students familiar with belly breathing and being in touch with emotions

Mats if lying down

Bell and inviter recommended

Steps

Start

• Find a comfortable, relaxed, stable sitting or lying position.

• Invite one sound of the bell.

Notice you are breathing

• Become aware of the in- and out-breath.

• No need to change the breath, just be aware of it.

Belly breathing

• Put your hands on your belly, aware of it rising and falling.

• Become aware of the length of each breath.

Aware of painful feelings

• Aware of difficult feelings in mind or body, e.g., physical pain, anger, sadness

• Breathe with it, say hello to it, and embrace it.

The tree

• You are a tree—your belly is the trunk, your arms are the branches.

• Your strong feeling is like the storm making your branches sway.

• Become aware of your belly—become stable and rooted.

• Come back to your breath and stay with the rising and falling of the belly:

> Breathing in, I calm this strong feeling.
> Breathing out, I can even smile to this strong feeling.

• Though the emotions are still present, stay with your breath.

• Soon the storm will pass.

Bell and ending

- Invite a sound of the bell.
- Continue breathing mindfully.

Reflection questions

- How do I feel now?
- What is the effect of the practice on my mind, body, and breath?
- How easy or difficult did I find the practice?
- How and on what occasion can I use this practice to help me take care of my emotions in my daily life?

Teaching notes

Tree image helps: strong and stable trunk while emotions shake the branches.

Works well with younger children.

Can be practiced in difficult and calm moments.

Be ready to hold space for strong emotions.

Focus on just one emotion at a time.

....

pebble meditation

Why?

Touch freshness, solidity, calm, and freedom within.

Become aware of the conditions of happiness that are already there.

Cultivate stability as a base for taking care of strong emotions.

Calm and relax body and mind.

Prep and materials

Space for class in a circle (chairs, cushions, tables, desks)

Four pebbles for each person

Bell recommended

Steps

Start

· Introduce the practice.

· Invite them each to choose four pebbles: one each for a mountain, a flower, still water, and space.

· Have them put the pebbles down on the ground to their left.

· Invite one sound of the bell.

First Pebble: Flower

· Pick up the flower pebble and place it in the palm of your hand.

> Breathing in I see myself as a flower.
> Breathing out I feel fresh.
> Flower, fresh

· Invite one sound of the bell and breathe in and out three times while saying:

> Breathing in: flower
> Breathing out: fresh

· Put the pebble down on the ground to your right.

Second Pebble: Mountain

· Pick up the mountain pebble and place it in the palm of your hand.

> Breathing in, I see myself as a mountain.
> Breathing out I feel solid.
> Mountain, solid

· Invite one sound of the bell and breathe in and out three times while saying:

> Breathing in: mountain
> Breathing out: solid

· Put the pebble down on the ground to your right.

Third Pebble: Still Water

· Pick up the still water pebble and place it in the palm of your hand.

> Breathing in I see myself as still water.
> Breathing out I become calm. I reflect things
> as they truly are.
> Still water, calm

- Invite one sound of the bell and breathe in and out three times while saying silently:

> Breathing in: still water
> Breathing out: calm

- Put the pebble down on the ground to your right.

Fourth Pebble: Space

- Pick up the space pebble and place it in the palm of your hand.

> Breathing in, I see myself as space.
> Breathing out I feel free.
> Space, free.

- Invite one sound of the bell and breathe in and out three times while saying silently:

> Breathing in: space.
> Breathing out: free.

- Put the pebble down on the ground to your right.

End

- Invite one sound of the bell to close.
- Collect the pebbles or leave them with students.

Reflection questions

- How do I feel now? What effect does this have on my mind, body, breath?
- How easy or difficult was it?
- How and where can I apply this in my daily life?

Variations

- Make a bag to keep the pebbles in (and decorate it).
- Carry the pebbles in your pocket to remember to cultivate these qualities.

Teaching notes

Cultivates qualities for happiness: flower-freshness, mountain-solidity, water-calm, space-freedom.

Works well with all age groups, especially young children.

You may like to sing the song "Breathing In, Breathing Out" as a way to introduce the practice.

Can be taught gradually, spread out over several sessions.

....

circle sharing

Why?

Learn to talk about thoughts and feelings openly and authentically.

Develop deep listening to benefit from each other's insights and experience.

Develop loving speech to share experiences, joys, difficulties, and questions.

Help us to feel seen, heard, understood, valued, and that we belong in the group.

Build a sense of connection with ourselves and others, and realize our problems are not unique.

Prep and materials

Gather chairs or cushions and mats in a circle so everyone can see each other.

Bell and inviter (optional but recommended)

Steps

Explain the basic process of sharing.

- Explain the method of sharing (bowing in, talking piece, etc.).
- No interruptions after bowing in or while holding the talking piece.
- Anyone can pass and just listen.
- Respect the role of teacher as facilitator.
- Ground rules: deep listening, loving speech (see above), no giving advice, maintain confidentiality (what is said here stays here).

Start

- Three sounds of the bell, three mindful breaths between each
- Introduce the topic (light and easy at first) to open the sharing.
- Invite the group to share.
- From time to time, invite a sound of the bell so everyone can breathe together.
- Allow silence, but if it's too long, pose a question or further topic to stimulate sharing.

End

- Sing a song together to bring the session to a close.
- Facilitator reflects on the sharing, expresses gratitude.
- Invite three sounds of the bell, enjoying three mindful breaths between each sound.
- Remind them as they leave: confidentiality, kindness, the teacher is available to talk privately.

Reflection Questions

- How did the practice affect me—mind, body, breath?
- How do I feel right now?
- How did it feel to use loving speech? Different from my normal speech?
- How did it feel to practice deep listening?
- How did it feel to be listened to by the group?

Variations

- Over time, explore more significant, personal and emotive topics.
- Some medium intensity topics: my practice over the past 24 hours, what makes a good friend or colleague, show how we care, something that made me cry, get mad, get scared, feel really happy.

Teaching notes

Teacher decides sharing method: bowing in, talking piece, etc.

Deep listening: fully present, no judgment; facilitator model

Loving speech: respect feelings of others, talk about oneself, no advice, blame, opinions. Only talk about what you are comfortable with (teacher takes care that students are not made too vulnerable too quickly).

Start light, over time balance lighter and more serious topics (students can offer ideas).

Find the right balance between maintaining the guidelines and contributing to a light, joyful rapport in the group.

....

beginning anew

Why?

Practice authentic communication: deep listening and loving speech.

Build a sense of connection with ourselves and with others.

Create harmonious and safer communities: in classrooms, staff rooms, and with families.

Learn ways to show our appreciation of one another, to express regrets and hurts, and to ask for support.

Learn a structured way to resolve difficulties and conflicts.

Prep and materials

Teacher well prepared in the practice

Chairs or mats in a circle

Plant or flowers in the middle of circle (recommended)

Bell (recommended)

Notes on the Steps

Step One: Flower watering (showing appreciation)

- Flowers need water to stay fresh, so we begin our sharing by finding some refreshing things to say and hear about one another.

- Flower watering can bring a lot of joy.

- Share concrete, specific things that the other person did that brought you joy.

Step Two: Expressing regrets (taking responsibility)

- Make sure to have first watered the flower of the other person.

- We express regrets about our own mistakes, weaknesses, or unskillful actions.

- When you apologize for something you regret, the hurt of the other person may be completely dissipated by your apology.

Step Three: Expressing a hurt

- Usually carried out one-on-one with another person present.

- We express a hurt we feel someone has caused us.

- Start by saying "I feel hurt because I perceived you said or did this or that."

- Focus on our own feelings and perceptions, and what support we would like to have—no blame.

- The other person listens deeply without interrupting—even if they hear something they feel is not true.

- If strong feelings arise, quietly practice to recognize, embrace, and calm our own feelings by breathing with them.

- Listen to develop compassion in our hearts for the other person.

Step Four: Asking for support with difficulties and hurts

- Here we express how we would like support for a difficult situation.

- Asking for support can happen at any point in beginning anew; need not follow the order of the other three.

- Skillfully asking for support helps participants clarify how they are feeling, and helps those who are listening to feel positive about how they might offer support.

Steps

- Sit in a circle, invite the bell three times, three mindful breaths between each.

- Remind the group about how to practice deep listening and loving speech.

- Explain we are here to show our appreciation and to resolve difficulties.

- Let everyone know which steps below we will practice, and what is the order and nature of each step (see the notes above—you may choose not to do all).

- Invite one more sound of the bell, and enjoy three mindful breaths.

- Model the first sharing yourself.

- One person indicates they want to speak; pick up the flowers and put it in front of them.

- Speaker begins with flower watering, and then optionally, continues with the other steps.

- The speaker, when finished, bows out or returns the flowers to the center.

- Others may take a turn.

Bell and ending

- You may like to share a brief heartfelt reflection as facilitator.

- Three sounds of the bell, each followed by three mindful breaths.

- If appropriate, sing a joyful song or hold hands and breathe for a minute.

- How do I feel right now—mind, body, breath?

- How did it feel to have your flowers watered? And to water others' flowers?

- How can we begin anew inside and outside the classroom?

Teaching notes

Pick a time when everyone feels calm and ready to listen.

Participation is voluntary.

Each person proceeds in order through the steps in the course of their sharing: begin with flower watering, followed by expressing a regret, and then expressing a hurt; make sure they don't skip a step.

Include plenty of flower watering: what we genuinely like, appreciate, or value about the other person—not flattery.

There is no rush in moving through the process. You may decide to only do one or two steps.

Decide beforehand how you will allow people to speak in turn (e.g., bowing in, passing the flowers).

Set a tone of ease and lightness.

Variations

Just do flower watering to build good relationships, or just flower watering and expressing regrets.

Use pictures for flower watering. Ask students to write something positive about one another on paper flower petals. Then each student sticks their petals and sticks them onto a card to make a flower.

appendix b
the five mindfulness trainings

The Five Mindfulness Trainings represent the vision for a global way of living and ethic. They are a concrete expression of the path of right understanding and true love, leading to healing, transformation, and happiness for ourselves and for the world. To practice the Five Mindfulness Trainings is to cultivate the insight of interbeing that can remove all discrimination, intolerance, anger, fear, and despair. If we live according to the Five Mindfulness Trainings, we are already on the path of a happy and free person. Knowing we are on that path, we are not lost in confusion about our life in the present or in fears about the future.

1. reverence for life

Aware of the suffering caused by the destruction of life, I am committed to cultivating the insight of interbeing and compassion and learning ways to protect the lives of people, animals, plants, and minerals. I am determined not to kill, not to let others kill, and not to support any act of killing in the world, in my thinking, or in my way of life. Seeing that harmful actions arise from anger, fear, greed, and intolerance, which in turn come from dualistic and discriminative thinking, I will cultivate openness, nondiscrimination, and nonattachment to views in order to transform violence, fanaticism, and dogmatism in myself and in the world.

2. true happiness

Aware of the suffering caused by exploitation, social injustice, stealing, and oppression, I am committed to practicing generosity in my thinking, speaking, and acting. I am determined not to steal and not to possess anything that should belong to others; and I will share my time, energy, and material resources with those who are in need. I will practice looking deeply to see that the happiness and suffering of others are not separate from my own happiness and suffering; that true happiness is not possible without understanding and compassion; and that running after wealth, fame, power, and sensual pleasures can bring much suffering and despair. I am aware that happiness depends on my mental attitude and not on external conditions, and that I can live happily in the present moment simply by remembering that I already have more than enough conditions to be happy. I am committed to practicing right livelihood so that I can help reduce the suffering of living beings on earth and stop contributing to global climate change.

3. true love

Aware of the suffering caused by sexual misconduct, I am committed to cultivating responsibility and learning ways to protect the safety and integrity of individuals, couples, families, and society. Knowing that sexual desire is not love, and that sexual activity motivated by craving always harms me as well as others, I am determined not to engage in sexual relations without true love and a deep, long-term commitment made known to my family and friends. I will do everything in my power to protect children from sexual abuse and to prevent couples and families from being broken by sexual misconduct. Seeing that body and mind are one, I am committed to learning appropriate ways to take care of my sexual energy and to cultivate loving kindness, compassion, joy, and inclusiveness—which are the four basic elements of true love—for my greater happiness and the greater happiness of others. Practicing true love, we know that we will continue beautifully into the future.

4. loving speech and deep listening

Aware of the suffering caused by unmindful speech and the inability to listen to others, I am committed to cultivating loving speech and compassionate listening in order to relieve suffering and to promote reconciliation and peace in myself and among other people, ethnic and religious groups, and nations. Knowing that words can create happiness or suffering, I am committed to speaking truthfully using words that inspire confidence, joy, and hope. When anger is manifesting in me, I am determined not to speak. I will practice mindful breathing and walking in order to recognize and to look deeply into my anger. I know that the roots of anger can be found in my wrong perceptions and lack of understanding of the suffering in me and in the other person. I will speak and listen in a way that can help me and the other person to transform suffering and see the way out of difficult situations. I am determined not to spread news that I do not know to be certain and not to utter words that can cause division or discord. I will practice right diligence to nourish my capacity for understanding, love, joy, and inclusiveness, and gradually transform anger, violence, and fear that lie deep in my consciousness.

5. nourishment and healing

Aware of the suffering caused by unmindful consumption, I am committed to cultivating good health, both physical and mental, for myself, my family, and my society by practicing mindful eating, drinking, and consuming. I will practice looking deeply into how I consume the four kinds of nutriments—namely edible foods, sense impressions, volition, and consciousness. I am determined not to use alcohol, not to gamble, and not to use drugs or any other products that contain toxins, such as certain websites, electronic games, TV programs, films, magazines, books, and conversations. I will practice coming back to the present moment to be in touch with the refreshing, healing, and nourishing elements in me and around me, not letting regrets and sorrow drag me back into the past nor letting anxieties, fear, or craving pull me out of the present moment. I am determined not to try to cover up loneliness, anxiety, or other suffering by losing myself in consumption. I will contemplate interbeing and consume in a way that preserves peace, joy, and well-being in my body and consciousness, and in the collective body and consciousness of my family, my society, and the earth.

appendix c
the five contemplations before eating

1. This food is a gift of the earth, the sky, numerous living beings, and much hard and loving work.

2. May we eat with mindfulness and gratitude so as to be worthy to receive this food.

3. May we recognize and transform unwholesome mental formations, especially our greed, and learn to eat with moderation.

4. May we keep our compassion alive by eating in such a way that reduces the suffering of living beings, stops contributing to climate change, and heals and preserves our precious planet.

5. We accept this food so that we may nurture our brotherhood and sisterhood, build our sangha, and nourish our ideal of serving all living beings.

Adaptations of the Five Contemplations for Children

1. This food is the gift of the whole universe: the earth, the sky, the rain, and the sun.

2. We thank all the people who have brought this food to us—the farmers, the people who work in the shops, and the cooks.

3. We only put on our plate as much food as we can eat. We chew the food slowly so that we can enjoy it.

4. We eat in a way that nurtures our compassion, protects other species and the environment, and heals and preserves our precious planet.

5. This food gives us energy to practice being more loving and understanding.

6. We eat this food in order to be healthy and happy and to love each other.

appendix d
what next?

resources to develop your personal practice and your teaching of mindfulness

The following section points to further resources that you might use to deepen your personal practice, inform your teaching, and engage with the wider Plum Village community. All relate to the Plum Village tradition in particular.

online resources

The Wake Up Schools
website: www.wakeupschools.org

This website is a major resource and hub of communication for Wake Up Schools—the network of educators, teachers, and practitioners cultivating mindfulness and applied ethics in education based on the teachings and practices of Thich Nhat Hanh and the Plum Village community. The website provides links to resources, including films and case studies, and an up-to-date list of books, films, talks, and events.

You can support Wake Up Schools through volunteer work and submissions to the website or to the journal *The Mindfulness Bell* (see below).

Plum Village: www.plumvillage.org

The Plum Village website provides core information about the community's activities and teachings, offering a selection of core texts and videos, including talks and articles by Thich Nhat Hanh and senior teachers. There are pages dedicated to the practice center's history, descriptions and tips for daily practice, and information about the many branches of this worldwide community.

The website provides information about local and international retreats and monastic tours, and is the registration portal for those wishing to attend retreats at Plum Village in France. There is also a growing list of apps to help cultivate mindfulness.

Wake Up: www.wkup.org

Wake Up is an active global community of young mindfulness practitioners, ages eighteen to thirty-five, inspired by the teachings of Thich Nhat Hanh. Started in 2007, this community comes together to practice mindfulness to nourish happiness and to contribute to building a healthier and a more compassionate society.

Wake Up has flourished around the globe, and Wake Up groups can be found on every continent and in many countries. They gather weekly or monthly to practice together. They organize mindfulness events and retreats, and visit meditation practice centers together. Many groups also organize events such as music evenings, large group meditations, picnics, and hikes.

Plum Village Online

The Plum Village community has a strong international presence online. Below are some of the main resources.

Facebook: There are currently 1.5 million followers on Thich Nhat Hanh's Facebook page: **www.facebook.com/thichnhathanh**

Twitter: Over 350,000 followers on Twitter: **@thichnhathanh**

YouTube: Plum Village's YouTube Channel has hundreds of videos and clips, including talks and footage of Thich Nhat Hanh, senior dharma teachers teaching around the world: **www.youtube.com/plumvillage**

The website **www.tnhaudio.org** regularly posts audio recordings of talks given by Thich Nhat Hanh and senior dharma teachers from around the world. The recordings are available free for download.

The Mindfulness Bell:
www.mindfulnessbell.org

The Mindfulness Bell is a magazine of the art of mindful living, published three times a year. It serves as an inspiration and teaching resource for those practicing mindfulness in daily life. Each issue features a teaching by Thich Nhat Hanh and stories and teachings by teachers and practitioners. The journal often includes articles that reflect on practicing with children and young people.

International Sangha Directory:
www.mindfulnessbell.org/directory

The International Sangha Directory provides a list of local groups practicing in the Plum Village tradition. This website includes a map with pin drops pointing out locations where established and budding groups are meeting.

Plumline: www.plumline.org

Plumline is a support center for those wishing to establish, build, and maintain an online mindfulness practice group. It is a place to share ideas and resources as online groups are being set up and developed.

The Mindfulness in Education Network:
www.mindfuled.org

The Mindfulness in Education Network began in 2001 as an email list to keep seventy-eight educators who attended Thich Nhat Hanh's two American retreats that year connected with each other. As of 2016 this global network's list has nearly two thousand participants from a variety of mindfulness traditions. MiEN has held an annual conference in the United States since 2008. Its website includes videos of past conference presentations and an invitation to join its growing list of subscribers.

Earth Holders Sangha:
www.earthholder.org

The Earth Holder Sangha is an affinity group within the Plum Village International Community of Engaged Buddhists, founded by Zen Master Thich Nhat Hanh. First created in the United States in 2015, the Earth Holder Sangha is guided by the ethics of the Five Mindfulness Trainings and Fourteen Mindfulness Trainings.

The purpose of the Earth Holder Sangha is to:

Build a community of Plum Village Earth Holders, bringing like-minded sangha members together for support and inspiration, and to develop Earth Holding practices inspired by Thich Nhat Hanh's teachings.

Engage in mindful action locally, nationally, and internationally.

Support sustainable communities, in particular Plum Village monasteries, lay practice centers, and local groups.

The Earth Holders create educational materials, host local gatherings, and organize online events.

ARISE:
www.pvracialequity.wordpress.com

Awakening through Race, Intersectionality, and Social Equity (ARISE) is committed to understanding and transforming racial, systemic, and social inequities. The website helps groups and individuals looking to connect online and in person around racial justice, cultural healing, and mindfulness—a living legacy of the close friendship between Zen Master Thich Nhat Hanh and Reverend Dr. Martin Luther King, Jr.

books and other resources

Guidebooks

Planting Seeds: Practicing Mindfulness with Children. Thich Nhat Hanh and the Plum Village Community, Sr. Jewel (Chan Chau Nghiem), ed. Berkeley, CA: Parallax Press, 2011. Clear teacher-friendly guidance aimed at first schools.

Everybody Present: Mindfulness in Education. Nikolaj Flor Rotne and Didde Flor Rotne. Berkeley, CA: Parallax Press, 2013. As described by the authors: "The book aims to help all educators transform feelings of inadequacy into experiences of abundance to set in motion a revolution of stillness, allowing each individual the sense of interbeing, inner calm, and joy. It contains clearly explained clinical studies, stories, and helpful tips for cultivating a personal practice and mindful teaching."

The Mindful School Leader: Practices to Transform Your Leadership and School. Valerie Brown and Kirsten Olson. Thousand Oaks, CA: Corwin, 2015. Explores the role of mindfulness in supporting thriving and compassionate leaders and building empathy, equity, and peace within schools. Based on secular mindfulness approaches and practical firsthand experience and examples.

The Mindful Teen: Powerful Skills To Help You Handle Stress One Moment at a Time. Dzung X. Vo. Oakland, CA: New Harbinger, 2015. Written directly for a teen audience by a pediatrician who works with adolescents inspired by Plum Village, MBSR, MBCT, and other mindfulness-based interventions. www.mindfulnessforteens.com.

Teach, Breathe, Learn: Mindfulness In and Out of the Classroom. Meena Srinivasan. Berkeley, CA: Parallax Press, 2014. By an international educator with several years of experience as a classroom teacher and school leader. Based on her own experience in the classroom, this book contains lesson plans and several resources about social and emotional learning and sharing mindfulness in the Plum Village tradition. http://teachbreathelearn.com.

Teaching Mindfulness Skills to Kids and Teens. Chris Willard and Amy Saltzman, eds., with a foreword by Susan Kaiser Greenland. New York: The Guilford Press, 2015. This volume includes Betsy Rose's essay "Mindfulness with a Beat: Embodied Practice in the Key of Song."

Tuning In: Mindfulness in Teaching and Learning: A Collection of Essays by Teachers for Teachers. Irene E McHenry and Richard Brady, eds. Philadelphia: Friends Council of Education, 2009. "I am delighted that the contributors to this book have come out to share how mindfulness and concentration can be a pleasure to learn as well as teach. This is an important book for teachers, school administrators, parents, and all others concerned with the well-being of the next generation." —Thich Nhat Hanh

Books for Children

MINDFULNESS IN GENERAL

A Pebble for Your Pocket. Thich Nhat Hanh. Berkeley, CA: Plum Blossom Books, 2001. A comprehensive pocketbook for older children with stories, simple explanations of the practices, and basic teachings on mindfulness.

Charlotte and the Quiet Place. Deborah Sosin. Berkeley, CA: Plum Blossom Books, 2011. A children's book with watercolor illustrations about Charlotte in a noisy city and the beauty of mindful breathing and silence.

Each Breath a Smile. Sr. Susan (Thuc Nghiem). Berkeley, CA: Plum Blossom Books, 2001. A colorful children's book for introducing mindful meditation to young children based on Thich Nhat Hanh's teachings.

MINDFUL MOVEMENTS

Mindful Movements: Ten Exercises for Well-Being. Thich Nhat Hanh and Wietske Vriezen. Berkeley, CA: Parallax Press, 2008. Short illustrated guidance for children on mindful movements. Includes DVD.

STRONG EMOTIONS

Anh's Anger. Gail Silver, with illustrations by Christianne Kromer. Berkeley, CA: Plum Blossom Books, 2009. An illustrated children's book about how a young boy meets and learns to embrace his anger as a fierce but fun and friendly character.

Peace, Bugs and Understanding: An Adventure in Sibling Harmony. Gail Silver, with illustrations by Youme Nguyen Ly. Berkeley, CA: Plum Blossom Books, 2014. An illustrated children's story about how the practice of loving kindness can resolve difficulties and strong emotions.

Steps and Stones. Gail Silver, with illustrations by Christianne Kromer. Berkeley, CA: Plum Blossom Books, 2011. The sequel to *Anh's Anger.* When Anh is hurt by his friend at school, Anger appears in disguise with ideas of revenge, but Anh discovers how walking meditation brings transformation.

PEBBLE MEDITATION

A Handful of Quiet: Happiness in Four Pebbles. Thich Nhat Hanh. Berkeley, CA: Plum Blossom Books, 2012. Short illustrated guide to pebble meditation with a description, drawing exercise, guidance, practice sheets, and more.

LOOKING DEEPLY

The Hermit and the Well. Thich Nhat Hanh. Berkeley, CA: Plum Blossom Books, 2003. A true story about Thich Nhat Hanh's inner discovery while visiting a hermitage as a schoolboy.

Is Nothing Something? Kids' Questions and Zen Answers. Thich Nhat Hanh. Berkeley, CA: Plum Blossom Books, 2014. A colorful illustrated collection of simple but profound answers to over thirty wide-ranging questions from children.

The Sun in My Belly. Sr. Susan (Thuc Nghiem). Berkeley, CA: Plum Blossom Books, 2007. A colorful children's book about interbeing and the healing power of relationships and nature.

ETHICS

The Coconut Monk. Thich Nhat Hanh. Berkeley, CA: Plum Blossom Books, 2009. An illustrated children's story about a monk and his friends—a cat and mouse—who live together peacefully during the Vietnam War.

Books for Young Adults

Basket of Plums Songbook: Music in the Tradition of Thich Nhat Hanh. Collected and arranged by Joseph Emet. Berkeley, CA: Parallax Press, 2013. The lyrics, musical score, and chords for forty-eight Plum Village practice songs.

The Dragon Prince: Stories and Legends from Vietnam. Thich Nhat Hanh. Berkeley, CA: Parallax Press, 2007. Fifteen traditional stories retold for youth and adults exploring questions of togetherness, responsibility, and conflict resolution.

The Stone Boy and Other Stories. Thich Nhat Hanh. Berkeley, CA: Parallax Press, 1996. Eleven traditional stories and short fiction written for youth and adults.

A Taste of Earth and Other Legends of Vietnam. Thich Nhat Hanh. Berkeley, CA: Parallax Press, 1993. Twelve traditional stories retold for youth and adults exploring questions of togetherness, responsibility, and conflict resolution.

Under the Rose Apple Tree. Thich Nhat Hanh. Berkeley, CA: Parallax Press, 2002. A pocketbook for early teens about the practice of mindfulness and the story of Siddhartha Gautama as a child.

Audio: Songs and Music

Wake Up Schools webpage: www.wakeupschools.org/songs. Song lyrics, sheet music, and recordings of classic Plum Village songs.

Betsy Rose, *Calm Down Boogie: Songs for Peaceful Moments and Lively Spirits* (2008). Lively and calming mindfulness songs for children. www.betsyrosemusic.org.

Betsy Rose, *Heart of a Child* (2006). Songs that support the heart and spirit of the educator or parent.

Betsy Rose, *In My Two Hands* (2011). Songs from the Plum Village tradition, supporting breath, awareness, and care for self and the earth.

Joe Reilly, *Children of the Earth* (2007). Joe and his friends herald environmental stewardship. www.joereilly.org.

Joe Reilly, *Touch the Earth* (2009). Music to strengthen community while embracing diversity and interbeing with each other and the environment.

Wake Up London and Friends, *Peace Sounds I* (2012) and *Peace Sounds II* (2016). Mixture of songs recorded by Wake Up London, a community of young adults who meet to support the work of Thich Nhat Hanh and Plum Village. www.peacesounds.org.

Films and Video

Thich Nhat Hanh's talks for educators are posted on the Wake Up Schools website: www.wakeupschools.org/video.

Los Educadores Felices cambiarán el Mundo (2016). With footage from the educators' retreat at Barcelona in 2013, this film tells of the transformative power of the mindfulness practices. In Spanish with subtitles in other languages. www.wakeupschools.org/educadores.

A Lotus for You, a Buddha to Be (2009). A film based on the educators' retreat led by Thich Nhat Hanh in 2008 at The Doon School, India, along with some footage of his pilgrimage thereafter. www.wakeupschools.org/lotusforyou.

The Five Powers (2014). Drawing from their collaboration with Martin Luther King, this animated film tells the story of Thich Nhat Hanh, Sr. Chan Khong, and Alfred Hasler and their nonviolent activism during the Vietnam War. www.the5powersmovie.com.

Happy Teachers Will Change the World (2015). A forty-minute film documenting inspirational experiences of an educators' retreat in Canada offered by Thich Nhat Hanh, the Plum Village monastics, and lay teachers. www.wakeupschools.org/happyteachersfilm.

Planting Seeds of Mindfulness (2016). An animated feature-length film aimed at younger viewers that tells the story of young people incorporating Plum Village practices into their lives after a move to a new town. www.plantingseedsofmindfulnessmovie.com.

A Visit to the Dharma Primary School (2015). A thirty-minute documentary exploring the impact of a visit from Plum Village monastics to a Buddhist primary school in the United Kingdom. www.wakeupschools. org/dharmaschool.

Vivir Despiertos (2016). A film about the practice of mindful living in which Thich Nhat Hanh and the monastics of the Plum Village community share the practice of mindfulness with communities in the Spanish-speaking world. www.wakeupschools.org/vivirdespiertos.

Wake Up Schools in India (2013). A fifteen-minute video showcasing workshops with Plum Village monastics at schools in India. www.wakeupschools.org/india.

Walk with Me: On the Road with Thich Nhat Hanh (2017). A meditative and intimate insight into a community of Plum Village monks and nuns who practice the art of mindfulness and the teachings of Thich Nhat Hanh. www.walkwithmefilm.com.

retreats and training

Practice Centers

Mindfulness Practice Centers in the Plum Village tradition provide opportunities for individuals, couples, and families to deepen their practice alongside monastics and lay residents. These centers attract people from across the globe who wish to cultivate mindfulness and contemplation in the context of simple communal living and a peaceful and refreshing environment.

All the centers offer retreats, talks, days of mindfulness, and time and space for rest. Retreats in the Plum Village tradition are not done all in silence, but offer the opportunity for participants to experience a wide range of the mindfulness practices shared throughout this book. It is possible to make day visits to enjoy the grounds, activities, and company, or to stay for longer retreats or courses. Some centers offer opportunities to volunteer or to undertake an internship. www.wakeupschools.org/centers.

Tours

The Plum Village community also goes on tour, holding talks, group meditations, and retreats in locations across the globe, including educators' retreats. You can find information about upcoming tours and related retreats through the practice centers, the Plum Village website, and the Wake Up School website, www.wakeupschools.org/events.

The Five Mindfulness Trainings

Those who have participated in a five-day retreat can then choose to receive one or more of the Five Mindfulness Trainings. Those who receive the trainings practice and study the trainings, which include reverence for life, true happiness, true love, loving speech and deep listening, and nourishment and healing. These five trainings are intended to be concrete reflections of how to live each moment in a way that can transform suffering and cultivate happiness in ourselves and in the world.

The Five Mindfulness Trainings are available on the Plum Village website: www.wakeupschools.org/5MT.

Wake Up Schools Teacher Training Commitment Program

If you would like to commit to training as a Wake Up Schools teacher, you do not need to wait: you can start right now. With this book in your hands, you already have the core practices and wider guidance you need to bring the practice into your own life and to share it with others.

You might also like the support of others, and Wake Up Schools trainers around the world offer the rich opportunity to study and practice with mentors; this can be a powerful way to develop the aspect of practicing in community by coming into contact and sharing with other teachers interested in engaged mindfulness and applied ethics. A network of Wake Up Schools trainers has grown up over the past few years, most of whom are established teachers already in the Plum Village tradition. For a current list of Wake Up Schools trainers, see the Wake Up Schools website for the most current information: www.wakeupschools.org/training.

Programs, Teachers, and Consultants

Many laypeople host retreats, workshops, or other events in the Plum Village tradition, and some may be able to come to your school or community as consultants and trainers. We list some who are actively available to help you below, many of whom have contributed their stories to this book. OI members are part of the Order of Interbeing, a community of monastics and laypeople who have committed to living their lives in accord with the Fourteen Mindfulness Trainings, a common set of ethics.

Note: We are aiming here to be illustrative rather than comprehensive, so this list does not include many excellent programs hosted by practice communities and individual practitioners. The list is for information only and is not a recommendation—at present the Plum Village community does not have an accreditation process for trainers and consultants, although they issue certificates of completion for certain retreats. These listings will change over time; you may be able to find more up-to-date information on the Wake Up Schools website: www.wakeupschools.org/teachers.

Ahimsa Trust (India) represents Thich Nhat Hanh and his community in the Indian subcontinent. It aims to spread the consciousness of peace and love through alliances and programs in the areas of mindfulness in education, community building, responsible tourism, and sustainable livelihoods. Ahimsa organizes workshops and retreats for teachers on Cultivating Mindfulness in Education, days and evenings of mindfulness, teachings, and fundraisers partly through pilgrimages "In the Footsteps of the Buddha." Ahimsa is setting up a Mindfulness Practice Center in the foothills of the Himalayas. It is spearheaded by Mindfulness Teachers and OI members Shantum and Gitanjali Seth: www.ahimsatrust.org.

Escuelas Despiertas (Wake Up Schools) (Spain), in collaboration with the University of Barcelona's Instituto de Ciencias de la Educación (ICE), offers a program dedicated entirely to the Plum Village approach to mindfulness in education. It is taught by **Pilar Aguilera**, an OI member. It grants credit through the Continuing Professional Development Plan of Catalonia's Department of Education: www.escuelasdespiertas.org.

Wake Up Schools France (France) is a wide network of Francophone teacher-practitioners who coordinate local sanghas, host workshops, and share experiences: www.wakeupschools.org/fr.

Vivir Despiertos (Ecuador) meets weekly at the Universidad San Francisco de Quito. Professor Andrés Proaño Serrano helps organize the group's weekly meetings to study and practice sitting, walking, and eating meditation: www.facebook.com/vivirdespiertosEcuador.

The Center for Mindfulness and Consciousness Studies at the University of Pittsburgh in the United States was inspired by the teachings of Thich Nhat Hanh and is directed by Tony Silvestre, an OI member and dharma teacher in the Plum Village tradition. The Center includes practitioners from both Buddhist traditions and MBSR and organizes its activities around scientific research on mindfulness, bringing mindfulness into schools, and service to the community: www.mindfulnesspitt.org.

Minding Your Life (MYL) (United States) was founded by Plum Village dharma teacher, OI member, and educational consultant Richard Brady. Richard is also a retired math teacher from Sidwell Friends School in Washington, DC. He leads retreats for educators. MYL has a website that includes his articles and newsletters on mindfulness in education: www.mindingyourlife.net.

The Mindfulness Institute offers programs for professionals, including teachers, administrators, school counselors, school psychologists, school social workers, and others in the kindergarten through twelfth grade and college settings. These programs are designed to help educators integrate mindfulness into their own lives and learn how to introduce simple, research-based mindful awareness practices to students. The Mindfulness Institute also focuses on how to work under pressure and how to build and strengthen collaborative relationships: www.floridamindfulness.org/MI.

Larry Ward and Peggy Rowe Ward from the United States are dharma teachers in the Plum Village tradition and OI members, and have supported school systems by integrating mindfulness into the curriculum. They facilitate in-service workshops and retreats for students, parents, and teachers. Peggy is completing her book for teachers and parents titled *Down to Earth*. They can be reached at www.thelotusinstitute.org.

Kaira Jewel Lingo from the United States is a lay dharma teacher, OI member, and mindfulness educator, leading retreats and offering mindfulness programs to educators, parents, and students in connection with the Wake Up Schools program in the United States and Europe. She was an ordained nun from 1999 to 2015 in Thich Nhat Hanh's Plum Village community. As a teacher of color, she also offers retreats for people of color, artists, and activists and focuses on a mindful response to climate change. She lives in Washington, DC: www.kairajewel.com.

Michael Ciborski and Fern Dorresteyn (United States) were ordained monastics at Plum Village Practice Center in France from 1996 to 2003. They are both OI members as well as dharma teachers in the Plum

Village tradition. They founded MorningSun Mindfulness Center and Community in New Hampshire, which hosts days of mindfulness and retreats. They also organize activities for parents and families at local schools: www.morningsuncommunity.org.

Michael Schwammberger (Spain and United Kingdom), former Plum Village monk (1997–2012), now a lay dharma teacher within the OI lineage, leads and co-leads retreats in the Plum Village tradition in Europe, including family retreats and retreats for schoolteachers within the Wake Up Schools program. He also visits schools sharing Thich Nhat Hanh's teachings and practices to the children: michaelms@tutanota.com.

Valerie Brown is an OI member since 2003, international retreat leader, educational consultant, leadership coach, author, and principal of Lead Smart Coaching, helping educators apply and integrate mindfulness in daily life. She is also a member of the Religious Society of Friends (Quakers) and a certified Kundalini yoga teacher and mindfulness practitioner. She works holistically with school leaders to embody leadership: www.leadsmartcoaching.com.

Joe Reilly (United States) is an OI member, singer, songwriter, and educator. To quote his website, he "writes songs from his heart. Joe's songs are playful, clever, engaging, joyful, and always have something meaningful to say. The core of his message is an invitation to heal our relationships with our selves, with each other, and with the earth": www.joereilly.org.

Betsy Rose (United States) is a singer, songwriter, peace activist, and educator offering workshops, in-school programs and trainings, conference presentations and keynotes, and musical inspiration to spiritual and social justice groups. Her musical programs for children and educators focus on earth care, conflict resolution, diversity, and mindfulness. For all who are involved in the lives of children: www.mindfulsongs.org. Betsy's programs and music for peacemakers, women, and all working for a just and sustainable world: www.betsyrosemusic.org.

Terry Cortes-Vega (United States), a OI member and dharma teacher, created the Master School, a secular summer day camp inspired by Plum Village practices that supports the needs of gifted youngsters. It is a family-run camp and is now in its thirty-fifth year: www.masterschoolkids.com.

Meena Srinivasan (United States) is a program manager for the Office of Social and Emotional Learning (SEL) for the Oakland Unified School District in California. An OI member, she embeds Plum Village practices into her work with teachers and school leaders. Meena has developed a four-week online course about mindfulness and social emotional learning based on her book *Teach, Breathe, Learn*: www.meenasrinivasan.com. Meena and her husband, Chihiro Wimbush, also started A Lens Inside, a nonprofit that develops mindful media and films to create educational programs that promote SEL through the exploration of social issues: www.alensinside.org.

Julie Berentsen (United Kingdom) offers workshops and ongoing classes. She works with young people (first and high school students), parents, staff, and communities: www.weareinsideout.com.

Tineke Spruytenberg and Claude Acker (Netherlands) are both OI members and have created an educational program that offers six-week courses and ongoing support to teachers, school teams, school boards, and others working in education: www.HappyTeachers.nu.

Dzung X. Vo (Canada), an OI member, has developed a secular mindfulness-based intervention for adolescents, inspired by Plum Village, MBSR, MBSR-T, MBCT, and other mindfulness-based interventions. The website includes free mindfulness videos, downloadable guided meditations, blog, and excerpts from his book *The Mindful Teen*: www.mindfulnessforteens.com.

Katherine Weare (United Kingdom) is a professor and academic, a mindfulness teacher and researcher, writer, and public speaker. She works across the world in a range of mindfulness traditions with adults and young people, and including the Plum Village approach, MBSR and the Mindfulness in Schools program. She is joint author of this book and author of many other publications on mindfulness, social and emotional learning, mental health, and well-being. She can be contacted at skw@soton.ac.uk.

Marianne Claveau (France) works with OR2D and Clermont Ferrand University (École Supérieure du Professorat et de l'Education). Her research focuses on how mindfulness helps develop core skills in education for sustainable development and facilitate innovative and creative teachings. She offers workshops and ongoing classes to school teams, university researchers, and students: marianne.claveau@orange.fr.

Elli Weisbaum (Canada) is an OI member and mindfulness educator. She is an instructor at the University of Toronto's Applied Mindfulness Meditation certificate program. She offers in-school introductory workshops, days of mindfulness, and does public speaking and research: www.elliweisbaum.com.

Stillness Revolution (Denmark) was founded by Nikolaj and Didde Flor Rotne, authors of *Everybody Present* and offers training, counseling, and coaching both in person and online: http://stillnessrevolution.com.

Youth Mindfulness (United Kingdom) was founded by Michael Bready and delivers teacher training programs in curricula for first school through higher education and at-risk youth inspired by Plum Village, positive psychology, MBSR, and other mindfulness-based interventions. It also offers an in-depth one-year mindfulness teacher training program and an eight-week course for adults: http://youthmindfulness.org.

The Dharma Primary School (United Kingdom) has a long-standing relationship with Plum Village. This small first school practices mindfulness through a whole-school model. They run workshops on Mindfulness for Children and host Open Mornings three times a year: www.dharmaschool.co.uk.

notes

PREFACE: A VISION FOR EDUCATION

1   Thich Nhat Hanh, Dharma Talk, June 15, 2014, at 21-Day Retreat in Plum Village, France.

PREFACE: THE PLUM VILLAGE CONTRIBUTION TO
THE FIELD OF MINDFULNESS IN EDUCATION

1   World Health Organization, 2011, *Global Burden of Mental Disorders and the Need for a Comprehensive, Coordinated Response from Health and Social Sectors at the Country Level: Report by the Secretariat*, http://apps.who.int/gb/ebwha/pdf_files/EB130/B130_9-en.pdf.

2   S. David, I. Boniwell, and A. Conley Ayers. *Oxford Handbook of Happiness* (Oxford, UK: Oxford University Press, 2014).

3   J. A. Durlak, R. P. Weissberg, A. B. Dymnicki, R. D. Taylor, and K. B. Schellinger, "Enhancing Students' Social and Emotional Development Promotes Success in School: Results of a Meta-Analysis," *Child Development* 82 (2011), 474–501.

4   A. Vaish, T. Grossman, and A. Woodward, "Not All Emotions Are Created Equal: The Negativity Bias in Social-Emotional Development," *Psychological Bulletin* 134 (3:2008), 383–40, http://www.cbcd.bbk.ac.uk/people/scientificstaff/tobias/Vaish_PsycBull_2008.

5   D. Kahneman and A. Deaton, "High Income Improves Evaluation of Life but Not Emotional Well-Being," *Proceedings of the National Academy of Science, USA* 107:38 (2010), 16489–93, doi:10.1073/pnas.1011492107.

6   J. Kabat-Zinn, *Full Catastrophe Living: Using the Wisdom of Your Body and Mind to Face Stress, Pain and Illness,* revised edition (New York: Bantam/Random House, 2011).

7   D. M. Davis and J. A. Hayes, "What Are the Benefits of Mindfulness?" *Monitor on Psychology, the American Psychological Association* 43:7 (July-August 2012), 64, http://www.apa.org/monitor/2012/07-08/ce-corner.aspx.

8   N. J. Albrecht, P. M. Albrecht, and M. Cohen, "Mindfully Teaching in the Classroom: A Literature Review," *Australian Journal of Teacher Education* 37:12 (2012), Article 1.

9   K. A. Schonert-Reichl and R. W. Roeser, *Handbook of Mindfulness in Education: Integrating Theory and Research into Practice* (New York: Springer, 2016).

10 B. Khoury, T. Lecomte, G. Fortin, M. Masse, P. Therien, V. Bouchard, M. Chapleau, K. Paquin, and S. G. Hofmann, "Mindfulness-Based Therapy: A Comprehensive Meta-Analysis," *Clinical Psychology Review* 33:6 (2013), 763–71.

11 K. Weare, "Evidence for Mindfulness: Impacts on the Well-Being and Performance of School Staff," 2014, https://mindfulnessinschools.org/wp-content/uploads/2014/10/Evidence-for-Mindfulness-Impact-on-school-staff.pdf.

12 K. Weare, "Developing Mindfulness with Children and Young People: A Review of the Evidence and Policy Context," *Journal of Children's Services* 8:2 (2013), 141–53, https://mindfulnessinschools.org/wp-content/uploads/2013/09/Developing-mindfulness-children-young-people.pdf.

13 S. Zoogman, B. Simon, S. Goldberg, W. Hoyt, and L. Miller, "Mindfulness Interventions with Youth: A Meta-Analysis," *Mindfulness* (2014), doi:10.1007/s12671-013-0260-4.

14 C. Zenner, S. Herrnleben-Kurz, and H. Walach, "Mindfulness-Based Interventions in Schools—a Systematic Review and Meta-Analysis," *Frontiers in Psychology* (2014), doi:10.3389/fpsyg.2014.00603.

15 R. J. Davidson, J. Kabat-Zinn, and J. Schumacher, "Alterations in Brain and Immune Function Produced by Mindfulness Meditation," *Psychosomatic Medicine* 65:4 (2003), 564–70.

16 R. Davidson and A. Lutz, "Buddha's Brain: Neuroplasticity and Meditation in the Spotlight," *IEEE Signal Processing Magazine* 25:1 (2008), 176–74.

17 B. Hölzel, S. Lazar, T. Gard, Z. Schuman-Olivier, and U. Ott, "How Does Mindfulness Meditation Work? Proposing Mechanisms of Action from a Conceptual and Neural Perspective," *Perspectives on Psychological Science* 6 (2011), 537, doi:10.1177/1745691611419671.

18 H. Roth, "Contemplative Studies: Prospects for a New Field," *Teacher's College Record* 108:6 (2006), 1787–815.

19 D. P. Barbezat and M. Bush, *Contemplative Practices in Higher Education: Powerful Methods to Transform Teaching and Learning* (San Francisco: Jossey Bass, 2014).

20 CASEL, http://www.casel.org/social-and-emotional-learning/core-competencies, 2016.

21 M. Lawlor, "Mindfulness and Social and Emotional Learning: A Conceptual Framework," in K. A. Schonert-Reichl and R. W. Roeser, *Handbook of Mindfulness in Education: Integrating Theory and Research into Practice* (New York: Springer, 2016).

CHAPTER ONE: THE BREATH

1 M. Bell, former classroom teacher, United Kingdom, "The Wisdom of Ordinary Children," *The Mindfulness Bell* 54 (2010), 37.

CHAPTER TWO: THE BELL OF MINDFULNESS

1 R. Brady, "My Path as a Mindful Educator," *The Mindfulness Bell* 54 (2010), 17.

2 S. Murphy, "Equanimity in the Classroom," *The Mindfulness Bell* 54 (2010), 21.

CHAPTER FOUR: WALKING

1   Bell, "Wisdom of Ordinary Children," 38.

CHAPTER FIVE: THE BODY

1   Bell, "Wisdom of Ordinary Children," 38.

CHAPTER SEVEN: TAKING CARE OF OUR EMOTIONS

1   Brady, "My Path," 17.

CHAPTER EIGHT: BEING TOGETHER

1   Sister Chan Khong, *Beginning Anew: Four Steps to Restoring Communication* (Berkeley, CA: Parallax Press, 2014).

CHAPTER NINE: CULTIVATING MINDFULNESS IN OURSELVES

1   Thich Nhat Hanh, Educators' Retreat, Brock University, Canada, 2013, from the film *Happy Teachers Will Change the World.*

2   Brother Phap Luu, monastic, Plum Village, France, from the film *Happy Teachers Will Change the World.*

3   Thich Nhat Hanh, talk at the Path of the Buddha Retreat, the 21-Day Retreat in Plum Village on June 21, 2009.

4   S. J. Kein (formerly Sara Unsworth), University Teacher, United States, "Teaching the Student Within," *The Mindfulness Bell* 54 (2010), 20.

5   Thich Nhat Hanh, Question and Answer Session, May 11, 2014, at Retreat for Educators in Barcelona, Spain.

6   Thich Nhat Hanh, *The Miracle of Mindfulness* (Boston: Beacon, 1996).

7   V. Brown and K. Olsen, *The Mindful School Leader: Practices to Transform Your Leadership and School* (Thousand Oaks, CA: Corwin, 2014).

CHAPTER TEN: CULTIVATING MINDFULNESS IN OUR STUDENTS AND CLASSROOMS

1   B. Rogers, *Classroom Behavior: A Practical Guide to Effective Teaching, Behavior Management and Colleague Support,* 4th edition (Thousand Oaks, CA: Sage, 2015).

2   C. Willard, "Tending the Whole Garden," *The Mindfulness Bell* 54 (2010), 23. Excerpted from Christopher Willard, *Child's Mind: How Mindfulness Can Help Our Children Be More Focused, Calm, and Relaxed* (Berkeley, CA: Parallax Press, 2010).

3   Ibid.

4   D. Wilson and M. Conyers, *Teaching Students to Drive Their Brains: Metacognitive Strategies, Activities, and Lesson Ideas* (Alexandria, VA: ASCD, 2016).

5   D. and N. Flor Rotne, "Four Steps for Deepening Silence," *Everybody Present: Mindfulness in Education* (New York: Penguin/Random House, 2009).

6   Bell, "Wisdom of Ordinary Children," 38.

7   Thich Nhat Hanh, Question and Answer Session, April 17, 2012, at the House of Lords, United Kingdom.

8   J. Reilly, songwriter and environmental educator, United States, "Clap, Tap, Hum, Breathe: Mindful Songwriting with Children," *The Mindfulness Bell* 71 (2016), 23.

9   Thich Nhat Hanh, Our Cosmic Body," *The Mindfulness Bell* 68 (2015), 5.

10 R. Brady, "Mindfulness and Mathematics: Teaching as a Deep Learning Process," *The Mindfulness Bell* 38 (2005), 38.

CHAPTER ELEVEN: CULTIVATING MINDFULNESS
ACROSS SCHOOL AND UNIVERSITY COMMUNITIES

1   Thich Nhat Hanh, Dharma Talk, January 4, 2012, at Applied Ethics in Education Retreat in Plum Village, France.

2   Brother Phap Dung, monastic, Plum Village, France, from the film *Happy Teachers Will Change the World.*

3   Thich Nhat Hanh, Dharma Talk, January 4, 2012.

4   Judith Toy, mindfulness teacher, United States, "Generation to Generation," *The Mindfulness Bell* 55 (2010), 18.

5   Willard, "Tending the Whole Garden."

6   Brady, "My Path," 18.

acknowledgments

We would like to thank many people for their invaluable help and support with this book. We cannot hope to thank all the many people who have been involved, and many people had multiple roles, including advising, liaising, and reading drafts. We apologize for anyone we have missed. We also cannot sadly thank the very many people who have supported the wider Wake Up Schools movement across the world, on which the book is based.

Brother Phap Luu (Brother Stream), for being the main cowriter, heading up the monastic and lay team who worked on the editing of Thich Nhat Hanh's words and the content of the core practices, reviewing the overall content of the book, and piloting the practices. Yvonne Mazurek, for being the office anchor for the book, working closely with the Italian, French, and Spanish versions of the survey and the respondents, interviewing teachers, transcribing, and categorizing replies and talks, and coordinating the volunteers. Elli Weisbaum, for her early vision of the book, preparing the survey in English, liaising with teachers from Canada and the United States, and transcribing and categorizing replies and talks. Sister Hien Nghiem (Sister True Dedication), for writing the preface. Brother Phap Linh (Brother Spirit), for being part of the early vision for the book, for editing two of the sections by Thich Nhat Hanh, and for ensuring that the book flowed and the practices fitted in with the Plum Village approach. Brother Phap Lai (Brother Ben), for contributing a practice (Tree in the Storm) and for advice on "What Next?" Brother Phap Dung, for being part of the early vision for the book, and guidance clarifying the vision of Wake Up Schools, including mindful ethics. Neha Kaul, for reading and categorizing articles from *The Mindfulness Bell*. Richard Brady, for constant support and reading drafts of the book in detail. Marianne Claveau for advising, liaising with teachers from France, Belgium, and Switzerland, and for translation. Miles Dunmore for advising, piloting the practices at Binley Farm, and reading drafts. Kaira Jewel Lingo for involvement in the early vision of the book and reading drafts. Valerie Brown, Tineke Spruytenburg, Mark Vette, Orlaith O'Sullivan, Willem Kuyken, and Brooke Dobson Lavelle for reading drafts. Margaret Alexander, Molly Keogh, and Natascha Bruckner for identifying articles in *The Mindfulness Bell* and other printed resources. Karim Manji for transcribing, categorizing talks, and working with Joe Holtaway to prepare audio and Web resources for the book. Earleen Roumagoux for interviewing, transcription, translation, and categorizing talks. Eva Maria Marin Ortiz for categorizing talks. Paul Bready, Jadzia Tedeschi, Peter van de Ven, and Doran Amos for transcription. Pascale Bernège, Eduardo Drot de Gourville, and Marta Fíguls for translation. Pilar Aguilera, Adriana Rocco, Gitanjali Seth, Shantum Seth, Christiane Terrier, Mario Torneri, and Sister Dao Nghiem (Sister Peach Blossom) for liaising with teachers across the world. Sister An Nghiem (Sister Peace) for being part of the early vision for the book, and for helping pilot the core practices. Sister Tri Nghiem for early advice and for contributions to the preface. Will Stephens and the 2014 retreatants at Binley Farm, United Kingdom, and the faculty, staff, and students of the Dharma Primary School in Brighton, United Kingdom, and the English-speaking staff at the 2015 Children and Teen's Program for piloting early versions of some of the core practices. The francophone staff at Plum Village's 2015 Children and Teen's Program for translation and piloting early versions of some of the core practices. Susan Lirakis and the Donaldson Foundation, who provided a grant to get this work in motion.

For completing the survey or sending a contribution by email, which helped our thinking but which we were sadly not able to use, through lack of space: Myriam Évelyne Amasse, Sivakami Ashley, Phe (Khoe) Bach, Lucia Bongiovanni, Lorette Bottineau, Brigitte Brugni, Miquel Cabrera Ortega, Gloria Castella, Guillaume Chave, Nikolai Chapochnikov, Miquel Colón Bofill, Francoise Cornu, Aura Costa, Terry Cortés-Vega, Martha Cullens, Antonia De Vita, Rose Dombrow, Frédéric, Sergio Gandini, Lily Gros, Charles Gross, Estelle Guihard, Jihad Hammami, Vicente Hao Chin Jr., Anh-Le Ho-Gia, Kiran Jamwal, Samantha Kemp, Bridget E. Kiley, Linda Kriynovich, Erica Plouffe Lazure, Stéphane Lecomte, Johannes Løssl, Barry Lucy, Manon Lusyne, L. M., Lindi MacFarlane, Susie Mackenzie, Elice Maldonado, Marie, Lindi McAlpine, Florence Migné, Zoe Miller-Sowers, Desislava Mineva, Evelyne Moinet, Mary Carmel Moran, Jacopo Mori, Nadia, David Nelson, Christine Ntibarutaye, Silvia Pinali, Ariadna Plans Raubert, Phil Dat Phan, Veronique Pochet, Brandon Rennels, Maria del Pilar Reyes, Sarah E. Robinson-Bertoni, Sol Riou, Jon Kristian Salunga, Baruch Shalev, John Snyder, Christine Szechai, Geoffrey Tan, Jadzia Tedeschi, Iris Thomas, Clara Torres López, Young Whan Choi, Sharon Weisbaum, Lynne Williamson, and Kelly Wye. Other educators also contributed but preferred to remain totally anonymous; we thank them too.

Finally, thanks to the staff at Parallax Press.

contributors to this book

The following is a list, in alphabetical order by last name, of the people we have quoted in the book. Based on their preferences, it includes their teaching role, their place of work, their affiliation with Plum Village, and country. OI members are those who have ordained as members of the Order of Interbeing, a community of monastics and laypeople who have committed to living their lives in accord with the Fourteen Mindfulness Trainings, a common set of ethics.

Pilar Aguilera, instructor and researcher, University of Barcelona Instituto de Ciencias de la Educación, OI member, Spain.

Sally-Anne Airey, former officer in the Royal Navy, professional coach and coach-mentor, France.

Betsy Blake Arizu, former chemistry teacher and school counselor, current educational consultant and mindfulness trainer, Mindfulness Institute, Tampa, Florida, OI member, United States.

Norma Ines Barreiro, social worker, physician, and childhood and adolescence human rights activist, Información y Diseños Educativos para Acciones Saludables AC, OI member, Mexico.

John Bell, consultant and mindfulness trainer for out of school youth, founding member of YouthBuild USA, Somerville, Massachusetts, lay dharma teacher and OI member, United States.

Mike Bell, former general studies and science teacher at a state secondary school near Cambridge, current educational consultant and mindfulness trainer, Evidence Based Teachers Network, OI member, United Kingdom.

Ruth Bentley, musician and mindfulness educator, France.

Julie Berentsen, elementary school teacher, United Kingdom.

Carmelo Blazquez Jimenez, educator, De Aldeas Infantiles SOS Cataluña, Spain.

Jenna Joya Blondel, college instructor, United States.

Gordon "Boz" Bosworth, educator and former US Forest Service Ranger, Utah State University and Uinta-Wasatch-Cache National Forest, and OI member living at Deer Park Monastery, United States.

Lauri Bower, Mindfulness teacher, St. Mary's Church of England Primary School in Barnsley, OI member, United Kingdom.

Richard Brady, retired math teacher, Sidwell Friends School's Upper School, educational consultant and founder of Minding Your Life, lay dharma teacher and OI member, United States.

Michael Bready, trainer and consultant, director of training, Youth Mindfulness, United Kingdom.

Paul Bready, education student and teacher in training, United Kingdom, and former intern at Wake Up Schools in Plum Village, France.

Alan Brown, grade dean and teacher at an independent high school in New York City.

Valerie Brown, international retreat leader, educational consultant, leadership coach, author, and principal of Lead Smart Coaching, OI member, United States. Coauthor of The Mindful School Leader.

Grace Bruneel, volunteer, Rosaryhill School, Hong Kong.

Barbara Calgaro, tutor and camp counselor, Centro Estivo di Sandrigo, Vicenza, Italy.

Carme Calvo Berbel, professional development trainer, Allô? Serveis, OI member, Spain.

Denys Candy, director, Jandon Center for Community Engagement, Smith College, Massachusetts. Consultant, OI member, United States, Europe, and Singapore.

Gloria Castella, English teacher, Escuela Can Manent in Cardedeu, Spain.

Michele Chaban, adjunct professor, founding and former director of Applied Mindfulness Meditation, University of Toronto, School of Continuing Studies, Factor-Inwentash School of Social Work, Dala Lana School of Public Health, Center for Bio-Ethics, Canada.

Sr. Chan Duc (Sr. Annabel; Sr. True Virtue), former classics and Sanskrit teacher in secondary schools and university, England and Greece. Now monastic dharma teacher and dean of practice at the European Institute of Applied Buddhism, Germany.

Br. Chan Phap Kham, monastic dharma teacher, Asian Institute of Applied Buddhism, Hong Kong.

Maggie Chau, researcher at Centre of Buddhist Studies, University of Hong Kong.

Fiona Cheong, novelist and associate professor of creative writing, University of Pittsburgh, United States, Europe, and Singapore.

Marianne Claveau, former high school and current university teacher, social worker and mindfulness trainer in community programs and Université de Clermont-Ferrand, France.

Bobbie Cleave, educator and former US Forest Service Ranger, Utah State University and Uinta-Wasatch-Cache National Forest, and OI member living at Deer Park Monastery, United States.

Anita Constantini, retreat leader, Campo di Felicità and TuscanWise Mindfulness Hiking Retreats, OI member, Italy.

Rosa Marina De Vecchi, educator and social worker, Cooperativa sociale l'Albero and local government agencies in Verona, OI Member, Italy.

Murielle Dionnet, kindergarten, elementary, and special education teacher in public elementary schools, lay dharma teacher and OI member, France.

Pascale Dumont, elementary school teacher in Nanterre, France.

Miles Dunmore, teacher of English literature, American School in London, United Kingdom. Member of the Heart of London Sangha and retreat facilitator.

Elia Ferrer Garcia, elementary school teacher, Centre D'educacio Infantil I Primaria Antaviana, Spain.

Didde Flor Rotne, meditation teacher and mindfulness mentor, Stillnessrevolution, Denmark. Coauthor of Everybody Present.

Nikolaj Flor Rotne, meditation teacher, speaker, and mentor, Stillnessrevolution, Denmark. Coauthor of *Everybody Present*.

Marcela Giordano, musician and volunteer, Plum Village Children's Program, Uruguay.

Julian Goetz, educator and administrator, Winterline Global Education, United States.

Sr. Hai Nghiem, monastic dharma teacher, Maison de L'Inspir, France.

Bea Harley, retired art teacher and former deputy administrative head, Dharma Primary School, United Kingdom.

Cara Harzheim, retired philosophy and languages teacher, Ludwig-Meyn-Gymnasium in Uetersen, OI member, Germany and France.

Derek Heffernan, teacher, Sir Guy Carleton Secondary School in Nepean, Ontario, Canada.

Goyo Hidalgo Ruiz, middle and high school teacher, Instituto de Enseñanza Secundaria San Isidoro in Seville, OI member, Spain.

Angelika "Anka" Hoberg, retired elementary school teacher, Worpswede, Germany.

Institut J. M. Zafra Educators' Sangha: Dunia Aparicio, Karina Grau, Carme Morist, Toni Pujades, Montserrat "Montse" Ramírez Sáez, and Rosa Rodrigo, middle and high school teachers in Barcelona, Spain.

Olga Julián Segura, professional development trainer, Spain.

Neha Kaul, adjunct assistant professor, School of Medicine, New York Medical College, United States.

Sara J. Kein (formerly Sara Unsworth), psychology faculty and chair of the Social and Behavioral Sciences at Diné College, United States.

Elizabeth Kriynovich, teacher, Delaware Valley Friends School in Paoli, Pennsylvania, United States.

Chau Li Huay, school trainer, government schools, Singapore.

Kaira Jewel Lingo, mindfulness educator and retreat leader, lay dharma teacher and OI member, United States and Europe. Editor of *Planting Seeds*.

Lyndsay Lunan, lecturer of literature and psychology, City of Glasgow College and Youth Mindfulness, United Kingdom.

Annie Mahon, author, blogger, mindfulness teacher, bodywork therapist, cofounder of Opening Heart Mindfulness Community and DC Yoga Week, OI member, United States.

Victoria Mausisa, retired business manager, retreat leader, and guest lecturer, United States.

Alison Mayo, early years leader, Dharma Primary School, United Kingdom.

Yvonne Mazurek, art history teacher, School Year Abroad and USAC in Viterbo, Italy, and volunteer coordinator for Wake Up Schools in Plum Village, France.

Sara Messire, elementary school teacher, France.

Constance Chua Mey-Ing, teacher and subject head for Character and Citizenship Education, Maha Bodhi School, Singapore.

Coreen Morsink, teacher and coach, St. Catherine's British School, Athens, Greece.

Kenley Neufeld, dean, lay dharma teacher, and OI member, Santa Barbara City College, California.

Nhu-Mai Nguyen, singer-songwriter and North American Wake Up ambassador, United States.

Gail Williams O'Brien, professor emeritus and former associate dean at North Carolina State University and yoga teacher, United States.

Jade Ong, middle and high school teacher at a school sponsored by the United Nations High Commissioner for Refugees, Malaysia.

Mack Paul, special education teacher, Irving Middle School in Norman, Oklahoma.

Christine Petaccia, occupational therapist at schools and KonaJoy therapy, United States.

Br. Phap Dung, monastic dharma teacher, Plum Village, France.

Br. Phap Lai (Br. Ben), monastic dharma teacher, Plum Village, France.

Br. Phap Luu (Br. Stream), monastic dharma teacher, Plum Village, France.

Jess Plews, former elementary teacher and lead instructor at the Outdoors Project, United Kingdom.

Mary Lee Prescott-Griffin, professor of education, Wheaton College, United States.

Morrakot "Chompoo" Raweewan, assistant professor of engineering, Sirindhorn International Institute of Technology, Thammasat University, OI member, Thailand.

Joe Reilly, singer, songwriter, and environmental educator, OI member, United States.

Susannah Robson, elementary school teacher, United Kingdom.

Adriana Rocco, mindfulness mentor, lay dharma teacher, and OI member, Italy.

Betsy Rose, singer, songwriter, mindfulness educator, and teacher trainer at schools, conferences, and retreats, United States.

Giorgia Rossato, educator and shiatsu therapist, afterschool programs, France and Italy.

Michael Schwammberger, mindfulness trainer and retreat leader, former monastic, lay dharma teacher, and OI member, Spain and United Kingdom.

Jasna K. Schwind, associate professor of nursing, Ryerson University, Canada.

Sara Martine Serrano, special education assistant at a Waldorf School and Camphill Community, lay Dharma Teacher and OI member, Switzerland.

Shantum Seth, senior advisor to the World Bank, Ahimsa Trust, lay dharma teacher, and OI member, India.

Ranjani Shankar, English teacher at a Catholic high school, India.

Gloria Shepard, independent mindfulness educator, United States.

Tony Silvestre, professor of infectious diseases and microbiology and director of the Center for Mindfulness and Consciousness Studies at the University of Pittsburgh, lay dharma teacher and OI member, United States.

Niki Smith, teaching assistant, Dharma Primary School, United Kingdom.

Matt Spence, high school teacher and coach, Providence Day School in Charlotte, North Carolina.

Tineke Spruytenburg, former special education teacher and current administrator, special education teacher, and cofounder of Happy Teachers, OI member, Netherlands.

Meena Srinivasan, former classroom teacher and current program manager for the Office of Social and Emotional Learning, Oakland Unified School District, OI member, United States. Author of *Teach, Breathe, Learn.*

Sr. Tai Nghiem, monastic, Plum Village, France.

Mariann Taigman, occupational therapist, United States.

Nisanart "Gift" Tavedikul, assistant director, American School of Bangkok, Thailand.

Christiane Terrier, retired physics and chemistry teacher, Lycée Edmond Michelet, Arpajon, OI member, and mindfulness trainer, France.

Judith Toy, meditation teacher, mentor, and author, OI member and former associate editor of *The Mindfulness Bell*, United States.

Br. Troi Minh Tam (Br. Heart), monastic, Deer Park Monastery, United States.

Chelsea True, executive director and mindfulness instructor, Joyful Mind Project, United States.

Katrina Tsang, university teacher, Hong Kong.

Mark Vette, lecturer, animal behavior specialist, zoologist, and founder of Dog Zen, OI member, New Zealand.

David Viafora, mindfulness teacher and social worker, United States.

Dzung X. Vo, pediatrician and adolescent medicine specialist, British Columbia Children's Hospital and University of British Columbia, OI member, Canada. Author of *The Mindful Teen.*

Peggy Rowe Ward, mindfulness teacher and retreat leader, lay dharma teacher and OI member, Lotus Institute, United States and Thailand.

Elli Weisbaum, mindfulness trainer and PhD candidate, Institute of Medical Sciences, University of Toronto, OI member, Canada.

Chris Willard, psychologist and faculty of Harvard Medical School, United States. Coauthor of *Teaching Mindfulness to Kids and Teens.*

Jennifer Wood, high school teacher and adviser, United States.

Caroline Woods, teacher, Dharma Primary School, United Kingdom.

Sarah Woolman, elementary and middle school teacher at a Waldorf School, United Kingdom.

Ross Young, elementary school teacher, United Kingdom.

About the Authors

Thich Nhat Hanh is one of the most revered Zen teachers in the world today. His best-selling books include *Planting Seeds* and *Peace of Mind*. He lives in Plum Village in southwest France. Nhat Hanh has been teaching the art of mindful living for more than seventy years.

Katherine Weare PhD is Emeritus Professor at the University of Exeter and Southampton in the UK. She is known internationally for long career in education, for her teaching, research and scholarship on the wellbeing of children and young people and those who care for them, now focusing particularly on mindfulness and compassion. Katherine advises various mindfulness projects, including the UK Mindfulness in Schools Project, the All Party Parliamentary Committee on developing mindfulness and well-being and is on the board of Mind and Life Europe. She is a trained and practicing teacher of MBSR and her own mindfulness and meditation practice draws on several traditions. She has three children and lives in Somerset, in the UK.

Related Titles from Parallax Press

Awakening Joy for Kids James Baraz and Michele Lilyanna

Everybody Present Nikolai Rotne and Didde Flor Rotne

Girls Rising Urana Jackson

Mindful Movements Thich Nhat Hanh

Parenting in the Present Moment Carla Naumberg

Planting Seeds Thich Nhat Hanh

Teach, Breathe, Learn Meena Srinivasan

Monastics and laypeople practice the art of mindful living in the tradition of Thich Nhat Hanh at retreat communities worldwide. To reach any of these communities, or for information about individuals and families joining for a practice period, please contact:

Plum Village
13 Martineau
33580 Dieulivol, France
plumvillage.org

Blue Cliff Monastery
3 Mindfulness Road
Pine Bush, NY 12566
bluecliffmonastery.org

Magnolia Grove Monastery
123 Towles Rd.
Batesville, MS 38606
magnoliagrovemonastery.org

Deer Park Monastery
2499 Melru Lane
Escondido, CA 92026
deerparkmonastery.org

The Mindfulness Bell, a journal of the art of mindful living in the tradition of Thich Nhat Hanh, is published three times a year by Plum Village.

To subscribe or to see the worldwide directory of sanghas, visit **mindfulnessbell.org**.

A portion of the proceeds from your book purchase supports Thich Nhat Hanh's peace work and mindfulness teachings around the world. For more information on how you can help, visit www.thichnhathanhfoundation.org.

Thank you.

PARALLAX PRESS

Parallax Press is a nonprofit publisher, founded and inspired by Zen Master Thich Nhat Hanh. We publish books on mindfulness in daily life and are committed to making these teachings accessible to everyone and preserving them for future generations. We do this work to alleviate suffering and contribute to a more just and joyful world.

For a copy of the catalog, please contact:

Parallax Press
P.O. Box 7355
Berkeley, CA 94707
parallax.org